. . . .

. . . .

. . . .

. . . . **Address**

. . . . **Name**

. . . . Other subjects of interest

☐ YOGA		☐ WESTERN MYSTERY TRADITION	
☐ MYTHOLOGY		☐ SUFISM, ISLAM	
☐ CHRISTIANITY		☐ PSYCHOLOGY	
☐ NEW SCIENCE		☐ FICTION	
☐ EARTH MYSTERIES		☐ QABALAH	
☐ WOMEN'S STUDIES		☐ HINDUISM	
☐ BUDDHISM, TAOISM		☐ PHILOSOPHY	
☐ HEALTH & HEALING		☐ ASTROLOGY, TAROT	
☐ NATIVE AMERICAN		☐ ANCIENT WISDOM,	

Please tick the subjects that are of particular interest to you

Thank you for choosing this book. If you would like to receive regular information about Element titles, please fill in this card.

is the book to have.
stimulates intellectu-

I., A.D.T.R., M.S.W.

ok at myself with fresh

Jonathan Fox, M.A.
The Essential Moreno

ogether and unified for

Joe Cassius, Ph.D.
uthor of *Body Scripts*.

ten in a way that brings
e.

Baum, Ph.D., A.B.P.P.
Bioenergetic Analysis

Rhythmic Integration

Rhythmic Integration

Finding Wholeness
in the Cycle of Change

Ronald Robbins, Ph.D.

P•U•L•S•E

A P.U.L.S.E. Book, published by Station Hill Press, Inc., Barrytown, New York 12507

Distributed in the United States and Canada by The Talman Company, 150 Fifth Avenue, New York, N.Y. 10011.

Library of Congress Cataloguing-in-Publication Data

Robbins, Ronald, 1938-
    Rhythmic cycle of change]
    Rhythmic integration: finding wholeness in the cycle of change; Ronald Robbins
    p. cm.
    Reprint. Originally published: The rhythmic cycle of change. Poughkeepsie, N.Y.; Neshama Publications, ©1988.
    Includes bibliographical references.
    ISBN 0-88268-099-4
    1. Psychotherapy. 2. Change (Psychology) 3. Social change. 4. Ethnopsychology. I. Title.
RC480.5.R569 1990
155—dc20

Manufactured in the United States of America.

CONTENTS

To My Mother
and the Memory of My Father
First Teachers

PREFACE

When I started the work that led to this book, the sixties were just coming to an end. Society had gone through a rapid period of change. The speed of things was beginning to come down from a frantic pace. The title of Alvin Toffler's best selling book, *Future Shock* put the mood of the times in perspective: It seemed we were all a little dazed by what appeared to be an ever increasing escalation of revolution, riot and war.

Perhaps in response to this, I found myself in a period of meditative practice looking for quiet and serenity. The search to calm down my own wavering center felt good and right to me. It brought periods of peace in harried times. The difference was noticeable. My friends wondered at my relaxed and peaceful state.

At a transpersonal psychology conference, one of my colleagues hooked me up to what was still a somewhat experimental device, a biofeedback machine. He told me to relax, something which by now I was getting pretty good at, and he noticed as the needle dropped to the lowest reading. He adjusted the scale downward and watched the needle hit the baseline again. Going through the process twice more, he commented, with amazement in his voice, "Perhaps you've died?"

Maybe some part of me had, but this death was full of life, inner light and excitement. I passed through the classic signposts of meditative experience: the visions and vulnerabilities, the raptures and enlightening moments that brought rushes of new insights in their wake. Somewhere though, in the silence of empty reflection, it came to me that by watching myself too much I was perhaps growing too self-absorbed, too caught in my own experience. My time could be directed in ways that could touch and be meaningful to others.

A subtle shift occurred. Rather than attending to the daily minutia of my thoughts—the aims, strivings and emotions passing before my awareness between periods of silence—I began, in my sessions, to watch the process of change itself. I slowly became aware of a regular progression of moods as I moved from a beginning wish "to know" to an achievement of that goal.

Gradually, I gained a new perspective on what was going on in myself. It was to affect my understanding of my work as a psychologist, and of the world.

In the particular experience of my meditation I saw that the process of change could be viewed as six distinct stages: dreaming, creating, communicating, inspiring, solidifying, and achieving. Each expressed a different potential of psychological experience. Each was critical in order to move through a complete cycle and each had its own unique moods, emotions, passions, and pitfalls.

I found this cycle of change outside of myself too, underlying each developing process I observed. Being thinner, obtaining a new job, coming up with a fine meal: each began with the wish of a dream and had to move, one phase integrated into the next, through the series for completion to be reached. When life did move in this way, it was indeed a dance, following the music of an inner rhythm that made it full of worth and a valued quality of realness. This living quality could occur even during the pains that attend life's most difficult trials.

But in my practice as a psychotherapist, I often saw that anywhere along the path a different kind of pain, a recycling pain that stopped change's unfolding, could occur. Change could arrest, become stifled or even gratingly dissonant. This brought with it a type of suffering that signalled the inner disruption of a life course and ineffective living. It provided the ground where psychopathology could root.

Judy, a dancer, dreamed of choreographing beautiful productions. She could never go farther than dreams until she allowed herself to accept the necessity of the struggles and tension of the creative phase, the point where inner dreams emerge to meet the realities of what is outside. The result was an all too often felt malaise.

Stan was inspired to take off weight and, through the aid of a diet drink, did so. But as with many things in his life, he failed to solidify his progress by developing new habits. Here they were needed to buttress a normal eating pattern that he could live with day in and day out. Without it, and with growing and familiar shame, he quickly regressed to where he began.

Looking outside of the clinical setting it was apparent that along the course of change each of us has sticking points we like to stay in. Productive or not, they are a home base. Psychological theory tells us this place is established in early life. But stay in them too long and we disrupt the change cycle and experience negative consequences. Often the flow of life becomes blocked at one stage or another. And at times merely having the insight that any such stage is a normal part of the change process, which only to be moved through, can pull us out of a self-defeating pattern.

The familiar phase or phases, however, that tend most to mark a person's life are not simply something negative or a challenge to overcome. The sheer frequency of experiences each of us has with such a phase can provide the opportunity to develop it into an area of excellence from which to move forward, a place of character and style that can shape the best of our individual expression.

Dreamers, for example, who carry their dreams through the full course of the change cycle bring poetry and sensitivity into an accomplished, often beautiful way of life. For creators who live through their struggle, the creative impetus matures until it reaches the fulfilled expression of what is truly original. Each of the other phases—communicator, inspirer, solidifier, and achiever—similarly offers its own potential to be fulfilled by those who become master of its way.

I have always experienced myself as committed to living a deep, full life. "Deep" in the sense that I actively look for the underlying meanings and strive to experience the subtle feelings behind the rush of events. "Full" in that I am interested in knowing the variety of life possibilities that my own existence can bring me.

I used the insights of the Rhythmic Cycle to strengthen my own weak areas, phases in me that were underdeveloped. I strove hard to find the poetry (dreaming) within and worked just as hard to make solid the prosaic (solidifying) which in the past I might have ignored. The personal development I've enjoyed, integrating the varied way-stations on the long cycle of change into a meaningful whole now culminating in this book, has been a great source of satisfaction to me.

To gather information on how other people found the way to deal with and integrate their own difficult phases, I had to move outside of myself. At first I approached several noted writers and artists, but I found that though they obviously expressed themselves through their work, it was not easy for them to talk directly about what was going on within, the how and the why of their own process of change. Then it struck me: there could be no better subjects than therapists from whom to gather reflections about the inner process. Their occupation was to be attuned to the discovery and expression of what went on "inside." And of course their training itself often involved searching out their psychological dynamics.

I talked to some of the leading therapists, giants of the time, about the course of change that marked their lives and the phase of the cycle that characterized their contribution. I visited J.L. Moreno, the genius that gave us psychodrama and role-playing; Albert Ellis, who argued people out of their neurosis; and Jacqui Schiff, who lived with schizophrenics in her home in order to bring them to healthy productive living.

I spoke with Carl Rogers about his sit-and-reflect technique that moved people forward. Virginia Satir, the popular family therapist, shared with me the can-do approach that marked everything she attempted. And Alexander Lowen emphasized his commitment to the body as the key to understanding his work and the achievements of his therapeutic approach.

There were others: Carl Jung, R.D. Laing, Fritz Perls, and Wilhelm Reich. I studied their lives from their writings, traced in the text how one or another phase of change marked the development of their personality and shaped their therapeutic contribution. I learned how they too moved through the process they followed on the path toward fulfillment. The confirmation of my thoughts and experiences was personally rewarding. These were exciting times.

I carried my studies beyond the individual, looking at different peoples, how they dealt with and manifested a particular phase of change that somehow characterized their culture. Among them were the tribal societies of the Pygmies and Bushman; the spiritual communities of Tantric Buddhists and 18th Century Chassids; the national cultures of middle Europe; and the more complexly defined groupings and sub-cultures based on sex-role behaviors.

But for me, and I hope for the reader, this work offers something more than a study and a new theoretical viewpoint. Though it isn't a "how to" book (the actual practice of Rhythmic Integration will require a separate volume), it is written in a way. that should help provide opportunity for growth. The reader is taken on a journey through each of the phases of change, helped to "know" change through personal experience and through immersion in its various way stations.

Thus the writing invites one to lightly enter into each phase. Toward this end I deliberately used a variety of styles, from the poetic and meditative to the logical and straightforward.

Each phase—Dreamer, Creator, Communicator, Inspirer, Solidifier, and Achiever—has its own chapter, designed to call up its particular mood; to teach of its development, dynamics and issues; and to illustrate it by way of people whose lives exemplify it.

Readers should of course supplement what is written by working for insights into their own process of change, noting phases that are familiar and exploring those that are unfamiliar. Private reveries and personal applications can prove useful, in suggesting one's areas of strength and pointing to those where personality might be developed further.

These insights about change can be carried beyond the therapeutic or personal growth setting as well. Politics, culture, society at large—all mirror the very processes that govern our intimate development.

Whether a reader's interest in change is theoretical or practical and whether it derives from the spiritual or therapeutic, the social or the individual, my aim is to stimulate awareness of the Cycle of Change itself and suggest a way toward integrating its various phases—to move us closer to fuller, wholer living.

Ronald Robbins, PhD

ACKNOWLEDGMENTS

This work has been a long project, necessarily made longer as the writing of one of its examples required waiting for the completion of a recent course of political history.

Many people are to be thanked for their help along the way. Some were there consistently offering service and encouragement. Others were there, though more briefly, at the right time to carry me over a difficult period or to suggest a refocus or contribute a valuable point or service.

Of the latter I would like to thank Liz Dunn, Holly Edelman, Andrea Grumbine, Shep Jackson, Bob Mitchell, Zerka Moreno, Leo Opdyke, Martha Opitz, Mel Robbins, Sol and Rae Rosenbloom, Myron Sharaf, Carolyn Scheer, Milton Teichman, and Edith Waller.

Of the former, special appreciation for my colleague, Don Grumbine, whose many readings and encouraging responses were a constant source of nourishment. Thanks to my good friend, Marty Fishgold, whose professional knowledge about books and publications and the complex ways of life were freely given to me and helped in countless ways.

For their assistance in editing, thanks to Win Bottum and Beverly Kaufman who put in long hours reviewing the text, searching out errors and wielding red pencil. Their astute criticisms and gentle but firm ways added to the quality of the text. Craig Wolf provided final copy editing. His experienced and professional way made going through the text still one more time an easy and worthwhile experience. Thanks too to Vaughn Winkler who helped me with such steadiness and warmth through the early struggles and pains of mastering the use of the computer.

Special mention has to be made to the therapists who allowed me to interview them for this project. Albert Ellis, Alexander Lowen, Jacqui Lee Schiff, and Virginia Satir: each responded to my request for personal-history information so its relationship to their work could be appreciated. Each was gracious and full in their sharing and my experiences with them have been both memorable and special delights for me. I was briefly able to interview the late Carl Rogers and this too was a pleasure. I regret that time constraints did not allow a longer period for us to work together.

My first interview with a therapeutic leader was with the late J. L. Moreno. This was done at the request of Dr. George Mora and under the auspices of the American Psychiatric Association's collection of taped biographies of outstanding contributors. I am very grateful to Dr. Mora for beginning me in this direction. Moreno was my first mentor in a specific psychotherapeutic approach. The time spent interviewing him deepened my appreciation for the link between life history and therapeutic contribution and led me to explore it further. I studied directly with both him and his wife, Zerka, over a period of several years and still continue to feel the power of their influence in my work.

I would like also to express my appreciation to my colleagues in the International Institute of Bioenergetic Analysis for providing me with the opportunity to serve as a trainer of developing therapists and to the New York, Rhinelander and Argentine Societies for opportunities to present Rhythmic Integration concepts as they developed and pertained to Bioenergetic topics.

Special thanks is due to coordinator Freddie Sabghir and the members of the Albany Rhythmic Integration Training Program for their consistent support and stimulus to the development of the concepts and methods of Rhythmic Integration over the past decade.

I want to especially thank those people who have been my clients. To be able to share in their totality, their pain, their growth, their sorrows and joys has been again and again a deeply moving, ever-humanizing experience. To know oneself must surely be one of the fullest and most daring tasks of life. For me to be able to be with others in their quest toward this aim has been to gain in respect for the searching out of life and to come to honor those that delve after its truths as they find it in their experience. The learning I have gotten from them has been immeasurable.

Finally, it is difficult to find words to express the depth of my gratefulness to my family. This work and the background development of it have occupied me for over 15 years. In that time I have watched my children, Joel and Michele, move from childhood to early adulthood. Their growth has been a constant wonder for me - a stimulus again and again to find delight in the process of change.

My son Joel's maturing scholarship gradually grew to a point of profundity recognized and valued by those who teach and know him. The depths of understanding and caring concern for the work of his father deeply moved me for its own sake as well as in its providing a living testament to the power and meaning that can lie in the experience of fatherhood.

My younger daughter, Michele, brought another element to my work. The sparkle and delight of her perceptions and activities time and again brought needed refreshment when the work process got too heavy and I became bogged down. In her last year of college, I eagerly await with anticipation the next steps in the unfolding of her life course.

Fullest appreciation goes to my wife, Gloria. Whisper-jet, archtypical woman, she has aided me in many ways, made space for my work and shared in my struggles. A powerful therapist, her comments have been astute and sensitively given, in ways that moved things on. She had the capacity to know when to be silent as well as when to intervene when the course seemed too consuming. She has brought real witness to the words of Proverbs 31:

When one finds a worthy wife,
her value is beyond pearls.
Her husband, entrusting his heart
to her, has an unfailing prize.

A Requiem for Psychotherapy

A sinking quiet came over Modern Psychotherapy. She went down slowly, almost unnoticed. Her day was done. The span of her years had been long, full of excitement, often glorious.

She was born over a hundred years ago, conceived from a series of penetrating analyses, by a searching Middle European, Dr. Sigmund Freud, who probed deeply into the lives of hysterical patients. The patients shared a neurotic symptomology that was rampant in those times, a symptomology formed under the Victorian blanket of sexual repression. Sigmund, with one foot in his day and the other moving toward the unknown, was drawn toward them.

To relieve the psychic suffering he saw, he explored and learned of the depths of the mind and the structure of the personality. His work emphasized sexual urges, traced their development in the first years of life. His analyses of memories, metaphors and dreams - run through with the crimson tinge of sexuality - met immediately with powerful resistance.

Almost as immediately, the energy of Freud's laser-like insights moved the creative elements of the avant-garde to new orientation. Myth, poetry, drama, education and social understanding: all felt the influence of what was occurring in the new field of Psychotherapy. Psyche, conscious and unconscious, had been brought forward toward life's center stage.

As the first generation of Freud's students matured, protest against his patrimony grew strong. Jung and Adler cried out and broke away to offer different understandings, new analyses to alleviate mental and emotional suffering. With a more strident voice the sound of Psychotherapy communicated to distant quarters.

Her spread was extensive. She crossed the ocean and took root in America, the land of opportunity. Her theory and practice intertwined with the times, fired the inspirations of the "Roaring Twenties." She was used to support libertine excesses as the social body whirled beyond the limits with its own enthusiasms. "Down repression - up libido." Id reigned supreme. Excess was the mean.

With the Great Depression, things came down hard. Therapy's work settled into a long period of solid, often prosaic service. A certain steady prestige was established. In the charge of Medicine, she was expensive, patronized only by those few who could afford her.

With War, the possessive high-priced grip of Medicine was loosened. Psychotherapy was needed for the common soldier at the front. More therapists were required. The door was opened for the scientific discipline of Psychology to grow clinical, shift its manpower into her service and treat the war shocks of world conflagration.

Peace brought return to steady work, but now, more and more, the secrets of the office came to be peeked at and pried upon. Research delved into Psychotherapy's workings, asked all manner of questions of her. She proved a fickle respondent, gave back all manner of inconsistent answers. For two decades Science probed, only to come up with mixed findings.

In the early 1960's a clinical researcher reported he had reviewed the results and boldly claimed that Psychotherapy, as she was known to be, was a fraud. She brought no results. He offered a new behavior-oriented approach that promised real differences, and scientific respectability as well.

Suddenly, as if a gate was open, a parade of identities strove forward. Each in its way claimed to have achieved "the" place, fulfilled "the" promise, of the "real" Psychotherapy. Some had roots in Therapy's youthful period of Anti-Freudian rebellion. Others seemed new to the moment.

Wherever they came from, the line was long. There was Behavior Therapy, Bioenergetics, Non-Directive Therapy, Ego Therapy, Existential Analysis, Family Therapy, Gestalt Therapy, Hypnotherapy, Jungian Therapy, Primal Therapy, Psychodrama, Rational-Emotive Therapy, Reparenting, Reality Therapy, Reichian Therapy, Transactional Analysis and others of lesser or less memorable note.

Each was costumed in an array of apparel fashioned from a number of attractive elements: emotion, mind or behavior; body or soul; individual, group or milieu; long term or short term; scientific or humanistic; etc., etc. Each strutted proudly, striking a series of seemingly quite original poses. Each appeared a well developed accomplishment, complete with leader, school, method and followers.

It was quite a time. Modern Psychotherapy's glamour caught the imagination of the entire society. Everyone wished to be seen with her. She was regularly mentioned in the newspapers. Meccas offered therapeutic smorgasbords so that the public could sample the variety of her wares. Book shelves growing pregnant with her new issues gave more and more room for her concerns.

The Rhythmic Cycle of Change

Therapy was omnipresent. Dancers danced with her. Musicians played with her. Joggers ran and masseurs stroked for her. The spiritual meditated for her, while even lovers did their thing for her. It was all called "good therapy". Bottom-line hard-nosed corporations, too, bought her technology. Sensitivity training, encounter groups, and growth methods proliferated.

Psychotherapy was out of the Doctor's office, beyond the hospital. Her application was no longer simply for the "patient." Her practice was applied to "clients," "persons," "relationships," "families," "systems" and even "humanity" itself. With suffering and disease at its etymological core, the term "patient" was now just too limiting.

Modern Psychotherapy had moved far from her source in the lives of the pained and disturbed. Everywhere she was calling for growth, the maximizing of potential for all who came to her. And results were occurring. People could be seen changing. They were more expressive and self-directed, better able to live with their feelings and understand their background. They tried new behaviors, gained energy, expressed more life. Research gave support to Modern Psychotherapy's new technologies.

Success widened the field. Religion jumped on board. Priests, ministers and rabbis took up Pastoral Counseling. Educators became counselors. Social Work, a whole profession, jumped en masse on Therapy's bandwagon.

Soon, untrained people began doing her work. "Do-it-yourself" technical manuals grew in popularity. Self-help groups proliferated to solve problems: "lose weight;" get off booze;" "face your divorce;" "ease bereavement;" "stop wife, child and parental abuse;" "overcome schizophrenic alienation." Modern Therapy's methods, grown simple, had become the province of everyday life and the common man.

Then slowly, hardly noticeably, Psychotherapy began to lose her grip on the nation's imagination. A cycle of change was ending. Bookshelves were given back to other things. Publicity subsided. Magazines and Meccas sold themselves to other purposes. Insurance cut back its payments and moved to force a shortening of the length of her application. The market and its power were moving elsewhere. Damned as narcissistic, her glory days were fading.

There were twitches at the end, strong ones, but now in her less dynamic condition, necessarily brief. Still they were not without attraction. EST marketers charged thousands for a one-group, two week course said to provide Mastery Level as a psychotherapeutic practitioner for all those professionals who would pay the price. A group of Family Therapy theorists proffered a course of therapy that could make the difference in one session. Neuro-linguistic Programmers sold a clear and easily learned copy program that could reproduce the important components employed by the great therapists in anyone who wished to acquire them.

Psychotherapy's delivery system could count less and less on her waning energy. Radio reduced her to half-minute solutions to ease a caller's pain, providing both a bit of entertainment and high audience ratings.

A little lady with a heavy Middle European accent became a TV superstar, chirping nightly about all kinds of sexual problems. Freud's concerns were surely in the past. Sex had come out from under the blanket. Repression, it seems, had been done away with. Orgasm for all.

The end was approaching. In December of 1985 the New York Times headline spoke of a party in Psychotherapy's honor:

"Psychotherapy, at 100, Is marked by Deep
Divisions on Approaches." (Daniel Goleman, 1985)

Over 7000 of her practitioners attended the gathering. The rigidities of her old age were there to be seen. Her health was poor,

The Rhythmic Cycle of Change

her corpus divided. For those who could see, it was evident that her day was passing.

> "Psychotherapy, after a century of existence, had splintered into factions so diverse that there is little agreement on exactly what psychotherapy is, how it should proceed or what it should accomplish. And despite the best of ecumenical efforts, the deep divisions seem to be getting even deeper." (Goleman, 1985)

Many of the Old Masters were present: Carl Rogers, R. D. Laing, Rollo May, Bruno Bettelheim, Virginia Satir and others. Many of the old issues were reiterated. They were:

> "... as basic as whether the therapist should actively direct the patient toward change or should simply guide him to insight; whether therapy should delve into the past or focus on the present; whether it should be long or short; whether it is science, art or religion." (Goleman, 1985)

Whether "science, art or religion?" Therapy's compassion for intra-psychic suffering, the reason at the core of its conception, was not mentioned. In the course of change, healing had been lost or forgotten. Missing too was Therapy as education, a way to a growth producing knowledge.

Modern Psychotherapy's controversies too, showed the effects of age. The old fire had lessened. The protagonists, many who had never before met each other, had less drive for the battle of polemics, more desire for easy meeting.

> "Despite serious differences in opinion over how therapy should be done, the masters were, for the most part civil with each other - even displaying those marks of the good therapist, warmth and empathy." (Goleman, 1985)

Sensing Psychotherapy's failing, The Times, in quoting one of the participants, concluded its report with a hope for something more whole.

> "What you have among us speakers is parallel monologues, not dialogue," said Dr. Minuchin. "We are each prisoners of our own dogma. The integration will be made by the 7,000 therapists in our audience. They are, I hope, flexible enough to see that each of these approaches has something to offer." (Goleman, 1985)

With the passing of Psychotherapy as we have known her, the corpus falls apart and a new integration becomes possible. The cleansing tears at her loss allow fresh eyes to see in perspective the proportions that make even blind men know elephants again as elephants, rather than just as a discontinuous aggregate of parts. Man's quest for unity, wholeness, is eternal. Its failure lies at the heart of psychic suffering and stifled growth. The way is cleared for new beginning.

The purifying wash of time cleans and smooths the jagged edges of the relics of the past. It allows for better fitting, makes room for a new coming together and spawns the conception that brings rebirth. Standing, waiting, are those involved with the quest, those longing for the healing, those delighted with the possibility of new ways to enter into the experience of the river of life.

The Rhythmic Cycle of Change

Modern Psychotherapy, you have served us well, touched our souls, moved us closer. You have given love, been loved. As we have known you, you will be missed.

Rhythms - an Introduction

Change, Change, Change.
Always the same - constantly different.
A profusion of rhythms
Each moving to its own end.

THE FLOW

Strange - to begin with the end, to have started with a requiem for psychotherapy. Surely the phoenix does rise from the ashes, and, from the point of view of change, every end brings only a new beginning. Still, one expects a book to start with a start, not an end. Then too, should one seriously consider psychotherapy, if only in its modern terms, to have passed away?

But look what's occurred. Death brings memories, a new look at the past. Things get topsy-turvy. Returning to psychotherapy's psychoanalytic roots, the stirring of old diggings has resulted in new twists to well-worn theories. No longer is Analysis's classic application narrowly restricted to people with Oeidpal problems. In the area of of the Borderline Personality, with its emphasis on loss, a new focus on old issues has led directly to the treatment of more primitive psychic concerns. (Kernberg, 1975; Masterson, 1972)

The return to archaic concerns is also replicated, outside of psychoanalysis. A spiritual psychology is emerging. It too is built on sifting the relics. It asks, "Why do bad things happen to good people?" (Kushner, 1981). It deals with questions of good and evil. (Peck, 1983) It uses altered states to seek out and restructure old inner worlds. (Harner, 1980) It has spawned new Mystery

THE RHYTHMIC CYCLE OF CHANGE

Schools, which draw on the ancient wisdoms of long-dead seers to effect new healing and growth.

These moves backward, backward to go forward, only underline the fact that the life, the thrust, the straight forward generative growth of the "modern" period of psychotherapy has passed. The time of psychotheraputic heroes, when a long line of explorers brought radical new views and methods to the search into the psyche, has gone.

Still, even if this is true, the question remains: "Why start this work with end?". The answer: ends, and their association with both past and new beginning, bring us the space, the time, the opening to be vividly aware of change.

Change is this work's subject. At times of endings we feel change in our bones, know it as it exists. Touched by the death of someone, the end of a life for example, we are shaken. The shells of fixity, in which we enwrap our life-worlds, crack apart. We experience them falling away in our minds, in our very bodies. Once gone, the processes of change pop vividly into awareness. We are in contact with them. For a time, we see them closely. In these moments, we can glimpse their workings and their meanings.

Ends bring change into focus. With ends, we know change most immediately, through experience, through its highlighting in our consciousness, through its sudden registration on and in our body. The time, now, is ripe to use what we have learned from the recent period of therapeutic exploration to deepen our understanding of the process of change.

Human change, and its rhythmic cycle, follows a clear course. From energy moving along a sequence of bodily systems, a progression of qualities develops to provide change its psychological base. The human capacities to Dream, Create, Communicate, Inspire, Solidify, and Achieve are called out.

This succession of capacities results from the flow of energy's movement as it excites a corresponding, underlying sequence of physiological structures. Each energized structure provides a phase, a phase which contributes to a whole, to a Rhythmic Cycle of Change.

When we live totally, an increasing quantity of energy moves us through these psycho-physical phases, each in its turn, until a climactic high point is reached. Then, no longer containable, energy spills over in release. From the pause that ensues, a new Rhythmic Cycle begins.

In the late 1960's I became a student of Bioenergetics, a psychotherapeutic method that combines work on the body and its energy with psychoanalytic theory. (Lowen 1958, 1975) I was fortunate to begin this study by entering therapy with its founder, Alexander Lowen.

At that time Bioenergetics was not well known in therapeutic circles. Where we lived, my wife and I were its only practitioners. Few members of the public believed that the body, with its energy and physical tensions, had anything to do with well-being or mental health.

People were understandably skeptical when I suggested they work with their physical and emotional tensions by hitting a bed or stretching over a specially designed bench. "What does the body have to do with the things in my head?," was the common question. They would have to gain personal experience to know the connection.

Now things are easier. A transformation in knowledge has occurred. The idea that our physical state relates to our emotional and mental well-being is commonplace. The body has been rediscovered. Millions jog, do yoga, have taken up sports or dancing. The "Holistic Health Movement" and the "New Age" have brought the mind-body relation into the public's awareness. The

THE RHYTHMIC CYCLE OF CHANGE

Bioenergetic approach is not as strange as it once was. On the surface, it is much more easily understood.

I studied Bioenergetics intensely, learning to acutely observe the body to see where muscles impede free movement. I became adept at reading the body, noting tension patterns, seeing how blocked areas related to each other and correlated with earlier life events that led to their formation. I saw how they continued to cause difficulties in living.

When I trained other therapists in Bioenergetic Analysis, demonstration of these learnings would often prove astounding. Relating significant facts about a person's history and functioning after a brief look at the body appeared awesome. Such "wisdom," so seemingly miraculous, was only the application of what was to them an unfamiliar knowledge. With time and practice, they too could develop similar facility.

While training, I became particularly interested in the flow of movement, the progression of physical changes that moved through the body. This could be seen in small muscle movements and changes in skin color. It could be felt in variations in temperature as different parts of the body became active. I would watch with fascination as energy changes took place in individuals while they did something as simple as lying quietly on a mat. (For Bioenergetic work clients are asked to wear shorts or bathing suits in order for observation of body changes to be made.)

As the stream of energy activated different parts of the body I noted that the expression of the person changed. It became evident that areas of energetic excitement underlied the content of consciousness. Different bodily zones, different physiological systems provided a different play to being and behavior. Thus an excited colorful face and head would be accompanied by a flood of varying ideas. Movement of the pelvis would precede talk of a sexual nature.

The Merriam-Webster Dictionary (1974) defines "process" as, "A natural phenomenon marked by gradual change that leads toward a particular result." The process of energy change that I was observing followed the design of the human form and was the foundation of the course of changes that took place within the individual's consciousness and behavior. Its study could have broad implications for living.

Certainly the relationship of energy to developmental processes had been previously described. Freud had traced the path of bodily energy as it developed in our early years. He called it "libido" and outlined its primal effects on the psyche. Oral, anal and genital zones all were seen as centers of libidinal activity. Each developed in its time and could contribute to the pathological shaping of the growing personality.

In Bioenergetics a somewhat similar sequence of development is pointed to as the source of a progression of a number of character structures, any of which can be locked into early in life. "Character Structure," in Bioenergetic thinking, is responsible for fixed pathological attitudes that negatively affect the way we perceive and behave whenever they are active. Bioenergetics labels the character structures in terms of the psychopathology to which they relate. There are the Schizophrenic, Schizoid, Oral, Psychopathic, Masochistic and Rigid types. (Lowen, 1958)

Both Psychoanalysis and Bioenergetics developed out of attention to pathology. Both focused on the history of early positions as they disturbed the functioning of later life. Both emphasized the fixity that resulted from trauma.

I was interested, however, not in the abnormal but the natural aspects of the course of energy movement. Though energy's movement did indeed show the imprint of early events, I was struck by the total course of its flow, its continued omnipresence and cyclic repetitiveness. Life repeatedly was spun out against the background of energy change. Different body areas in their time gave different tones to what was happening. Emerson knew of it and he wrote:

> "Life is a train of moods like a string of beads, and as we pass through them they prove to be many-colored lenses which paint the world their own hue, and each shows only what lies in its focus."
> (Emerson, 1950)

Each phase of the Rhythmic Cycle, it became evident, gave rise to its own characteristic point of view and aroused its own way of being. "Character," as Lowen (1975) pointed out differed from the fixed rigidities of "Character Structure." This suggested it had positive as well as negative aspects.

The initial excitement stimulated by what I was seeing moved me to study within myself the process of energy movement and its phases. It proved possible to arouse and maintain the level of energy at various points in its growth. This arrest of energy, Freud pointed out, happens unconsciously in the development of neurosis. In Bioenergetics, too, unconscious arrest is viewed as central. It is the source of the pathological development of character structure.

However, by consciously rather than unconsciously controlling energetic arrest, I found any phase of the Rhythmic Cycle could be focused on in a way that could prove not pathological, but of value. In a sense each way-station along the course of energy change could be lit up and highlighted, used and expressed.

I spent a number of years immersing myself in each of what came to be called the Phases of the Rhythmic Cycle:

Dreamer **Inspirer**
Creator **Solidifier**
Communicator **Achiever**

Each phase proved to be a world unto itself as well as a gateway to other worlds (ie., manifestations of subsequent phases). Each could be the center-point of a way of life for an individual, at times positively fashioned into a real asset for living, at other times misused to escape life's necessities. I found the effect of this immersion effort deeply meaningful in transforming my own processes as well as useful in developing my understanding of the general principles and phases of energy movement.

It became apparent that all the phases of change are required for whole living. Every process we undertake must undergo the sequence of the Rhythmic Cycle if it is to yield full fruit. Even the simplest undertakings, we shall see, begin with the vague stirrings of spirit that stimulate our dreams. As energy develops they become capable of moving us, along the course of change, to the final fulfilling rewards of achievement and release.

It was evident that some processes of change, like life itself, take a lifetime to complete while others are completed in just a moment. Some are consistently frustrated, others diverted off course. Some sadly die out prematurely. Through it all the Rhythmic Cycle, being of our nature, is a part of everything we do.

My look inward was accompanied by a similar look outward. Using the orientation of the Rhythmic Cycle I studied various cultures, my own psychotherapeutic practice, and the lives and works of a number of therapeutic innovators who were then leading the field.

To see how the Rhythmic Cycle was manifest in collective behavior, I studied primitive, historical and contemporary cultures. It was clear that the process of change that energy incites within the individual manifested itself in a similar way to affect the course of cultural development. The Rhythmic Cycle could therefore be used as a key to understanding a culture's underlying expression and strengths as well as their development and arrest.

15

THE RHYTHMIC CYCLE OF CHANGE

Through my own therapeutic practice it became apparent that each phase of the Rhythmic Cycle provides its own rewards, dilemmas and pitfalls in the experiencing of life. Each could serve as a vehicle for healthy generativity as well as become the source of a pathological deadening.

As my understanding of the phases of the Rhythmic Cycle, the sequence of Dream, Creation, Communication, Inspiration, Solidification and Achievement, deepened, the interplay between the positive and negative aspects of the character of each phase grew clearer. Some phases were undeveloped in an individual. When life demanded their exercise, trouble was bound to occur. Other phases were the source of real strengths, strengths that, at times, even came to underlie areas of personal expertise.

From the therapeutic knowledge I was gaining, theoretical thoughts and practices relevant to therapy and growth emerged. Concepts and techniques were designed to help individuals gain an understanding of their own Rhythmic Cycle and to aid them in living with their own ongoing process of change in a conscious and integrated way. As these methods were tested and proven they were applied with clients, developed into experiential workshops, taught to professionals, and even used to profoundly improve the performance of athletes. (Robbins, 1984, 1985)

I have long been a student of the various schools of psychotherapy. Like many, I have been amazed as well as confused by the diversity of emphasis and approach they represent. Their leaders were my teachers, at times directly, at other times through their written work. I used the Rhythmic Cycle to study the lives of a number of these people, influential therapeutic innovators whose stars grew in prominence during the rapid growth period of psychotherapy that took place in the 1960's. Where possible I interviewed them personally. They willingly and graciously shared themselves in the effort to understand their lives and their contribution in the context of the Rhythmic Cycle.

Not surprisingly each innovator emphasized the particular phase of the Rhythmic Cycle that highlighted his or her own functioning. It was woven into their lives and for the most part was the major theme of their work. The reason for the diversity of approaches that led to my confusion became clear. Each, focusing on the individual phase of the Rhythmic Cycle most personally relevant to them, emphasized it in their understanding, practice and writings.

I came to see that my own approach came from a striving toward wholeness, an integration of parts. From this bias, it was apparent that to understand the totality of the therapeutic process required viewing the field in all its facets, to see the elephant, not just its parts. From this vantage point each therapeutic innovator and therapy was seen to take an appropriate place as part of a larger whole, a place highlighting one or another of the phases of the Rhythmic Cycle.

It is my intention in this work to draw on the experience and knowledge I have gained through my studies to introduce the Rhythmic Cycle and its way-stations in a full and rounded fashion. The delineation of a life fundamental, which I have experienced the Rhythmic Cycle to be, has many and broad implications. I have briefly suggested some above and will do so more concretely at this work's end, but this book is meant to be mainly descriptive. It is not its purpose to trace these implications out fully.

It is my hope that the readers will be stimulated to be aware of and appreciate the Rhythmic Cycle of Change in their own lives and begin to use its insights in a way to understand and aid both themselves and others. I also hope other professionals will be motivated to learn and develop the clinical aspects of the work further and that the theoretical perspectives presented here will be found useful for scholarly work in fields concerned with human endeavor.

THE RHYTHMIC CYCLE OF CHANGE

In the sections that follow, we will look at each of the phases of the Rhythmic Cycle in depth. Each is illustrated in a series of divisions. They set the mood of each phase, tell of its energetic dynamics and trace its early human development. They show its application in therapy as well as its function in the patterning of a culture. To accomplish the latter the Tibetan Buddhists, Philippine Pygmies, African Bushmen, 17th and 18th century Jewish mystical communities, contemporary Mid-European societies and male—female identity principles are considered.

In the final section of each chapter a manifestation of the phase of the Rhythmic Cycle being considered is traced through the interweaving of the character and contribution of a relevant therapeutic leader. Carl Jung, R. D. Laing, Albert Ellis, J. L. Moreno, Jacqui Lee Schiff, Carl Rogers and Virginia Satir and Alexander Lowen are each considered in their turn.

Before beginning this exploration of the phases of the Rhythmic Cycle some basic concepts need to be presented in a way that will provide an overall view of how they will be employed. To do this, introductory notes on energy, character structure and therapy as well as an illustrative overall example of the Rhythmic Cycle as it has been lived in the political history of the United States over the last generation are presented.

I have endeavored to make the initial discussion of these concepts simple and have chosen illustrations that are close to things we are aware of in everyday experience. The Rhythmic Cycle, however, as it will be seen, also underlies the fullest and most profound aspects of our experiencing.

ENERGY DYNAMICS OF THE RHYTHMIC CYCLE

The basis of the Rhythmic Cycle of Change lies in the movement of energy through our bodies. The body is where life energy is produced and where the first channel for its flow is carved. Its production depends on a number of things. Sleep, stimulation, food, oxygen, movement and hormonal chemistry contribute to its increase.

The increase of energy, however, does not simply result in more of the same. Rather, it proceeds to build in a number of stages, each of which adds its own very definite qualities, potentials and concerns to the psychological functioning of the individual. It is like moving from sleep to full wakefulness. Along the way, as energy builds, we pass through markedly different moods, phases and events.

The energetic phases of the Rhythmic Cycle are quite specific and part of each of us. As individuals, some we know well and others, because of our history, are less consciously familiar. A brief descriptive overview of each phase can highten our awareness.

DREAM PHASE

The Cycle begins with a low level of energy during a period of natural quiet. Such beginnings, with their gap in energetic excitation, are closely associated with sleep, meditation or pause. From these states the visions, sounds, and sensory awarenesses of the Dream Phase emerge.

CREATIVE PHASE

In the next phase, the Creative Phase, the body stirs. Nerves cause muscles to contract in short-lived jerks that reorient the body, bringing new things into view. Similar kinds of movements are seen during the restless struggle of the artistic moment, as well as, more prosaically, in the leg-bouncing of a student creating a response to a difficult examination.

COMMUNICATOR PHASE

A third level of energy is experienced in the Communicator Phase. At this point the musculature of the digestive system, the inner tube that runs from mouth to anus, activates. The body is stimulated to reach, through sound and/or movement, to make a claim on the environment. A bond is sought through which the nourishment necessary for a further increase in energetic potential can be obtained.

INSPIRER PHASE

At the fourth level of energy the chest expands and raises to increase the amount of oxygen taken in with each breath. The metabolic flame is fanned. Energetic potential, gathered in the Communicator Phase, ignites into actual energy. The result is the heady rise of excitement characteristic of the Phase of the Inspirer. It can be seen in the deep breathing politician rousing the crowd and felt in the words of the preacher lifting the spirit.

SOLIDIFIER PHASE

An ability to contain this new level of excitement develops during the next phase, the Solidifier Phase. Overt movement slows as energy is used to contract, tighten, firm and build muscle. Through this isometric-like exercise, the body develops a storehouse of energy. Muscle walls grow thicker. They hold against, dampen down and prevent impulsive release. They enhance the development of a steady dependable energy expenditure. The Solidifier Phase is seen in the strong muscular body of the laborer.

ACHIEVER PHASE

A gradual working free of bodily holdings in the Solidifier period ushers in the Achiever Phase of the Rhythmic Cycle. Muscular contraction is now matched by muscular extension. A stylish expressive display of contraction and extension activates, excites and plays through the whole body.

The result of such physical play is an increase in expressive power throughout the organism, an increase matched by a capacity for ease, grace and flow in movement. The beauty that flowers in this phase is displayed in the presence of the accomplished, the stance of the leader, the glow of the star.

As the Achiever Phase moves toward completion, contraction and extension rhythmically pump the body towards its limit. Excitement increases to the peak of endurance. When one or another area of the body floods with energy, a threshold of control is passed. In an instant of instability, a climactic reflexive release occurs pouring out hormones and fluids that change the body's chemical balance.

From this point of spilling over, the charged energetic level of the Rhythmic Cycle weakens and subsides. The body returns to the place of quiet from which energy again renews its climb. A new Rhythmic Cycle begins.

CHARACTER PHASES, BOUNDARIES
AND THE RHYTHMIC CYCLE

Energy progression, buildup and release, is rarely smooth and even. A continuing impediment to its coursing causes an individual to express himself again and again in a similar way. Because we all have such impediments, we come to associate any given person with one or another specific phase of the Rhythmic Cycle. Its qualities define their character. We recognize the way they function by their particular character style. For example:

Dreamers take us aback by their uncanny reflections on life's deeper meaning. **Creators** constantly come out with new and original points of view. The **Communicator's** verbal fluidity has an appeal that motivates us toward giving.

Inspirers inflame our hopes, lift us onto paths of new possibility. **Solidifiers** are there, dependable bulwarks in difficult times. **Achievers** model. Their stance and action make life feel graceful and pleasurable.

In ancient Greece the word "character" designated a marker or boundary sign used to divide the land to control its development and function. (Leonard, 1966) For humans the word character has a related meaning. We too are subjected to the placement of boundaries that shape the way areas, in this case, areas of our body, develop to mark out our functioning. These marks determine which phase or phases of the Rhythmic Cycle become characteristic for us as individuals.

Two types of boundaries can form in a person's body to break or divide energetic flow. A held area, caused by tight muscles, dams energy movement. A flaccid area, where the musculature lacks tone, dissipates it. Each impedes energy flow through the rest of the body and highlights the dynamics of its physical location in the total pattern of functioning.

Character boundaries most often develop when physiological systems are first patterned into behavior. At these times, whether early in life or at the onset of a new learning, the body is particularly vulnerable to experiences that disrupt harmony and control. The boundary formation that ensues is the body's natural attempt to reestablish energetic integrity.

In the moment of formation boundaries limit the effects of trauma from moving through the entire organism. Later, however, they repeatedly alter the flow of successive Rhythmic Cycles distorting the progression of energy off its simplest and most natural course. This can lead to numerous types of outcomes exemplified in everyday events.

In one outcome, a body area relevant to a particular activity (in the following description, the long inner tube of the Communicator Phase) can be so central that an entire Rhythmic Cycle develops around its function. For example:

> A good discussion (a motif from the Communicator Phase) can move from the stimulating excitement of a number of ideas (Inspirer Phase), to the meaty development of one or two facets (Solidifier Phase), to a telling point that brings the conversation to a conclusion (Achiever Phase). With the end comes a release of energy and a fall to silence. There is no more to be said.

Here the Rhythmic Cycle moves to completion in one phase, the Communicator Phase. The boundary around this area was not so unyielding as to block energetic buildup and flow throughout the individuals invbolved. The end-point results in good feelings, feelings that reinforce the positive use of the phase employed. This kind of pleasurable experience motivates repetition. Through it individuals gain skill in the employment of the phase, expertise that can be used positively in other situations.

More powerful disruptions to energy flow, however, prove less beneficial. For example, the phase where a barrier is located can be maintained so long that it arrests both passage and release.

> Richard, an Inspirer, was asked to give road directions to a faraway city. He began telling the twists and turns of a familiar routing. Then he suggested another way that might be shorter. Growing more excited he added a possibility that had

scenic advantages. In the midst of giving a fourth set of directions, one that passed an excellent restaurant, the confused and impatient questioner threw up her hands and shouted furiously:

"Never mind!" At this rate I'll never get anywhere!"

In the rush of ideas Richard never passed the Inspirer Phase. The problem of how to get to the city was not worked out. Nothing solid was ever established and so Richard's eager help, became a source of upset and the contact ended unpleasantly.

Another disruptive possibility occurs when so much energy is spent in one phase that little is left for advancement.

Edith labored hard through an extended Solidifier Phase. Hours were spent tightening the nuts and bolts of a report. Tired, but finished at last, she took the opportunity before a meeting, to casually drop her work on a table in front of where her manager would sit rather than to take the trouble to give it to him personally.

When her manager arrived he noticed the report, leafed through its first pages and placed it in his briefcase. The meeting proceeded without a nod or a mention from him.

Later, Edith had a feeling of being unappreciated. The Achiever Phase of the Rhythmic Cycle had passed without allowing for any reward or pleasure in her accomplishment. Edith was left feeling bitter, wondering if her efforts were worth it.

The weak way Edith moved through the Achievement Phase of the Rhythmic Cycle caused her to miss a real meeting and clear conclusion with her manager. The results were feelings of disappointment and a lack of meaning.

Yet another way the Rhythmic Cycle can be disrupted is through dissipation. The leaking away of energy lowers excitement until there is a regression to an earlier phase.

As had become typical, John was fantasizing about making love to Mary. (Dream Phase) This time he decided to do something different, to move to make his dream real. (Creative Phase) Filled with trepidation, he talked to Mary to arrange a dinner, an evening at home. (Communicator Phase)

Mary arrived. Dinner came and went but John could go no further. He hemmed and hawed uncertainly, trying to suppress the panicky discomfort of an unfamiliar rapidly growing excitement. (Inspiration Phase) As he did so, he felt his energy frittering away and sensed himself growing weaker.

By the time Mary left, John felt empty and helpless. Soon he was back to fantasy, far from the discomfort of the reality he had been through. (Dream Phase)

John's return to an earlier state brought momentary comfort, but with it came a vague sense of impotence, feelings of failure and the frustration that occurs with an inability to mature.

THERAPY AND THE RHYTHMIC CYCLE

Psychopathology occurs when we don't move beyond or are continually drawn back to a particular position, the phase that marks our character. The familiarity, the homelike feeling of this place gives a sense of safety and control but a price is paid for it. Drives remain frustrated and unfulfilled. Functioning becomes distorted.

Pain occurs when life's difficulties divert the Rhythmic Cycle too far from its natural course. When stress bends us too far or too long out of shape, the integrity of our life-flow breaks down. When balance is lost, being may be injured.

The Rhythmic Cycle comes into play in all therapeutic approaches. Any successful change results in more integrated and harmonious energy flow. It shows in improvements in aliveness, feeling and functioning.

Psychotherapy works to free an individual's energy so that it can move to fulfill basic drives. It attempts to relieve the difficulties that a period or a life style of errant functioning causes. In its more ambitious forms it aims to permanently alter a disturbed pattern of energy flow, returning it to a smoother, more natural course.

Though each phase of the Rhythmic Cycle has its positive aspect, it can also clearly give rise to its own form of pathological distortion. Each phase is marked by its poles:

> In the **Dream Phase** of the Rhythmic Cycle, sensory illusions, visions, voices, and fantasies give clues to our body's drives and provide a magical, even sacred, power to our motivations. If the phase is maintained too long however, the conscious border between dream and reality begins to disappear. What is real becomes contaminated by what is imagined. The meaning of the outer world fades away.

> In the Rhythmic Cycle's **Creative Phase**, quick energetic bursts of movement repattern orientation providing new outlooks and choices. But too constant a bombardment of choices makes advance impossible, and a "no exit" situation occurs.

The result is nervous agitation, non-participation with the world and feelings of alienation.

In the **Communicator Phase** there is a request for what is needed. However, if the need is denied, or what satisfies isn't taken in, development withers. The organism weakens. Low-grade depression ensues.

The physical uplift of the **Inspirer Phase** brings the enthusiasm and promise of great hopes, but grand heights without boundaries result in mania. When the balloon bursts, its rapid fall brings despair.

In the **Solidifier Phase** movement slows, steadies, and becomes purposeful, anchoring one against the capriciousness of life. If the holding is maintained too long, though, it becomes an oppressive burden. Immobility and stagnation cause feelings of misery and long-suffering.

The **Achiever Phase** brings the prize of status and success. If these become their own ends, an endless effort to defend and advance the favored position develops. Humanity, even life itself, can be sacrificed to purposes far out of touch with basic living processes. Personal pleasure is lost. Bitterness ensues.

Knowledge of the Rhythmic Cycle offers a number of benefits that can aid in the process of therapeutic change. It can help point out and delineate the underlying issues of a problem phase, indicating timing and techniques of ameliorative intervention. Equally significant, it gives an appreciation about when things should best be left alone. It points to the signposts that demonstrate whether healthy or unhealthy changes are occurring.

THE RHYTHMIC CYCLE OF CHANGE

There is a therapeutic part in each of us that attempts to reestablish full functioning when it is known to be lost. This is an outgrowth of the curative powers built into our being. A conscious knowledge of the difficulties caused by tension and dissipation strengthens our awareness when things are amiss. Familiarity with how energy development can be thwarted along the various way-stations of the Rhythmic Cycle aids our capacity to help ourselves at troublesome points.

AMERICA AND THE RHYTHMIC CYCLE

The changes that take place along the Rhythmic Cycle affect not only the individual but also the collective human endeavor. Societies and cultures follow the path. Arnold Toynbee used a phase analysis similar to the Rhythmic Cycle to organize his understanding of history. The recent American political progression provides a clear example of a course of the Rhythmic Cycle, one easily recalled by those who lived through it.

It was against the background of silence, the quiet sameness of the Eisenhower years in the late 50's, that the **Dreams** and visions of John F. Kennedy and Dr. Martin Luther King Jr. were forming. Through the energy of their vision the quiet was broken. The country was shocked into awakeness by a new mood of **Creative** change. Wild drug trips as well as polarizing rebellions by the disenfranchised, struggling against the status quo to make their existence known, marked the birth pangs of a new Cycle of Change.

Dialogue ensued. The Hippie Flower Child sang about a life style of innocent love. Angry protesters raged against the nation's injustice with screams for a better, fairer, and stronger America. Societies' weak and undernourished made their needs known. The poor found their voice and the way to Washington. "**Communicate**" became the the pop-word of the day.

Lyndon Johnson **Inspired** the nation's hopes. He forwarded grand designs for a "Great Society." Model Cities and Head Start handed out funds to give a leg up along the path. Patterns of politics, education, sex, prejudice, religion and so forth were looked at with an eye to making possible "The Impossible Dream." Excitement reached riotous proportions.

With Nixon the nation quieted. The Silent Majority took over. Containment bounded enthusiasm. Pie-in-the-sky disappeared. The extensiveness of the feeling of change lessened. The Vietnam War was worked to a quiet, almost nondescript end. Diplomacy forged a new relationship with China.

Watergate shame put the finishing touches on expressions of excess and ebullience. What had been accomplished, **Solidified** into the bedrock of American society, under the plodding bulwark style of Gerald Ford.

In the mid-70's, Jimmy Carter offered a new level of excitement. With his genteel Southern style, he promised personal grace and honesty, a soothing return to dignity. A political unknown, he came from nowhere to **Achieve** the Presidency.

Carter's gentle soft way helped him personally win an Israeli-Egyptian settlement. The achievement was rewarded with a Nobel Prize but was not enough to sustain the public's confidence against the hard challenge of an Iranian fanatic who held the Nation hostage.

During the week of the 1982 election it was announced that the American captives would be released. The seemingly endless days of waiting had brought success for Carter's policy of patience.

There was little pleasure though, in this achievement. Rather it stimulated a powerfully negative emotional reaction against Carter who was blamed for the return to another period of national shame and humiliation, a momentary return to the Solidifier Phase.

The voters equated the long wait for the hostage release with Carter's personal weakness. They, along with their President, had again found themselves bogged down. Feelings of impotence were assuaged at the ballot box. In the sudden massive turnaround of voter opinion that followed the announcement that the hostages would be released, Reagan beat Carter by a landslide.

Reagan, like Carter, was a graceful **Achiever** but the soft approach was now replaced by a hard-driving one. Emphasis on an easy going, warm, feminine-like receptivity was supplanted by emphasis on the power of muscular assertion. Aggression, strength, and driving competition were heralded as the supreme values.

Reagan capitalized on the moment of his victory. Rather than acknowledge the emotions that caused it, he claimed it as confirmation for what had been until then, his very unpopular conservative views. Seizing the advantage, in a way acting very unconservatively, his sword struck swiftly.

In a period of rapid legislative activity, Reagan's forces strove to emasculate the social programs of the past 50 years. The poor, old and weak faced the loss of previous gains. Jobs and farms were lost. Attitudes hardened.

A new psychology emerged. A combative style pushed for bigger bombs and looked for adversaries to attack, for new victories to be won, new conquests to reward the expression of the hard-driving, assertive masculine component of the Achievement Character. Many people began to feel both tougher and better.

The drive grew to frightening proportions. With bomb fears, military maneuvering and talk of Armageddon, the future moved toward an inevitable time of climax, the end of this period's Rhythmic Cycle.

A Democratic congressional victory, revelation about Irangate, the promise of a Nicaraguan peace treaty, a stock market spasm - the unchecked drive of the Achiever Phase was over. In a little more than a generation, from the nation's youngest President to the nation's oldest, the country came full cycle.

The 1988 Presidential Primaries, as the Rhythmic Cycle would predict, brought in its wake the signs of a new period of silence, a time, like the Eisenhower years before, when the backdrop occurs for a new Cycle of Change.

Mike Dukakis and George Bush, sharing the non-excitement of their personalities, appeared to settle into their selection as their party's candidates in party races that quietly and anti-climactically seemed to end long before the finish line. One called a milque toast, the other called dull, each appeared to bring with him a return to the silence of the gap, the time even before dreams.

SUMMARY

We have seen that the Rhythmic Cycle is part of us. Built into our physiology, it permeates all of our lives. Its structure underlies what we perceive and do. A phrase like "History repeats itself," refers to the underlying continual cycling of the flux and flow of events. Experiences of mistiming, "A good idea expressed too soon" or "having had its day," can serve to make us wiser as to when and where things are appropriate and connected.

Recent popular writings in psychology have emphasized the fact that events follow a process, a movement through a progression of phases. "The Mid-Life Crisis" emphasizes how our life-span moves in systematic stages. The resolution of grief, we are told, courses along a regular sequence. Knowing this helps in self-understanding and acceptance of it attunes us to signal points for the development of new psychological growth as we encounter the differing demands of differing life periods.

But the Rhythmic Cycle is more omnipresent than the process of a feeling or a life stage. It continually lives within and through us. It is the process of the changing levels of excitement as it climbs, from what seems like nothing, to its highest peak and back again to the silence of beginning.

The Rhythmic Cycle of Change

As energy flows through each of these levels, new body parts bring new psychological and social attributes into play. Graphically, one might picture it as a giant wave of strength building upon itself. (See Fig. 1) From out of the silence of the energy gap, six steps can be delineated along the way. They mark the phases of The Dreamer, The Creator, The Communicator, The Inspirer, The Solidifier, and The Achiever.

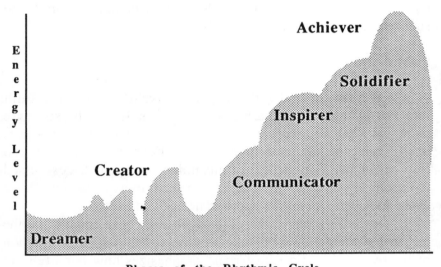

Phases of the Rhythmic Cycle
Fig.1 Relationship of rhythmic cycle to physical energy level.

Readers will find their own pattern of the Rhythmic Cycle accompanying them as they move through this work. The organization and style of the writing carries the phases into focus. Paying attention, caring about and working with your reactions along the way can prove useful in the enlargement of self-knowledge and can stimulate personal growth in relation to the everpresent process of change.

The journey begins in a different mood from where this introductory chapter has been. The world of dreams emerges from another place. Time slows down, moves more quietly, expands into eternities. Space fills the boundaries between moments, providing the infinite vacuum, the silent backdrop of the reveries through which the changing forms of the hidden become conscious.

Dreamer

He came and I saw,
I saw him see
and it reflected me.

THE MOOD

There are pools within us - watery pools that are the birth of our stuff. We are born out of the watery sac and are permeated with water throughout our lives. Waterless, dried out, we would shrink to only a fraction of our weight. Watery liquid fills out our substance.

Our dreams reflect the liquid movements of our body. If a drop of water falls on a dreaming person's skin it will make its way into his fantasies, perhaps as rain, perhaps as a waterfall. In some symbolic way the experience will appear in consciousness.

Dreams are like an intangible liquid flowing through consciousness, at times moving us deeply. Filling out the story of our character, dreams can be complete analogues for our life's dynamics in any given moment. (Robbins & Robbins, 1980) From them we can learn who we are as well as what we must do to maximize ourselves. A dream enacted leads to our most powerful expressions; a dream come true leads to our most golden moments.

Dream processes produce symbols, metaphors and memories. Mystical moments as well as everyday reflections and fantasies result from them. They are responsible for our sense of mystery and our appreciation of life's poetry. They are the source of our vision and spur us to move toward remote, even unbelievable, ends.

The Dream State comes to us spontaneously but it can also be induced. In therapy, a quiet relaxed state can stimulate free association and fantasy production or in hypnosis, the individual is moved into a deep state of quiet, from whence memories and images can be stirred. With drugs, the body's physiology is artificially altered, allowing an easing of the ego's vigilance and the rolling through of fantastic imagery.

On mystical paths the Dream State is induced by demands for asceticism - fasting, intense concentration, sleeplessness and compulsive exercise. Each of these is capable of leading to the state of physical exhaustion and muscular collapse in which the waking Dream State occurs. The body's message then cries out to consciousness for a response.

The Dream's symbols, conscious images stimulated by the body's inner movements, seem to come from the darkest and most hidden aspects of existence. They are often attributed to the forces of other worlds in operation - the gods, the demons, past lives, unknown realities. When heeded, they can be interpreted as signs and portents of things unknown to the outwardly observing eye.

The force behind the clearest of these messages can have an intensity that provides passionate impetus. Some who have only briefly felt such moments have given their lives to the experience, dedicating their being to them. They have used their visions as a point of reference to guide their choices and behavior.

Powerful dreams have the force to affect the lives of others. Masses have been moved by them. Generations have followed their rallying cry, hallowing their motivating and organizing power with religious sanctity. Society's great principles come from these origins.

The Dream Quality is the force underlying all faiths, the mystical underpinning giving the unconscious truth to the core of their expression. A dream's truth, emanating from the common structure of the body, echoes a universal meaning that we can all understand because all share the potential for its physical dynamic.

Beauty also emerges from the Dreamer within - poems, rituals, stories, myths, edifices, even many institutions give testament to deeply internal events. They are actualizations of the Dream State giving expression to movements close to our core. Their production requires the use of other aspects of our personality, aspects that originate further along on the Rhythmic Cycle. Once formed they can carry us back to the magical beauty of our dreams, reminding us of deeper values.

But the Dream State can also become captured by its products. Rigid attachment to the symbol on which the truth rides into awareness can and does cause great human difficulty. The unconscious truth from which a dream develops is a shifting sand. Growing out of the moment it is best dealt with in the moment.

Too tight an allegiance to a symbol in fact stops the free flowing process, the dream work around it. The symbol gradually becomes removed from its source in our nature and is reworked into a rallying cry for position. The protective structures built around the symbols of our dreams gradually encase them. They become heavy, outdated and lifeless, no longer in touch with the vital core of their origin. Attempts to revivify them often lead to zealous distortions tinged with inhuman madness. Their living connection with the inner source is lost.

The Rhythmic Cycle of Change

Dream symbols, once they become rigidified, don't pass away easily. Incursions into the power structure with which they become intertwined are warded off. New possibilities, new dreams and new expressions that might be more timely, more relevant as replacements, are fought against. We then hang on to dreams that have lost their meaning, living lives directed by old fantasies appropriate in our past but not attuned to our needs of the moment. When such dreams finally reach fruition we find the effort expended to fulfill them leads only to illusion.

The Dream State presents other dangers besides those that occur from too rigid allegiance to symbols. There are nightmares.

The hellish forces of our body's binding blocks can stop powerful dream-creating urges from moving to release. The dream is left incomplete when emotional tumult arouses the sleeper. Incomplete emotion can be destructively acted out in waking life in an attempt to purge the disturbed drive. Dreams can then become surrounded by evil interpretations with all the power of black magic.

Hitler provides an example. (van der Post, 1975) In a rain-soaked trench during the First World War he dreamt he was being engulfed in muck and mud, in danger of being pulled down into an obscene death. The dream's terror broke him from sleep. Fighting feelings of suffocation, he stumbled out and away from the filthy pit. As he did, a shell landed, killing those he left behind.

Hitler's response to the death around him was not a feeling of tragedy but rather of exhilarating expansion. This, he thought, was a personal salvation. Magic moved his mind. He linked his escape from real death to the muddy engulfing symbols of his dream. Together he saw them as a providential sign. He was saved to save Germany, raise it out of the glut and filth of commonness.

Dream symbols relate to the body's dynamics and reveal attitudes toward them. Hitler's driving illusion can be seen as growing from his ambivalence toward what he considered the gross within himself - the "dirty," the "ugly," the "foul," the waste that his own body created. Hitler was obsessed with commonness and filth. At one level he rejected it while on another level he was attracted to it. He dwelt on the color brown. His troops were "brownshirts," his headquarters the "brownhouse," his mistress Eva Braun (Braun' translates'Brown').

Conflicted about his own functions, Hitler, it could be said, dramatically attempted to rise above his own feces as he had risen out of the muddy stench of the trenches. In the process he pulled his country after him. The result was futile. It led, ironically, to the laying waste of those he involved. The actions that grew from his interrupted dream led to his own destruction in the dream's terms. Hitler died amidst the rubble.

Because of the dangers the Dream State presents many mystical methods that rely on awake observation of illusionary processes forbid their path to the young.

Yoga traditions often demand reaching the age of forty, after having successfully worked and raised a family, before beginning the mystical quest. Jews, under thirty, are warned not to spend too much time on the symbolic Biblical story, Ezekiel. Primitive tribes reveal their life secrets slowly, with only the elders having the sum of available knowledge.

A Jewish mystical warning places the difficulties in perspective:

> Four reached Paradise - one died, one went
> insane, one led others astray, and only one, Rabbi
> Akiva -- the great and holy master, was able to enter
> and return unharmed. (Scholem, 1974)

Only the whole and complete can safely give up their ties to reality, dip into the source of their unconscious core and return sanely enriched, able to meaningfully share the wealth they have found.

The Rhythmic Cycle of Change

The Traditions teach that with age and the completion of life's more energetically focused tasks, the time for mystical pursuits gradually emerges. The body then naturally lets down, softens and becomes open to the internal freeing required for easy aware passage to and from the Dream State. The mystical encounter becomes safer, more natural.

The mystical path grows out of the Dream State but differs from the way to madness in that the course is <u>deliberately</u> chosen. It does not spontaneously emerge as a result of stimulation by daily events. It comes rather from conscious desire and effort to contact and merge with the spiritual images themselves, and to know from them the core energies that move us. Success in such a striving requires entering into the dynamics that underlie the character of the Dreamer.

CHARACTER OF THE DREAMER

The Dream State marks the psychological beginning of the Rhythmic Cycle. The first conscious phase, it is the source of magical worlds, of symbols, illusions and metaphors. Tied closely to the senses, it produces visions and voices, sensations and intuitions that seem to come from faraway paranormal places. Though we all regularly move through these places, the Dreamer's energy dynamics often settle in the Dream State. Dreams fill their consciousnesses. They are comfortable with them.

With its sensory involvement, the Dream State relates to the earliest modes of individual life. It provides a protective cocoon. Rich in itself, it tends to keep the individual from direct assertion to meet needs. Through it, another world, an inner world develops. Within its symbols, urges and tensions are expressed and dissipated.

The Dream State becomes highly developed under conditions that don't allow for motor outlet. An asleep person dreams. An uninvolved student fantasizes. A lonely child is absorbed in a world of pretend. For each, excitement and release are handled internally, seemingly uninfluenced by contemporary outside events.

Often a person who becomes a Dreamer has learned to experience motor assertion as dangerous. Danger may be reacted to by either fight, flight or freeze. When all these possibilities are associated with the expectation of overwhelming disaster, movement through the world may come to a standstill. The situation has been called one of double-bind. In truth it is one of triple-bind: can't move forward, can't move backward, can't stand still. At this point, tension and conflict can only be resolved by the dissipation of energy. As it is spent, a symbolic but seemingly more livable world is formed.

The life flow of the Dreamer often takes place within this context. It has its definite advantages. A magic that lessens the stress of seemingly unbearable conditions emerges into consciousness. Within it the deepest parts of the organism are easily touched and poetically expressed. Sensitivity to inner and outer vibrations heightens and allows for an intuitive reading of developing trends. There is an experience of totality.

The formative experiences of this sense of totality that characterizes the Dreamer and the Dream State comes before muscular usage can take place. A paradigmatic period occurs prior to birth when the fetus uses the musculature of the mother as its protective shield. During the first months in the womb the unborn is totally united with the emotional upheavals of the mother. There is a full union between them, an experiential oneness.

As mid-pregnancy approaches, movement becomes possible. The new body quivers with life. The eyes move rapidly in ways that will be repeated whenever dreams are viewed. The fetus kicks and flails to relieve tension and discharge energy.

With quickening, the new being bumps into the mother's body and begins to gain experience with the limitations to movement imposed by the boundaries of an outer reality. It is an experience of difference, the end of totality, the start of differentiation. During this period the fetus's only salvation if in difficulty, is to let go, yielding all resistance, returning to the flow of undifferentiated unconsciousness.

We know little directly of these processes. They occur before birth. We lack potent research tools to study such phenomena. We do know that early experiences affect the growing baby. Conditioning of the neonate's movements and responses to outside stimuli have been scientifically demonstrated. Mothers who take drugs are known to pass their addiction on to the fetus, necessitating a period of withdrawal after birth when the drug is no longer available to the infant.

Oxygen deprivation, which may be related to stress reactions in the mother's body, can cause fetal death and abortion. The carrying mother's temperature and body tone can undergo vast changes, the result of unconscious emotions, which affect the developing fetus. To diminish such stresses, folk traditions warn: "Protect the unborn child - avoid evil influences."

The sense of safety that can accompany early intrauterine conditions during more relaxed times is suggested by closely observing Dreamers in stress. In group therapy, when free to assume any physical position, Dreamers often move to a womb-like fetal posture if strong affect is released by others. They describe this position as providing a protected space away from the danger they sense around them.

Deeply disturbed chronic psychotics, Dreamers with little reality connection, are seen in a similar position in the back wards of our mental hospitals. Society unwittingly induces and supports their sleeplike escape by tending to their needs, functioning like an all-giving protective womb rather than engaging them in the creative struggle for survival. Society has overplayed the malingering symbiotic connection, insuring the maintenance of the regressed state and avoiding the more troublesome responsibility of aiding in the struggle toward life.

Many people assume a similar fetal position of inner security in sleep. Even awake people when placed in the fetal position typically let go of breathing tensions, quickly and deeply reestablishing a sense of harmony through a deep, full respiratory rhythm.

The Dreamer's fantasy productions, too, suggest the relationship between their energy dynamics and the womb situation. Enclosures and containers; closets, caves and underground passageways symbolically represent the womb, a place of security and incubation. Entering them can begin a trip into rediscovery and renewal - a contact with basic urges and energy resources. Symbols of water and fluid motion have a prototype in the gentle rocking motion of the fetus in the intrauterine watery sea - the primal substance of our first home.

ENERGY DYNAMICS

The Dreamer's refuge is a lack of tension. It is achieved by dissipating energy, going flaccid, in either all or part of the body. This leads to distorted reality perception, changes the experiencing of danger and incapacitates the ability to respond. The metaphoric counterparts of the senses grow in influence. The outer world is distorted as if looking through water or as reflecting off of a wavy mirror.

The Dreamer's body recreates the fluid softness of the fetus. Areas of the body lacking muscle tone provide the locus of the physical dynamics of their character. Pressing in these places with the hands results in a marked yielding. Even bony structures such as the chest can show such fluid give.

It is easy to understand the Dreamer's sensitivity to external vibration when one feels the softness of these unprotected areas.

The Rhythmic Cycle of Change

The vulnerability of such persons, when even their inner organs are so available to external incursions, is marked. They are without the protection and reality connection that an alive musculature provides. Even subtle stimulation causes ripples through their organism.

Though their thin protective coating gives little physical defense it does allow immediate contact with the "vibes" from within and without. Sensory awareness is high. The organs of touch, taste smell, vision, sound, and kinesthesis send their message to consciousness without competition from motor demands. They are received in a pristine form. They stir the imagination into consciousness.

The magic of the imagination lies in its juxtaposing strange combinations of symbols. (Robbins 1984) Things appear together suggesting a cause and effect while hiding their true relationship. In this way dreams follow the same principle a Magician uses to produce an illusion. The Magician shows the empty hat. Magic words are said. A wave of the wand and "Poof!"- a rabbit appears. The true connection between the empty hat and rabbit's appearance is hidden. The mystery lies in the magic of juxtaposed perceptions.

Dreams work similarly, juxtaposing symbols in kaleidoscopic ways. One appears to cause another. In truth, it is the flow of energy movement through the body that provides the unseen link that weaves together signs that have historically or metaphorically come to be associated with different body areas.

The initial impetus to this inner energy movement comes from biological urges as well as from the vibrations begun by external stimulation. The resulting unitary flow is interfered with by flaccid as well as by tightly contracted places in the body. These blocks give a structure to the organization of the symbols. As a barrier is released or passed, new bodily areas come into play weaving new symbols into the evolving pattern of dream consciousness. (Robbins & Robbins 1980)

The whole process of dream emergence, though seemingly random, follows the rules that pattern the Dream State. The dream's symbols give clue to the areas of the body that are stimulated. The dream's structure reflects the body's pattern of physical holdings. The dream's force tells of the strength of the energetic movement.

The Dream State moves into consciousness when part or all of the outer musculature acquires a weakly shielded putty-like undercharged quality. Though dreams are often experienced as loaded with energy excitement, the amount of energy involved is often less than that required simply to walk. At times of a partially or totally asleep musculature, one unavailable to dampen down the body's small and subtle currents, energy can be powerfully perceived in consciousness in symbolic ways.

THERAPY

The Dreamer is a visionary, a prophet, because he or she has the capacity to see with his or her being in an intuitive way that brings a more immediate kind of information than simple reason can provide. It is the artist's and poet's source, the way of metaphor.

Without influence from the other aspects of the Rhythmic Cycle, however, the dream component can and does drown the individual in fantasy, cutting off the realities of the body, the community and the ongoing rhythms of the larger Nature. They are left afloat in a sea of schizophrenic images.

For the Dreamer, the dream product can easily become an escape from what is necessary. An inability to integrate the symbol into a realistic relation to the larger reality leaves one in great danger.

Dreams can lubricate the psyche to slide over the confrontations necessary for growth. A dream believed can literally replace the view of reality needed for full contact and living. As the Dreamer's feelings are symbolized, they are robbed of the outlet necessary to struggle through the discomfort and pain of the moment to travel the course of the Rhythmic Cycle. Instead there is an unseen compromise, with the price incompletely known and continually being paid. The devil's due is frequently collected when life's pains are dreamily avoided.

Under stress, illusion and delusion offer a valley of clouds, plunged into for respite. At these times the dream may not be used as a vision for strength to move forward in life, but rather may grotesquely exaggerate the destructive power of fear.

> Jean, a Dreamer, came to her therapy session following a visit to the dentist for a chipped tooth. The accident had been repaired by layering on a substance that held fast to the tooth to fill the gap. Jean is terrified that the layers will slowly come loose, carrying with them her existence, leaving her nothing, but she is equally terrified to give vent to her emotion.
>
> Her delusion drives her to pick away at her own skin. She is cut off from outer reality. Verbal reassurance is futile. She fears an annihilation she can't escape. My gently touching her face leads to terrifying screams of release. She is not destroyed. The illusion dissolves in emotional discharge through a human contact with a physical reality beyond her own imagination.

When one is locked within the Dream Phase "what-is" is shrouded in the symbols of "what-is-needed" or "what is feared." The external world is experienced unrealistically. Illusions and delusions develop as a way of dealing with life, as a stimulus to avoid strongly driving on. The mirage distorts clarity, control and direction.

The challenge for the Dreamer is to set this gift within the larger framework of the total, to carry dreams into realistic contact with the outer world, to move them through the Rhythmic Cycle.

THE TIBETAN BUDDHISTS

The Buddhists of Tibet wove the processes of the Dreamer into a rich spiritual culture that reflects their history and geography. The assimilation of Buddhism and local religions indigenous to their land resulted in a unique amalgam that organized an entire society around the Dream State.

Enlightenment or "awakeness" was reached, after a hard search, by the Indian Prince Gautama - the Buddha. It is said that he was raised by wealthy parents in perfect luxury, isolated from the ravages of the greater humanity around him to ensure that he would know only happiness, contentment and pleasure.

As a young man, however, he looked out from the protective walls of the kingdom his parents had established. He had his first experiences with the painful aspects of life.

He saw four things: an old man bent and crippled by time; a sick man devoured and made loathsome by disease; a dead man who had been made lifeless and spiritless by life's universal destiny; and a monk, both serene and blissfully aware.

Gautama was so moved by the tragic plight of his fellow man that he left his previous life to search for the answer to human suffering. His journey brought insight and guidance in the ways to free oneself of earthly woes - the "four noble truths" and the "holy eight-fold path."

Through the principles that Gautama discovered his followers give up the bonds of the senses, move toward, and eventually may even attain the blissful state of Buddhahood - the garden removed from all suffering. (Ballou, no date given)

Buddhist philosophy and method adapted and changed as it meshed with the belief systems of other lands. In Tibet, emphasis on dream aspects led to the flourishing of a unique and full synthesis.

One rarely reads of Tibet without encountering mention of the difficult conditions that the country's nature imposes on its residents. The cruel but beautiful natural environment makes for hard living. The weather can range from 80 degrees above to 40 degrees below zero. Cold winds, violent sudden blizzards and a short growing season have made this rocky, mountain-locked land of little interest to more advanced technological civilizations. It is a land where life battles nature, and death and destruction are always at hand. There is little escape.

To young growing life, the culture itself is said to add difficulties giving harsh tests to ensure that only the strong survive:

"..... I have seen little processions approaching.... a stream... . At its banks the procession will stop, and the grandmother will take the baby... . The baby will be undressed, and grandmother will stoop and immerse the little body in the water, so that only the head and mouth are exposed to the air. In the bitter cold the baby turns red, then blue, and its cries of protest stop. It looks dead, but grandmother has much experience of such things, and the little one is lifted from the water, dried, and dressed. If the baby survives, then it is as the Gods decree. If it dies, then it has been spared much suffering on earth." Rampa, 1964)

The difficult life makes the promise of release from suffering highly appealing. Tantric Buddhism, centering around the dream process and promising respite for its followers, flourished and developed for centuries undisturbed by outside influences. The entire culture, headed by a theocracy, was organized around the practice of its principles.

Tantra uses rites and rituals that are centered around the senses and the Dream Phase of the Rhythmic Cycle to demonstrate the illusory quality of consciousness. Visualization, for example, employs:

"... forces familiar to man only at the deeper levels of consciousness, which, ordinarily, people rarely become aware of except in dreams." (Blofeld, 1970)

In visualization the Tantric practitioner learns to consciously call up and experience a dream-like state at will. He begins by learning to focus his attention fully and completely at one point. He may choose to stare at a picture picked because its content is filled with psychological themes that are important for him. He memorizes it in every detail until it can be exactly reconstructed in his mind's eye whenever he wills.

This mastered image becomes meaningful as it relates to and is made vivid by the practitioner's emotions and thoughts. The image of the picture moves the flow of energy in his body. He merges with it and feels the power it stirs. It is as if his own internally directed movie is stimulated. Eventually, as with all good films, catharsis drains away the emotions that have been aroused.

The Rhythmic Cycle of Change

The mental image shrinks to nothing, leaving a silence, a state of void that in this case may last hours or even days.

The reader might experience the initial phases of this dream-like process by the following exercise:

> Close the eyes and spend several minutes focusing on letting go of all muscular tension. Start with the feet and then work through the other body parts, gently directing them to relax and let go. Notice the breathing deepen as the energetic pattern of the tension free dream-like state is approached.
>
> This completed, picture an animal. Let it come into the mind's eye, the "third eye". Pay attention to its color, shape and other physical characteristics and then watch to see what happens.

This exercise, in a rudimentary way, shows the underlying psychic dynamic of the visualization process. Once the Tantric practitioner has become proficient at this process, he uses it for further development. The image is employed to transmute feelings from negative to positive, and he will call upon his fantasy to protect and help him deal with troublesome moments, intentionally avoiding the present by focusing instead on the image.

With time, typically after many years, the practitioner will realize (REAL-ize, real - eyes), with a sense of truth, the transparency and transitoriness of all thoughts, images and feelings. He can then give up ego aspects that foolishly hang on to thoughts and forms as certainties and absolutes. He enters into the state of "awakeness" experiencing the totality of energy that underlies the earliest bodily states.

This experience is an energetic one, a realization through the senses, an immediate knowing of the core of being and of the unity of the "All" through its common energetic base. To know this, by living it, is to be enlightened, to be humble, to be at one. To be able to move easily into this state, to live there almost at will is to be an enlightened master, a master of the Dreamer elements, a master of one phase of the Rhythmic Cycle.

This discussion of Tantra is greatly simplified. In actual practice all senses, not just visual, are worked with in similar ways. This Eastern path has its counterparts in the West. All spiritual forms originate in the Dreamer Phase of the Rhythmic Cycle. Spirits are imagined contents. No matter how concretely we choose to believe in them they remain images in our mind, an outgrowth of the symbolizing process of the Dream State.

The Dream Phase of the Rhythmic Cycle provides a necessary and important contribution to our living. To spontaneously fall into this state and be unable to escape it, however, tears away our contact with reality. Our everyday view is overwhelmed. Elements in our being break out of synchronization with the rest of our personality and our world. Sensations and images can't be expressed in an integrated way. Chaos ensues.

If broken harmony and balance are to be reestablished it is necessary for the Dreamer experience to be lived out, born from our private being, shared with the world around us. Black Elk, the Oglala Sioux Indian is told:

> "Nephew, I know now what the trouble is! You must do what the bay horse in your vision wanted you to do. You must do your duty and perform this vision for your people upon earth. You must have the horse dance first for the people to see. Then the fear will leave you; but if you do not do this, something very bad will happen to you." (Neihardt, 1972)

The Rhythmic Cycle of Change

The dream, when born into the outer world and worked through, has both a curative healing power as well as a power to guide one in a life direction. Modern man tends to rely on his logical thinking, his ego or status position to give him a direction and a sense of choice regarding which way to focus his energy discharge. The commitment to a dream, with its contact with the deeper passions of life, is a more powerful, if less rational, mobilizer. Those who follow their dreams are more individualistic and less influenced by the molding effects of social reinforcers. They march to their own drummer.

CARL JUNG - THE DREAMER

A student asked his Rabbi, "Where is God?. Why doesn't He show Himself?"

The Rabbi answered, "God comes closer to mankind in some periods of time, and retreats from him in others. It depends on the readiness of man." (Bekritsky 1979)

God's appearance depends on man's readiness - readiness to perceive the world through magic eyes, eyes that resonate with the vibration of life's experience, eyes that see visions and miracles, eyes that suspend judgment and reason long enough to intuit the moment of immediacy. From this moment, this personal, autistic moment, God becomes known.

In the early 1960's, God's face and the experience of magic were far from the popular consciousness. Reason ruled the study of man. Psychology was the study of the order and control of behavior. Myths and meaning were irrelevant. What could not be measured was often believed to be non-existent. The irrational, the ground of dream and symbol, was discarded from the study of man. The work of Carl Jung, the Dreamer, wasn't required reading in the study of Man's personality. God was pronounced dead. Jung was in eclipse.

The mid-'60's brought turmoil to the American way of life. The power center of the civilized world underwent a split, and the core purposes that held it together fragmented into pieces. It started with the Black Revolution; a reasonable revolution guided by Martin Luther King, a peaceful revolution that hoped to modify injustice without escalating rage to destructive levels.

With the Vietnam War, the passions of the country could no longer be kept non-violent. The divisions in the country over the war destroyed a coherent purpose in America. The American myth that combined power with righteousness was shaken.

Mind-expanding drugs gave impetus to a counter-society. The Hippie Dreamers spoke of love and peace on the eve when all hell broke loose in America's institutions. A new search for meaning, for relevance, was begun. Religion revived. Science lost its place of power and Carl Jung reappeared in bookstores and college courses.

Carl Jung was a Dreamer and a magic man. He reworked the experiences and emotions of the moment into complex symbolic dream elements that he then used as the authoritative guide to his life. He consulted his night dreams for direction, and their meaning ruled his daylight decisions.

In his unusual autobiography, <u>Memories, Dreams and Reflections</u> (Jung, 1961), Jung ignored daily events - his family, his reality struggles, his successes and failures - in favor of those things that had symbolic meaning to him, those things that touched his imagination.

"Fate will have it - and this has always been the case with me - that all the `outer' aspects of my life should be accidental. Only what is interior has proved to have substance and a determining value. As a result, all memory of outer events has faded, and perhaps these 'outer' experiences were never so very essential anyhow, or were so only in that they coincided with phases of my inner development." (Jung, 1961)

"Coincided," in this context perhaps a strange term, one that denies interaction, denies cause and effect, denies unity. We must draw on our own experience of the Dream Phase if we are to understand the use of this word.

The Dream Phase denies an awareness of causality by its sense of immediacy and its seemingly random associations. Filling our consciousness, it gives no hint of material cause. It distorts time, place and logic with its nonsensical way of symbolizing. It seems unlimited by either the rules of common sense or those of the physical world.

In fantasy; images and illusions - memories and metaphors, are replete with magical associations derived from the subjectively experienced state of the organism. At least temporarily the objectively known cause and effect way of looking at reality is obviated.

In the matter of attention, Jung was quite clear about where he directed his focus - inward toward the dream source, toward the symbolic. At times he so withdrew from outer life that interaction was almost nil. The divorce between inner and outer realities, between spirit and material, could appear so great to him that he suggested they were two different systems, rolling along in "synchronicity," propelled together by some "other" force.

Reference to the "other" force provided an aura of authority to Jung's images. Events showed they were not without prophetic power. He dreamed of a world war years before it took place and after a brief trip to the United States in the 20's predicted the eventual rise of radical feminism in America. (Stern, 1976)

Jung's life though, as explicated in his own autobiography, is too logical, too understandable, for the observer to take synchronicity as the full truth. Life events clearly interacted with his physical personhood to mold his character and develop his imaginative capacities as a Dreamer while still allowing the vital connection to reality necessary to turn what was sometimes a degenerative defensive posture into the source of a positive productive way of life.

Jung, the Dreamer, has been called the Prophet of the Age of Aquarius, Aquarius the Water Carrier. Like most Dreamers, water seemed to draw Jung's being in a primal way. From his earliest years he recalls:

> "The lake stretched away and away into the distance. The expanse of water was an inconceivable pleasure to me, an incomparable splendor. At that time, the idea became fixed in my mind that I must live near a lake. Without water, I thought, nobody could live at all." (Jung, 1961)

Jung lived near water all his adult life, building unique circular womb-like homes on the shores of liquid bodies. He lived out the Dreamer's tie to water in his home and in his work. Eventually it came to characterize his reputation, "Prophet of the Age of Aquarius." He drew his meaning from the deepest sources, the wellspring of his being.

The first watery environment is intrauterine. The character of the Dreamer can be formed at this point by strong disturbing interactions during the period of pregnancy. These interactions are based on the physiological tensions in the hosting environment. Held and/or disturbed emotions have a strong effect on the developing process. They alter circulation, warmth and oxygen supply, and have long been believed to be the genesis of the schizophrenic processes, the pathology to which the Dreamer may fall victim.

Was Jung's mother so disturbing? His autobiography gives some clues about this unusual woman whose behaviors did indeed stimulate disturbing fantasies in him.

> "At night her "strange and mysterious" wanderings resulted in terrifying visions of her head repeatedly floating off her body."(Jung, 1961)

Other times her perceptions were uncanny but carried a force that was:

> "... archaic and ruthless; ruthless as truth and nature." (Jung, 1961)

Jung saw her, as he saw himself, as having two sides. A banal, conventional everyday personality and a strange personality close to the sources of existence from which came bald ringing realities that would stun him into trembling silence.

As an adult, Jung said this capacity to express stark truth came from the "Natural Mind." It "...wells up from the earth like a natural spring, and brings with it the peculiar wisdom of nature." (Jung, 1961) Those who possess it can strip away the defenses and the ego protection of others, baring the deepest core of their personality.

Therapists find this kind of raw, uncanny wisdom in schizophrenic personalities. Their strange and powerful intuitions are not tempered by exigencies of the external moment, not contained by the normal barriers of the body's musculature. They appear unbidden, often intensely, affecting others with little realization of the consequences.they cause.

The results of such activity on a vulnerable child's developing ego can be disastrous. Faced with the awfulness of adult truths, beyond the capacity to defend, unable to escape, the child develops a knowledge far beyond their years. This wisdom cuts them off from their peers and blocks contact with the playful simplicity of the "child's world." This world, still seen and known, is no longer easily entered. The child so affected is thereby aged.

Such was the early life of Carl Jung. His mother was reputed by the community to be mad, perhaps a "witch." (Private Comm., 1975) She shared her difficulties with her son, binding him close to her by "telling <me> everything she could not say to my father." (Jung, 1961) As a result, Jung developed an affinity for being "outside time." (Jung, 1961)

This affinity drew him toward certain experiences. Visions of ancient times and existences, stimulated by museum trips and the world of books, were woven into his consciousness. (Jung, 1961) From these experiences and the mood with which he entered them grew his later fascination with reincarnation, myth and mysticism.

Jung spent many childhood hours by himself. He had no friends. He played alone, in his own space, his own world, out of the purview of watchful eyes and negative intrusions.

His sensitivity brought a deep empathic immersion into what he saw, a resonating contact in which he swam into his experiences, fused and became one with them - in a "participation mystique," a union that recapitulated the dynamics of the womb and brought feelings of its tidal movements.

Immersion deepens oneness. It allows learnings and growth possibilities to come quickly, almost effortlessly. By vibrating in tune with outer movements, experience is brought through the pores into contact with our core organs. For Jung, experiences moved in so deeply they could be said to move his blood, to have illumined his very bone marrow. From there, they would slowly work their way out providing the content of his fantasies, dreams and images - "the flowerings of his rhizome." (Jung, 1961)

Immersion and fusion have life-affirming as well as life-destroying potential. They allow us to flow with rhythms other than our own, to participate in music, to be moved by film or theater, to be at one with nature, to merge in love, to get lost in a crowd. We can enrich and renew ourselves in these moments - moments that allow expansion by absorption.

However, if the rhythm we attach to is too foreign to our system, or too intense in amplitude or duration for our bodies to tolerate, we must defend ourselves to maintain our integrity, to protect the cohesiveness of our being from annihilation.

Deep absorption is a potentially annihilating process. What is absorbed can overwhelm the life processes of the organism. The individual, too long in such a state, may go mad, destroying the more prosaic learnings that protect against stress and allow contact with practical realities - realities that must be accounted to if a life is to survive. Early on, Jung showed the potential to ignore these realities:

> "I was crossing the bridge over the Rhine Falls to Neuhausen. The maid caught me just in time - I already had one leg under the railing and was about to slip through. These things point to an unconscious urge, or, it may be, a fatal resistance to life in this world." (Jung, 1961)

The waters below absorbed his consciousness, pulling him toward a harmonious union, a return to a womb-like existence. It was a tugging he would experience again and again. He "...yearned all his life for the mothering darkness and safety of a cloistered place." (Stern, 1976)

The adult Jung was keenly aware of the dangers that passage into these deep elements held. The stress following his break with Freud plummeted him into the Dream State. He knew that others, Nietzche for instance, had not come back from forays into the depths, and that such processes could easily end in madness.

Faith that he was following a process dictated by a "Higher Will" convinced him that he would make it through this stormy period. He was aided by the intensity of his own will, coupled with the practical desire to be responsible to his patients, wife and children which he called "...actualities which made demands upon me and proved to me again and again that I really existed." (Jung, 1961)

To fulfill the dynamics of the Dreamer, to bring them to fullest fruition, Jung needed to develop the capacity to tolerate the feelings of own creative independence. Aspects of his character that interfered with the flowing of his energies to creative outlets had to be loosened. His body had to become freer for discharge. Energy could not be so thoroughly absorbed in images.

Jung's relationship with Freud had provided the protection of a sustaining umbilical connection for his creative expression and fulfillment. Through it he focused his writing and productivity expressing, nurturing and amplifying his "master's" teaching.

Operating within the authority of another gives a cocoon-like safety to explore and to learn. Eventually, the growing student, if he is to reach personal fulfillment, must use the knowledge absorbed as a springboard for the expression of his or her own truth. At this point, another's authority is no longer acceptable.

The flaws in the teaching of another become evident when lived through one's own unique experiencing. Another's way doesn't quite fit. A struggle for separateness breaks the connectedness of the relationship. A new collegial relationship can form or, as in Jung's case, formal contact may end.

The Rhythmic Cycle of Change

Jung's time of separation began with a request by Freud for help in analyzing one of Freud's own dreams. Jung, in his role as analyst, asked his mentor for personal historical information that would assist the process.

"Freud's response to these words was a curious look - a look of the utmost suspicion. Then he said, `but I cannot risk my authority!' That sentence burned itself into my memory, and in it the end of our relationship was already foreshadowed. Freud was placing personal authority above truth." (Jung, 1961)

The crack in Jung's relationship with Freud was powerful and abrupt. It widened into a gulf that broke Jung and left him struggling in the Creative Phase of the Rhythmic Cycle for several years. Though he had analyzed the details of his earlier life through his work with Freud, this new emotional disturbance brought to him the knowledge that he was personally split. There was a disassociated part of himself, foreign to his identity. He realized that something was " ..still around and possesses a creative life which I lack." (Jung, 1961) He had to reclaim it to reunite his life flow.

The break with Freud left Jung out of touch with a stabilizing center. Freud had provided it. He didn't have it for himself. The result was a cacophony of tumultuous emotions. He struggled against "being torn to pieces." (Jung, 1961) His confrontation was with an ultimate split that could carry him permanently away from reality. It provided the impetus necessary to work with the pathology in his own being.

Jung dropped deep into himself, returning to early modes of functioning, to the Dream State. Terrifying fantasies rolled into awareness at times almost obliterating all ego control. Jung feared going crazy and feared the intense overwhelming feelings that came when he was immersed in emotion. To reestablish control he strove to contact his body. Then he used the Dreamer's mode of working feelings into voices and images so that he might gain the reassurance of clear vision.

> "I was frequently so wrought up that I had to do certain yoga exercises in order to hold my emotions in check. As soon as I had the feeling that I was myself again, I abandoned this restraint upon the emotions and allowed the inner voices to speak afresh." (Jung, 1961)

> "To the extent that I managed to translate the emotions into images - that is to say, to find the images which were concealed in the emotions - I was inwardly calmed and reassured. Had I left those images hidden in the emotions, I might have been torn to pieces by them. First I formulated the things as I had observed them, usually in high-flown language... even of bombast. It is a style I find embarrassing, it grates on my nerves, as when someone draws his nails along a plaster wall or scrapes his knife against a plate." (Jung, 1961)

Dream symbols provided Jung his own way of working with rampaging emotions. The process followed its own Rhythmic Cycle. It began with the sensation of movement within the body, moved inward to the production of images, and then evolved into words and categories.

The driving impetus underlying the development of this process was the sense of imminent annihilation: "I will be torn to pieces." From the creative struggle with this terror, the originally unreleased emotion continued its course through to creative embodiment. It resulted in the formulation of a theory and the framework of a life's vocation, the development of a psychological approach that mirrored his own inner unfolding.

For Jung, words brought the detachment of the Communicator's processes of intellectual pursuit and decision. Objective analysis and thought moves one away from the senses and the Dream State, away from violent surges of the creative struggle. The tight rules of logic replace rolling metaphor and uncontrolled energy.

Objectivity, the cold eye of Science, seeks to avoid contamination of what "is" by the lyric imagery of inner experience. It demands a determining control and focus to obtain a succinct and parsimonious point.

Jung's move from the fantasies of his inner eye and the creative struggle of his emotions to the objectivity and purposefulness of the rational approach was a natural progression. He reworked his deeply personal interest in dreams, myths and magic in a way that communicated to those academics who were attracted to his topic. His scientific style was careful, erudite, but often unbearably dry.

Later, in the section that focuses on the Communicator Phase of the Rhythmic Cycle, we will see the rational scientific aspect of life more richly and spontaneously developed by one who is more at home with it. For now, suffice it to say that communicating according to scientific strictures represented for Jung a strong movement away from the Dream Phase and the edge of madness.

As Jung's interest in the understanding of dreams, myths and rituals matured, his work, based on the personal truth of his experience, was built into a solid structure from which he could express himself. Still he needed the help of another to allow his energies to flow to full embodiment.

Full emergence from the personal chaos of this period of Jung's life only moved toward completion as he became intensely involved in a relationship with a woman. Tony Wolff was Jung's "'Eros' Winged Muse" (Stern, 1976), bringing Jung into play with his disassociated sexuality. It was an incestuous-like affair, one with a client. It grew into a relationship that included his wife and spanned decades. Through it, Jung moved toward deeper contact with his own physical nature, out of the labyrinth that had engulfed the totality of his being. With this, at last, he achieved an easier relationship with everyday reality.

Jung's break with Freud had set in motion a Rhythmic Cycle through which he reworked the meaning of his life experiences. Through the process he found the means to lead others through the dark journey of night into the illumination of conscious reality.

For Jung, work, imagery and the Dream State always remained primary, the beginning from which to move toward expression. For his own life integrity, it had been necessary to allow life's energy to move through his body and culminate in an expressive sexuality.

For much of his life sexuality remained tainted, not completely accepted. He symbolized it as the "dark side of the god image." (Jung, 1961). He might have known it as something more positive, the Crown of the God-head for instance, or like Freud he might have placed it at the center of his psychology, or even more realistically he could have accepted it as a natural bodily outlet that could be a source of pleasure.

In fact, the symbol Jung chose for sexuality ("dark side of the God image") summarized the negative setting and shame in which sexuality had been embedded in his early life. Releasing himself from this negative position, allowing the energies of sexuality to come forth and recognizing their personal and biological significance resulted in Jung's blooming, in mid and later life, into a new fullness.

The Rhythmic Cycle of Change

The Dreamer Jung was free and whole enough, so that his energies could be expressed and integrated, in his own way, throughout the Rhythmic Cycle. The main focus of his life work remained in immersion, and the Dreamer's intuition. He explored dream symbols and archetypes, both longitudinally, in terms of historic connections, and latitudinally, in terms of contemporary commonalities.

Jung pointed to Humanity's inner experience. Through his psychotherapeutic work he could help an individual move into that which was hinted at but incompletely known. From there it could be clarified and amplified, united with disassociated aspects of being, with the larger human spirit and with the totality of existence.

For Jung, as for each of us when we are immersed in the Dream State the risk is run of dissipating energies in an endless retrogression of reflections, mirroring the mirroring of mirrors. To flow into the next phase of the Rhythmic Cycle, the phase of the Creator requires a splitting away, a splitting like that which occurs in the birth process where with the final severing of the umbilical cord a new and separate creation comes into existence.

Creator

In the beginning the spirit of God created
Heaven and earth,
The waters above and the waters below,
The greater light - day, and the lesser light - night,
The fish of the sea, the birds of the sky, the creatures of the earth,
And in His own image, Man.

On the seventh day He rested from His work.

THE STRUGGLE

Split, division, break, from one comes two. The creation of existence has its impetus in division - a fragmenting of unity followed by a new synthesis. Human creations have a similar beginning.

As energy grows, the ensuing drive moves the Dream Phase to its end, to an existentially suspenseful, potentially creative moment. Then a split, a leading edge, a border of uncertainty, marked by a cliff-hanging instant when the impending direction of movement is unknown, swishes in the new. The potential for change charges with energy until in a tearing instant, the edge is crossed, the silence is broken and movement erupts through the surface to produce a creative spontaneous release.

Transition is part of the natural order of things, a part of the changing nature of existence. It is noted in time and marks out its epochs; it defines space and delineates boundaries; it separates life into its many forms. Man's being is set within nature's framework of quiescence and activity.

Transitions are everywhere. Rituals are created and then practiced to ease the pains of uncertainty that accompany them. Holidays are celebrated at the change of seasons. Human relationships are entered and exited in stylized ways that mark the passing between individuality and joining. Without ritual we fully experience the uncertainty of the new and struggle for a creative means to set the course.

The creative life shuns reliance on social ritual and constantly strives to create a new and unique form. The new form, once created, may also be left behind when the impetus for creative activity begins again. Such living demands full participation in the moment, abandons the past and is unmindful of the future. It causes life to be experienced in its fullest, starkest intensity.

The Creator lives a life of great risk, on the edge, not fully committed to the fulfillment of inner drives nor to the exigencies of the outer environment. The course begun is rarely planned through. It is full of surprises and uncertainties. Each moment is the stimulus for a new bit of creation rather than simply a point along a direction toward a known end.

For the Creator, security and satisfaction are anathema, restlessness is prevalent. There is no clear goal or end point to fasten down movement. Yet there is often a rush of activity that carries the energetic process to a new and unexpected conclusion and then - an ending in exhaustion. This way of living requires and reflects a capacity to split drive from action and mind from body.

We can learn to emphasize the excitement and passion of the creative edge by forming and maintaining the split within. Man is a bag of separate bones and muscles, different tissues and fluids held together in a whole. For any individual at any time the various parts may be integrated and coordinated or they may be divided and at odds, moving in different directions and at different purposes.

Humans are not alone in the animal kingdom in their capacity to learn to act out in a divided way. A distressed monkey can extend his arm, look at it as if it were an outside object and attack it. Energy flow separates until a part becomes foreign, sensorially disconnected from the rest of the body.

Humans, because of the development of their brain, have the potential for division and reunification to a degree unknown by any other animal. Mind and reason, culturally shaped, can flow harmoniously with the experience of the body or sit above, separate from and even at odds with the body's immediacy.

Humans are capable of delaying the instinctual drive, of channeling it into varied forms of expression. They can control and suppress urges for long periods as well as turn them against the larger life flow. They can focus and maintain physical attitudes to heighten or lessen the effect of the inner separation of unity. They can consciously delay or block development of a harmonious balance.

Unity between mind and body allows a harmony and wholeness. Duality leads to disharmony and dissynchronization and serves as an impetus to the creation of a new integration. These extremes of the flow-break or unity-duality continuum can be seen in the philosophies of the mystic as opposed to the scientific logic of the rationalist.

Mystical practice highlights the constant flux of the universe. Scientific method tends to overlook the totality of existence's ever-changing process. It focuses instead on the fixed points of the boundaries of change. Its concern is with the separation between things and events dividing them into unique items and categories for concrete manipulation by determined rules.

This difference in focus amplifies the two ways that man can know: the intuitive, pre-verbal and magical, or the rational, verbal and objective. One emphasizes the internal, the other the external. One speaks a language of the image, with its blurred meaning, the other of the fact, with its exact reproducibility.

The energy dynamics of the Creator Phase of the Rhythmic Cycle highlight the interface between these two approaches. Counting on nothing, the Creator constantly brings forward the original.

ENERGY DYNAMICS OF CREATION

From the pause to the brink and through, a bursting of eruptive energy, experienced in thoughts, movements, sensation and ideas, the creative moment is born out of an experiencing of energy flow that overcomes the body's holding.

This experience of overcoming can range from a gentle murmur to a violent overwhelming depending on the body's level of energy charge and the tenacity of its holding. Such moments serve as a source of renewal and creativity, aiding in the establishment of a harmonious connection between need and satisfaction.

The Creative Character develops when the emergence from the natural pause in the Rhythmic Cycle is profoundly disturbed by environmental shock. The sequence of rhythmic flow is thereby disrupted. The course of natural movement is broken. These effects recapitulate again and again when circumstances similar to the original shocking situation are perceived.

A young pet duck climbs some stairs. Shocked by a loud noise emanating from a radiator on the staircase landing, it pauses, tenses its neck and creatively comes up with a new way, widely arcing off its familiar course to avoid the noise-maker. From then on, for the rest of its life, it tenses and arcs whenever passing this place.

Environmental shock leads to hitches in the natural rhythm and throws the individual into an internal state of division and split. It introduces frozenness into the mobility of the organism, amplifying, expanding and rigidifying the natural separation that occurs in rhythmic flow. Energetic integrity is broken into separate components. The struggle to bring those components together lays the groundwork for the creative act, the new solution that frees and reestablishes harmonious energy flow.

Within the body there are zones of long energy flow, involving large muscles, and areas of shorter flow, where the continuity of energy is easily broken. These smaller muscle areas are crucially involved in the energy dynamics of the Creative Phase of the Rhythmic Cycle. In physical development they are the first areas in which control is gained. Through them the fetus is capable of jerking and twisting the body in the spasmodic contractions that aid propulsion through the birth canal; out of the belly and into life.

In the formation of the character of the Creator the small muscles of the spine slip out of line to hold the body defensively in an energetically broken position. The joints of the neck are particularly vulnerable because they connect to and support the heavy weight of the head. When weak or undercharged, the muscles that attach the head to the spine can be overwhelmed with little difficulty, shocking the bones they attach to out of position. As the muscles involved are small, surges of energy can reestablish unity with equal ease.

A crazed inconsistency results from disjointedness in energetic flow. The energy levels on both sides of a split can differ widely, sending contradictory urgings of approach and avoidance.

The Rhythmic Cycle of Change

On the one side there is an urge to move while on the other side to hold still. A struggle divides and twists the organism. The mind strives in two directions while seeking one way to release the disjuncture to reestablish union and strong flow.

Dynamically one can respond to the inner split in three ways. First, energy can be dissipated in a move toward relaxation, causing regression and a reestablishment of the Dream State. Secondly, in an attempt to contain the charge of excitement, the leading edge can be struggled against and maintained by stiffening other muscles, leading to a frozen state and giving a frozen look to the individual.

Freezing has its own danger. When energy builds against a leading edge that won't release, and no outlet can be found, the integrity of the body's fabric is challenged. Immobilization can be followed by a loss of physical cohesion. The emotional result is noxious terror, trembling movement without direction that often ends in sudden cathartic release, and a physical falling apart. Though relieving, it often causes a backlash of negative reaction.

A third, more productive resolution, involves a creative struggle to work through the split and give birth to the new. The Creative Character attempts through mind and will to struggle with the binding tension until it collapses, allowing energy to make a new whole of the disjointed, fractured parts - ending the inner conflict and reestablishing the broken integrity.

All characters have tension blocks, but the internal impetus to creation caused by the relative fragility and location of the Creator's blocks is such that the need to bridge the gap with creative breakthrough permeates a great deal of the Creator's life.

The disjointed framework shocked into the Creator's nature is a constant stimulation to the moment of creation. With release the pleasure of energy flow is reestablished and contact is felt with existence, life and the moment. The creative by-products left behind portray the result of the psychological struggle to feel life, integrated in the full human condition; or to touch death, broken and fragmented.

If energies are to be a source of creative growth and a core source of direction, rather than simply the impetus for restless actions fueling destructive release and a backlash in more intense holding, a conscious respect for internal movements and an orientation that tolerates and uses release constructively are required.

THE DEVELOPMENT OF THE CREATIVE CHARACTER

The life of the Creative Character focuses around the formation and resolution of the splitting edge. For them, early child-rearing trauma results in a continual struggle with the breaking point. A forcing of the edge experience leaves the life-flow stunned, and fragmented on the edge of explosive terror and/or creative breakthrough. Such a position continually and urgently searches for a new start, a new synthesis that leads toward wholeness.

Under stress, the Creator's movements appear like the first jerks that mark the quickening of life in the mother's belly. They are reminiscent of the newborn's reaction to irritation.

The birth experience itself can stamp in the pattern of the Creative Character. The fetus struggles through the birth canal, going from the inner world of the womb and its dream dynamics to life outside. But the ambivalent musculature of a rigid, inhospitable and unwanting parent - one who unconsciously rejects the fruits of sexual experience while consciously claiming to accept the child - does not contact harmoniously with the infant's struggling movements. The birth process attacks the child rather than working and massaging it through the passage, life's first transition.

After birth, the infant does best if the parent is with it in a flowing contactful way. A continual pattern of violation and disruption of the natural life rhythm, through birth and then beyond, prevents the later development of a smooth coordination in movement from the small to the larger muscles. For an individual who has repeatedly gone through this kind of trauma, the first line of defense remains quick, jerky, disconnected movement and the holdings of the small joint muscles.

There are many ways to touch, hold and interact with an infant. The parents who unconsciously repress their own irritation, who fail to acknowledge it and release it in consciously directed ways will communicate it with their bodies directly to the unprotected infant through rough inconsistent handling. The integrity of the infant's flow is intruded upon. The physical contact needed for development is given harshly, abruptly, even violently although at the same time words may exude a cover of gentleness and love. A divided message results in a divided organism.

The infant responds to what is happening. To defend against inconsistency and attack, it stiffly contracts the small muscles that can be controlled. Tension builds in the muscles that lift the head and mobilize the joints - areas that are developmentally capable of responding with contraction at early stages of extra-uterine life. When the holding reaches the breaking point, the infant flails uncontrollably to release the accumulated charge.

Release comes in cathartic outbursts, an antidote to the splitting discomforts of inner stress. For the Creator however, release brings the unwanted aspects of the infant's existence strongly into the rejecting parent's awareness. The parent's inner feelings of violence override the possibility of concerned response to the child's needs.

Instead, the abruptness of painful shock, hostile response, is used to stifle the cathartic process and cause the disjointed holding to be reestablished and maintained. As the infant moves through childhood it is taught that direct release is unacceptable social behavior - craziness.

Creative means must be found to express the crazed inner energy pattern. If not, the organism, blocked from discharge, moves to a state of no-flow, non-being, lifelessness - the not-seen, not-heard state, unconsciously desired by the parent.

Stagnation at the leading edge gives impetus to the battle to survive with all the terror it carries with it. Caught in passage, stunned into immobility, the individual loses contact with flow and being. "To be or not to be?" and, "Life or death?" become the questions. With the release of feeling, the resulting energetic union of head and body gives an experience of new existence and rebirth.

The body dynamics of the Creative Character are fixed early in life. The leading edge in life's rhythm becomes a place so habitual it is sought as a home, the point of new beginnings. Again and again dammed energies are either urgently struggled with in an attempt toward suppression or mobilized to move in new directions, to create paths of release. Channeled eruptions can take surprising and spontaneous directions, yielding new possibilities - the birth of a new way.

Breaking through the leading edge is an experience in being reborn. Vitality and spontaneity return. The existential question loses valence. Life moves on, to thrive rather than survive, until the edge tension reestablishes itself organically at the beginning of a new Rhythmic Cycle or is regressed to defensively. When the leading edge is simply part of life's natural rhythm, not faced grimly but put in proportion to its true meaning, the Creative Phase in the Rhythmic Cycle can be passed without an escalation of terror and desperation.

THE ARTIST AS CREATOR

The Creative Character necessarily leads a creative life. Every stress that disrupts the flow reestablishes the underlying physical dynamics for creation. To become an artist, the products of the character must be refined. The initial spark of creation must be strengthened, organized, shaped and expressed. The spark must be matured along the course of the Rhythmic Cycle.

Not all Creative Characters are artists, nor are all artists Creative Characters. But all artists must be able to tolerate the creative moment. They must endure the frustration of held energy, and then split and break through.

For the Creative Character this endurance is almost second nature. The process of creation has been repeatedly used for defensive purposes in response to stress and has become a welcomed, even sought after, excitement. Volatile, Creative Characters seek and enjoy the creative moment as a chance to feel the passion of existence.

For them creativity is "the" aspect of the entire Rhythmic Cycle. Like all characters they run the risk of becoming lost in this phase and not proceeding through the full course. Pathological consequences and disturbed one-sided functioning then result. The close relationship between the creative person and "crazy" behavior is well known.

Who better than Van Gogh to delineate the torture of an artist who needs the creative breakthrough for the reestablishment of personal integrity but instead is captured in a state of creative arrest:

> "..... a prisoner in an I-don't-know-what-for horrible, horrible, utterly horrible cage.....It is impossible for him to do anything.... Because he hasn't got just that which he needs in order to be creative. Because the fate of circumstances has reduced him to a state of nothingness. ... Yet.....he feels instinctively... . Something is alive in me: what can it be!" (Ghiselin, 1952)

Imprisonment is broken by the splitting edge that leads to a "...profound and thorough alteration of our inner life and of the outer forms in which life finds expression." (Ghiselin, 1952) The destruction of the old order produces a new form that brings one into a different relationship with the world.

In his book The Creative Process (1952), Brewster Ghiselin presents the reflections of a number of well known Creators on their own creative processes. His introduction and his selections, which include writings by Roger Sessions; A. E Housman; J. B. Yates; Vincent Van Gogh; Isadora Duncan; Wolfgang Mozart; Henri Poincare; Thomas Wolfe; Frederick Nietzsche and Henry Miller, provide examples that highlight the dynamics of creativity. They outline its source in the body, its struggle against split, and its release in breakthrough.

Creativity, no matter what its expressive form, has its source in bodily movements. Composer Roger Sessions (Ghiselin 1952) parallels musical impulses with "those primitive movements which are the very conditions of our existence." A. E. Housman (Ghiselin, 1952) calls poetry "more physical than intellectual". J.B. Yates (Ghiselin, 1952) finds art ..."unable to move us, if our thoughts do not rush out to the edges of our flesh."

Physical movement is primary to creativity but its blockage is also a necessary condition. Frustration checks the inner life in what dancer Isadora Duncan calls "a state of complete suspense."

This suspense can end in splitting. When mind observes the creative process it appears automatic and involuntary, not a result of a unified personality. Words, poems and ideas, when in this state, seem to emerge from a separate place, to be recorded and preserved.

Mozart, for example, heard his works spring whole in his mind. He didn't view himself as possessing a creative talent. In fact he credited memory as his greatest gift. Memory carried the deposits of his Dream State into a realized existence.

"[In] .... the bag of my memory
.... everything is ... already finished and it rarely

differs on paper from what it was in my imagination." (Mozart, 1952)

For Mozart the move from dream to reality appeared automatic. In some way he wasn't unified in the process. Outside of it, he was "just" a listener and recorder. At these times, though certainly not in the more reality-oriented parts of his life (Reiter, 1975), he was able to avoid directly experiencing the struggle.

For others creativity is more difficult and more totally involving. For them the struggle of creation has all the intensity of a difficult birth in which the Creative Character runs the risk of getting nowhere. Pushing and pulling at the same time the frozen block tightens. Letting go is crucial if push and pull are to be successfully alternated and movement is to carry through to breakthrough.

"Often when one works on a hard question nothing good is accomplished at the first attack. Then one takes a rest, longer or shorter and sits down anew to the work." (Poincare, 1952)

"One gets near to the heart of the truth....in the measure that he ceases to struggle, in the measure that he abandons the will." (Miller, 1952; Ghiselin, 1952)

Letting go allows the body's inner movements, the emotions, to be artistically born into reality.

"Only emotion can arouse the sub-conscious into action, can overwhelm the rational control of mind to leave the body to choose its symbols of creative release." (Lowell, 1952)

The amplitude of the release depends upon the amount of energy buildup behind the frustrating block. The catharsis can be brief:

> "As I went along thinking of nothing in particular there would flow into my mind, with sudden and unaccountable emotion, sometimes a line or two of verse, sometimes a whole stanza at once." (Housman, 1952)

or consuming,

> "It was a process that began in a whirling vortex and a creative chaos.... It seemed that I had inside me, swelling and gathering all the time, a huge black cloud, and that this cloud was loaded with electricity, pregnant, crested, with the kind of hurricane violence that could not be held in check much longer.... (Wolfe, 1952)

and then,

> "It was exactly as if this great black storm cloud had opened up and mid flashes of lightning, was pouring from its depths a torrential and ungovernable flood. And I was born along with it." (Wolfe, 1952)

The highly charged moment can be totally overwhelming. Nietzsche writes that during it:

> "Something profoundly convulsive and disturbing suddenly becomes visible and audible

with indescribable definiteness and exactness. One hears - one does not seek; one takes - one does not ask who gives: a thought flashes out like lightning, inevitably, without hesitation. I have never had any choice about it. There is an ecstasy whose terrific tension is sometimes released by a flood of tears, during which one's progress varies from involuntary impetuousity to involuntary slowness. There is the feeling that one is utterly out of hand, with the most distinct consciousness of an infinitude of shuddering thrills that pass through one from head to foot. There is profound happiness in which the most painful and gloomy feelings are not discordant in effect, but are required as necessary colors in this overflow of light. There is an instinct for rhythmic relations which embraces an entire world of forms (length, the need for a widely extended rhythm, is almost a measure of the force of inspiration, a sort of counterpart to its pressure and tension). Every thing occurs quite without volition, as if in an eruption of freedom, independence, power and divinity." (Nietzsche, 1952)

Sadly, for Nietzsche the stresses of the creative moment eventually led backward to a pathological engulfment of his personality - a constant home in the Dream's State. Reality was lost to lunacy.

There are other possibilities. Henry Miller grew to place the creative process, the split, the struggle, and the passion of release in its existential position and found a healthy personal balance within the world.

Miller began:

> "...a thorough novice, incapable, awkward, tongue-tied, almost paralyzed by fear and apprehensive-ness." (Miller, 1952)

The search for self, the path of self-discovery passed through the creative struggle ending only with the realization that he was:

> "... nothing less than nothing." (Miller, 1952)

> "I had to grow foul with knowledge, realize the futility of everything, smash everything, grow desperate, then humble, then sponge myself off the slate, as it were, in order to recover my authenticity. I had to arrive at the brink and then take a leap at the dark." (Miller, 1952)

Miller took the Creative State the full course of the Rhythmic Cycle. The final leap moved him again through the gap to connect in a wholer way with the world around him. With authenticity came reality and a new problem, the problem of "making a life in accord with the deep-centered rhythm of the cosmos... ." (Miller, 1952)

THE PATHOLOGICAL ALTERNATIVE

The bodily split in the Creative Character forms in early life. During therapy when a tensed Creative Character is asked to lie on a bed and swing their arms, legs and head, random disconnected motions like those that are seen in a newborn infant in stress often occur. Body parts appear to move independently, groping non-directedly - the head lolls and rolls. Small muscles seem to throw the body's parts in eruptive, random jerks. The body bumps along like an old-time movie.

Awareness of this fragmentation disconcerts the person who stops and tries methodically to gain control by thinking through coordinated movements. The attempt is unsuccessful - thinking about movements doesn't produce flow. The struggle must be relaxed, the split resolved, in order to let go to free movement.

Will had a complaint, which he stated quietly and matter-of-factly. He had lost enthusiasm for his work. He had been attracted to teaching because the life and spontaneity of children excited him. He loved their enthusiasm and greatly enjoyed the freedom that it elicited in his being. Now it was gone. He was unmotivated and disappointed.

This was part of a pattern - enthusiastic involvement followed by disengagement and deathly staleness. He sat before me with his head flushed and bright but the rest of his body from the neck down was pale and lifeless. He was struggling to end the split in his body.

A charged head, filled with obsessive recycling ideas, sat on top of an undercharged, white, gaunt and spastic body - a hung body that looked dead. The rigidity of the spinal muscles of the neck stopped energy flow.

I asked him to lie quietly on the bed and give up his directing ego. He was to do no problem solving, rational or directed thinking for two minutes. His first attempt failed. His head filled with directions: "I'll notice my body." "What's the best way to do this?" "What exactly is wanted?"

He was instructed to return to the task and strongly tell himself "Stop!," whenever he caught himself in directed thinking. After initial difficulty he succeeded. Soon a brief spontaneous realization about his life broke through but he immediately blocked the flow and avoided the rule. The obsessive defense reoccurred, was pointed out and he began once more.

Now the energy coursed more strongly through his body. He observed the bed moving. He puzzled over what was causing the shaking. Still split, he was unaware that his own restless movements were the cause.

Told it was he who was moving the bed, he reentered the assignment. This time sexual feelings came into conscious awareness. His head was reunited with his body. Momentarily he knew what he was experiencing but again quickly obliterated his feelings from consciousness by freezing up. Obsessive thinking returned. This time he was unable to get himself to stop.

He was told that sexual movements and feelings were part of the pattern of more totally integrated functioning. Flowing required awareness and acceptance of them.

He smiled happily with the allowance of his experience, wriggled around on the bed, and enjoyed the feeling of his skin and body. He was filled with the delight of renewed vitality. For the moment the split was gone. The flow moved through the pelvis into his legs. Energy ran through his whole body.

The Rhythmic Cycle of Change

THE PYGMY CULTURE

The Negrito Pygmy tribe (Stewart, 1975) in the Philippines is organized around the dynamics of the Creative Character. Though of course every individual is not of this character, accidents of history have served to make the culture's rituals manifest the creative process as an antidote to the overwhelming effects of terrifying natural circumstances.

The Negritos are subject to powerful typhoons: crashing, thunderous explosions accompany searing bolts of lightning. The violence of the storms and the destructive power of the wind-whipped rains are heightened in the consciousness of the people by a mythology that attributes nature's outpourings to the anger and fury of their god, the attacking Tolandian.

According to their belief, the vindictive Tolandian learns what transgressions a Negrito has committed from his messengers, the monkeys and earthworms, who see and tell everything that occurs. Like an unaccepting parent he does not like to hear of bad things. The Negritos use their own projections to decide what upsets their God and what must be done to make amends for the difficulties their acts cause.

Tolandian's independent and violent power underlies all natural events. He is dangerous to Man and must be constantly and alertly attended to and pacified. In response to such ever-present danger, the Negrito is typically in a state of heightened energy charge and awareness hoping to influence his God in favor of his survival.

In such survival consciousness, events are a "matter of life and death to everyone." (Stewart, 1954) Constant creation of repressing ritual is required if God is not to be angered. Even a simple misfortune as tripping on a root is seen as a sign from Tolandian that a wrong has been done. A ceremony of atonement asking the root for forgiveness and offering a goodwill token must be created and given. If not, the spirit of the root will haunt the offender by repeatedly tripping him up. He ascribes his fall to the root spirit rather than to his own error and whenever he encounters the root that brought him down he is obliged to repeat the ceremony.

The spirit images are viewed not as illusion, nor from within, but as powerful and real forces from beyond. Negritos give great power to the Dream element of spirit realities. But unlike Dreamers, who would choose to live as spirit entities themselves, flowing in an imaginary world, the Negritos employ therapeutic ways to exorcise the element that is seen as outside and against them fragmenting and terrorizing their lives.

The healing ceremony shakes out offending images so that the individual's world view can be reorganized without the disrupting element. The process requires the troubled individual to enter into a violent, agitated, trance-like state. Shaking and gyrating, he is worked into a frenzy with the assistance of a shaman. In moments of seizure like body contortions, of wild, fragmented physical movement, the small muscles of the body, those that mark the Creative Character, are tensely held against the high charge of energy. The catharsis occurs when the harmony-disrupting repressed terror is released.

The crazed images, which come to mind as the body throws off its energy and enters the dynamics of the Dream State, give insight into the source of the trouble. The element of consciousness that brought splitting disharmony to the organism comes into view. The vision might show a violation of authority, or the breaking of a taboo, or a frightening story or event. With the illusion exposed, its negative power can be overcome through the creation of yet still another ceremony of atonement.

Some Pygmies, those whose character and body is most easily suited to moving into trance, will repeatedly enter these states, becoming masters of this antidote to terror. Recognized as shamans, they are capable of moving through the gyrations at will.

They use the imagery they see to connect to others who cannot attain the cathartic state for themselves. Valued seers, they are able to bring back visions that speak of the life of the troubled one. With the image in the open, its disturbing power is lost and its chronic effects on the individual are transcended.

The illusion that there is an overwhelming authority represented by the angry, terrifying but pacifiable Tolandian is central to the Negrito's culture and lifestyle. If it were brought into the open and purged, the form supporting the culture's character would be destroyed. It is never publicly challenged.

The Tolandian rituals and their controlling effect on behavior keep the aura of terror close to the group and constantly stimulate its creative urges. Every event is potentially the source of destruction and can introduce the leading edge - the frozen fear that splits the energies of the person and yields the dynamic state necessary for the creation of a new pacifying ritual.

Survival consciousness, compulsive creation of ritual, terror and emotional outburst: all indicate that the Negritos are stuck in the issues of the Creative Character. Unable to question their view of God, they are unable to creatively evolve beyond their beliefs to new cultural phases on the Rhythmic Cycle.

The Creative Character as seen in the Negrito is not limited to primitive tribes. Its dynamics mark many fundamental religions such as the Holy Rollers, sects that speak in tongues, religious snake handlers, faith healers and others. The charged response to the emotional buildup of the evangelist requires only the touch of the healer to yield spasming, fragmented release and the bodily jerks characteristic of the newborn.

The therapeutic methods of Primal Scream, Rebirthing and parts of Bioenergetic therapy make use of cathartic release to aid the individual in re-establishing an easier flow of energies that unite the divided organism. For this free flow to be maintained, the sense of violence and intrusion that lead to fragmentation must be made conscious and seen realistically.

RONALD LAING - THE CREATOR

Ronald Laing is a poet, analyzer of madness, psychiatric revolutionary and Creative Character. His work grew and spread in the disruptive period of the Sixties when he served as the documenter of the collective insanity of the time. His character made him particularly fit to become the central figure in challenging the treatment of the severely mentally ill.

The stir created by his writings about the insane and his focus on the humanity of the mentally ill may have surprised those who might have believed mental health professions to be deeply human. Mental health had been built into a profession and, like all institutions, this one too could and had impeded human contact between people, replacing internally directed reactions with institutionalized role reactions.

Creative Characters do not respond well to roles and status. When not frozen, their bodies are unguarded and highly responsive to dimensions of genuineness and artificiality, truth and falsity, pleasure and pain. Since their larger muscles do not develop tensions to serve as armor and they lack the free mature use of counteraggression to ward off the insults of others, they depend on sensitivity and contact to measure the possibilities in relationship. Their intensity and passion raise the specter of instability to the establishment that rejects them as unfit because they challenge the rigid stance of rules and roles.

Laing wrote of the pathology of the Creative Character, the schizoid state. (Laing, 1959) He wrote of the treatment of an illness marked by the separation of head and heart, thought and feeling, and of a mental health technology that lacked human relationship because of its own insanity.

His descriptions of the schizoid condition moved readers to empathetic feelings with the insane and pricked the buried terrors of a fragmented sensibility in even those out of contact with that aspect of their experience. He pointed out that:

> "... we are all, in our fashions, truly mad, schizoid, doubly divorced, once from ourselves and once from virtually everyone and everything else."
> (Evans, 1976)

The Creative Phase of the Rhythmic Cycle belongs to each of us though it may or may not be our major focus.

Laing made major contributions to our understanding of the pathological aspects of the Creative Character in his writings on the schizoid state. His keen analysis presented the symptoms of the sickness that the Creative Character is prone to experience with its immobilization and alienation, its struggle for survival and its experience of terror.

Laing's creative writing style often moves in pieces from the existentially abstract to the awakening and shocking present, and then drifts back into the Dreamer state and the poetic and metaphorical. As a literary example of an inner flow process of the Creator it evokes in the reader the feelings of the process.

As a therapist, Laing presents neither a system nor a technique but, rather, a way of being. He does not claim to offer a therapy at all, simply a framework for experimentation. He talks of "what is" rather than "cure." He does not approach a client with "what-should-be" or "what-could-be" but senses the moment of the person and participates in their world view. The client's behavior is known as "expressive of his existence." (Laing, 1965)

To participate with the client, Laing writes, "The therapist must have the plasticity to transpose himself into another's strange and even alien view of the world. In this act he draws on his own psychotic possibilities, without forgoing his sanity... ." (Laing, 1965)

For a therapist who is not a Creator or a Dreamer, for one who is more secure about existence, "It is often difficult ... to transpose himself into the world of an individual whose experiences may be utterly lacking in any unquestionable, self-validating certainties." (Laing, 1965)

Establishment psychiatry, with its categories, classification, symptoms and medical regimens, is foreign territory for the Creative Character. Laing finds the difficulty within himself.

> "I have difficulty discovering the signs and symptoms of psychosis in persons I am myself interviewing." (Laing, 1965)

Laing's problem appears to come less from moral principles than from the difficulty of coming from and maintaining an integrated separate point of view. Participating from the point of the client, Laing is closer to the experience of the patient than to the role of the doctor. When at one with the schizoid and schizophrenic patient, he lacks the emotional distancing or independent point of view required to apply objective medical categories and definitions.

A base of integral selfhood from which to make judgments and understand their application cannot occur when there is a fragmenting split and a condition of stasis at the gap's edge. Participating in the patient's schizoid state calls for experiencing the physical dynamics of the Creator Phase of the Rhythmic Cycle, and whereas for Laing this approach at times might be a conscious choice, at other times it is likely to be an unconscious defensive reaction.

On a TV talk show, Laing could be seen moving from an integrated to a split state. The host, with a brash attacking style, was known to be attracted to the hidden and sensational in others.

He was infamous for encounters that brought the hidden into exhibition and could be said to appeal to his audiences' voyeuristic tendencies.

Laing had come to talk about his recent book and work, but the interviewer moved in on his personal life. Attacking a hint of sexual moralism, the interviewer repeatedly asked Laing, "Have you ever had an affair?" Initial evasions brought more aggressive badgering. The question was repeated again and again. Laing began to come apart. His voice quivered, his poise and acumen faded. He was visibly shaken.

His poetry suggests what he was experiencing:

"What is my face now? There are different kinds of feelings in the space where the mask was. The more I concentrate on them the more porous they become - they fade and dissolve into finer and finer dust. I thought I had a face." (Laing, 1976)

".. I'm sodden with terror
suffused with fear
a terrified sponge
I'm helpless
I can't move
It's meaningless to get out of it by
running away
talking
I'm quivering all over......" (Laing, 1976)

Laing's book Knots (Laing, 1970) can put the reader in the binding tensions of the Creative State. It is composed of logical poems of illogic, binds that can lead to a state of immobility.

Can logic, with its tight appeal to mind, be poem, with its arousal of emotion? Can a geometric arrangement of squares and rectangles be art? They are in the realm of modern art, and <u>Knots</u> is in the realm of modern poems. They appeal to the same constricted sense of motionlessness that is in abstract forms, and arouse the tension and sensation of fragmentation. They are the poems of modern mental science.

An example can create the tension of the Creative Phase of the Rhythmic Cycle for the reader:

"How clever is one to be stupid?

The others told her she was stupid. So she made herself stupid in order not to see how stupid they were to think she was stupid, because it was bad to think they were stupid.

She preferred to be stupid and good,
rather than bad and clever.

It is bad to be stupid: she needs to be clever
to be so good and stupid.
It is bad to be clever, because this shows
how stupid they were
to tell her how stupid she was."
(Laing, 1970)

To struggle for meaning when the answer appears meaningless leads one to lose contact with the experience of living. In infancy, Laing's living was attacked from all directions - a "no exit" situation. Later even the validity of his own experience was questioned. Childhood questions about reality brought unreal responses.

"I could not believe all of them, one of them,
or none of them." (Laing, 1976)

Upon his birth, Laing's mother became depressed. A nursemaid hired to nurture him in her absence:

> "..turned out to be a drunken slut and another woman was brought in. She was a drunken slut as well. Then my mother took over... ." (Laing, 1976)

Mother abandoned him to his father's violence. At three he heard his father tell his mother:

> "I am going to beat him within an inch of his life this time." (Laing, 1976)

Then:

> "...he began literally to smash me to pieces...I contracted to a point. There no one could get me. On the other side of that point was... where I came from?" (Laing, 1976)

He withdrew his energy leaving the musculature without the flow that gives it unity. Here, so reduced [("... within an inch of my life (Laing, 1976)], he felt safe, in control. He had experienced near—death and survived. From time to time, as an adult, the experience is recapitulated. He asks:

> "Who can say whether we are alive or dead?" (Laing, 1976)

Laing's childhood memories read like a horror story. Few came into his house. When they did there was apt to be physical violence. His own movements were contained. He was "led on a leash like a dog" until he was five. (Laing, 1976) Answers to questions about sexuality massacred the truth. Both parents agreed that:

> "... all sexual activity had ceased between them irrevocably before I was conceived." (Laing, 1976)

For Laing, early violent experiences led to the formation of the Creative Character. A total attack on the life-flow leads to fragmentation of energy. One is unable to move forward into the world for satisfaction because the bodily aggression to move out is lacking. Terrible dangers, the way things once were, are imagined to lie ahead.

Energy at these times can easily get captured in the head - "The person feels like a fetus in the womb of his skull, being fed by thoughts from his brain." (Laing, 1976) From this place the individual may move backward in the Rhythmic Cycle to the nothingness at the center of the gap, or to the place of illusion and dream that gives a sense of another world, or he may, if the assertiveness can be gotten to, move forward.

With the release of terror, the person moves into the next portion of the Rhythmic Cycle, the Communicator Phase. This movement is marked by expressions that demand that injustices be rectified and needs met. Here again, energy might be blocked. The throat tenses; words stream in an effort toward opening.

Laing's writings demonstrate his movement in both directions, backward into the Dreamer Phase and forward into the Communicator Phase. The move forward is evident in his work of the Sixties. The primal rage he felt in watching patients shocked, drugged and robotized was nourished by the rebelliousness of the times. His writing communicated his protest:

> "If I really wanted to put myself in the position of being driven crazy, then the best way I can think of going about it is to go into one of those psychiatric institutions, mental hospital, where psychiatric psychosis is in full swing, uncontested." (Laing, 1976)

Laing's move through the leading edge and into Communication was facilitated by the characteristics of the '60's. Communication and protest were the watchwords. His ideas were reinforced by events around him. He was a quasi-leader of a protest movement, part of the larger revolution that began against many of society's institutionalized practices.

As the social rhythm moved through this upheaving phase of its development, Laing's work lost popular following. The vast applauding audience was gone. In his writing his concerns drifted backward in the Rhythmic Cycle. From the leading edge, he returned to the Dream State.

In The Facts of Life (Laing, 1976), writing now in the Seventies, Laing talks of his struggle to experience, understand and dissect the psychological aspects of intrauterine events and birth, concerns that mark the Dream Phase. He presents autobiographical material and searches out the sources of his own personal pain in fetal development and birth trauma.

The book moves in Laing's characteristically creative way. It passes through the fantasy productions of the Dreamer Phase; the Creator presentation of memory fragments, role plays, syllogisms and logical arguments; and ends in a more formal Communicator piece, appropriately entitled, "A Lecture." There, he again presents his Sixties protest against the Psychiatric Establishment, adding new examples from personal experience to his earlier dissent.

Laing's book, as well as his work in general, does not move to full development. The Rhythmic Cycle is not carried through to completion. It falls short. A full, energetic Rhythmic Cycle goes beyond Communication into Inspiration, Solidification and the Achievement of an identifiable position that manifests the total integrity of the person's unique being, and their full human process.

Laing suggests his own lack of fulfillment. He is still seeking the sources of his difficulties, looking for answers to early questions:

> "I am a student of my own nature. I can only tell you how my own life has gone. Its been a very circuitous journey. I certainly would not propose it as a model for anyone else to follow. In a sense, I suppose its just the story of a mid-twentieth century intellectual. I suppose I'm one of the symptoms of the times.... . I feel my major contributions are yet to come." (Laing, 1976)

Communicator

Simple Song,
Simple feeling,
Touch my soul
Sets me reeling,
So I sing as I go,
Simple song I love you so.

THE TONE

Community - the simple sharing of mood and purpose - binds us together in oneness. The warm bond of contact overcomes separation. Longing is subsumed in feelings of belonging when we move together through the shared needs of our humanity. Give and take come easily when we are sympathetically in tune with each other.

Philosophers posit utopia, communities of lifestyle and purpose, gentle cradling havens that soothe stress with lullaby. They are places where needs are met by caring response and tender love. Simple rules follow from the easy justice of fairness. Life is sweet. Happiness abounds.

The philosopher's logic seems to make such good sense. But the complexity of the human animal doesn't fit neatly into the package. Other trends and patterns, emotions and strivings, which fill out the wholeness of man, introduce counterforces and emphasize principles that contradict the simple view of life which is formed in infancy when an easy relationship that fulfills needs is so important to full growth. If that relationship is denied, the character of the Communicator is formed.

The Communicator is acutely attuned to a withholding environment. He forms a variety of physical and behavioral strategies to communicate need. Charms or demands ranging from the subtle to the revolutionary are developed. Others are cajoled to provide, in the hope that the common bond can be reestablished.

The Communicator can have a softening effect on others, attuning them to the vulnerable side of life, humanizing by stimulating a loving and caring emotional response. At best they orchestrate a concern for warmth and justice like a Norman Rockwell painting, a Pete Seeger concert, or a Hippie flower child. Bundled in a wrapper of innocence and optimism, the Communicator appeals.

Initially, hostility and frustration are couched in humor and wit, made fluffy and softened by the "oh, so human" side of life. Through humor, difficulty is shared rather than lived in isolation. Togetherness in a common consciousness joins what has been separated. In unity there is strength to rectify wrongs and move forward in safety.

To change the world, though, may take a complaint. When charm fails to bring a response, rage rises to stir a reaction. Something is wrong. A need is not being met. Communication is begun in order to affect the environment - to make it respond. Rage demands a difference. "I am deprived." "I am denied." "I am cheated." "Look at me!" "Respond to me!" "Love me!"

Enjoined, the environment quickens to the challenge as the shout builds momentum. The request is heard. Harmony is sought. The environment changes. A response is given.

When the response is acknowledged the Communicator quiets for a moment but, when locked in the dynamics of personal character, what is given is not taken in. Left unsatisfied the protest resumes.

The process can thereby occur again and again and again. The bite persists. "Give me more." "Give me something else." "Not quite right." "I am not satisfied." The environment grows weary and attends elsewhere. The cry is no longer heard, the need goes unanswered. The Communicator retreats, denies his emptiness and lives around it. He returns to the passivity of charm to regain balancing connection to the world around him.

The history of protest follows this course. Those who yell and rage, or charm and manipulate for change, receive little when the change comes. They do not ask for what their body needs. They are distracted by the emotional outlet protest allows. The source of their tension however, is not affected. Satisfactions are not assimilated.

Aspects of the protest movement of the Sixties illustrate how a responsive ear encourages escalated demand and causes rage to expand to anarchistic proportions, shaking the interpersonal balance to its roots, leaving the Communicator demanding outrageously. It all started with a powerful but controlled attempt to right the horribly unfair wrongs of black suppression. Tactics were measured and defined. Non-violent methods were skillfully developed to fight an inhuman, racist establishment.

As success came and the rules and laws began to change, the tempo increased. Voices grew wilder. Gaining fuel from Vietnam War protestors, the country's mood repeatedly reached the flash point. Violence erupted, devastating outbursts occurred and led to ill consequences. Those already on the fringe felt the searing consequences of going too far as inner cities burned.

Lyndon Johnson listened to the longings of these protestors. With a strong Communicator component himself, he responded to the plight of the needy and the weak. Money and energy were poured into a War on Poverty. His sympathetic ear and generous response failed to satisfy. It stimulated only more requests, more demands.

When Nixon followed the listening ear was gone. This President would not meet with those who had demands. Pickets went unattended. Protestors were called "whiners." The establishment consolidated and would give no more. Denied a response, the sounds of protest faded rapidly:

> "Bye bye American Pie. Drove my Chevy to
> the levy but the levy was dry." (Mclean, 1971)

The end of the Communicator Phase came quickly. From it, from cries of protest, a society had responded. The establishment was changed. Safeguards were built in law to change the nation's more flagrant racist inhumanities.

ENERGY DYNAMICS

The Communicator maintains a physiologically deprived energy position. Intake is reduced leaving a mild but chronic sense of deprivation. A demanding attitude doesn't ease to receive and take in. The result is a hunger that drives sharp and critical attunement to any deficiency of the environment, a physical motivation to develop and maintain a behavior pattern that highlights these deficits, and a desire for abundance that is rarely satisfied. Formed by a sparse ungiving environment, the holding pattern that sets the organism in the Communicator pattern typically develops during the first months after birth.

The Communicator learns to hold within by constricting that part of the inner tube, which includes the mouth, lungs and voice box, as well as the stomach. These organs call for what is needed and process what is taken in.

Normally the infant cries in response to internal urgings. When crying consistently fails to communicate and bring what is needed from the environment, it stops. The oral tube holds and conserves what energy is available by restricting activity. While the feeling of pain is reduced by stifling inner movement, the capacity to assimilate any nourishment that might be received is also limited. Things don't function so well. Lack, the stimulus to longing, rage, denial and mild depression, prevails.

Lack shows in the Communicator's body. Deprivation is written into a lean undernourished appearance. The long hungry look physically portrays the frustrated reaching that patterned its growth. The chest is misformed with deep indentations and distorting malformations in the rib-cage. Posture is often slouched and collapsed, with the belly drooping, looking as if there is not enough life force to hold it up.

The voice and face often develop an appeal which calls out for contact and supplies. To enhance it, the Communicator may develop a resonant volume and pitch that seems to include the whole body. The voice belies the physical appearance. The surpisingly undernourished body of a beautifully toned radio announcer is an example.

The Communicator's charming youthful face that seems to never age is a constant stimuli for a tender nourishing response. But in the later years the face may wizen and the voice rasp and shout if the inner tensions haven't yet relaxed.

DEVELOPMENT OF THE COMMUNICATOR

From the receptivity of the Dream state to the splitting of the Creative moment, the infant moves to the Communicator Phase of the Rhythmic Cycle. He develops the capacities to call upon others for the stimulation necessary to gain strength and provide the interaction through which he eventually learns to take care of himself. The rhythmic flow of development in energy level at this point depends on input and reciprocal stimulation - a new era of bonding between mother and child.

Birth necessitates a new vehicle of connection to replace the umbilical cord. The new being brings with it the attraction of its rhythms. Warmth, color and tiny physical expressions are a charm to adults who reciprocate with their own warmth and tenderness to the vulnerability and softness of the baby.

The very existence of the young baby is a stimulus to change the environment. It cannot make it without response from others. It needs love and nourishment - contact that is meaningful to its need system - along with adult protection from overwhelming stresses. Communication provides the common bond of attachment between baby and parent.

When the back—and—forth of the relationship between infant and adult does not go easily, the Communicator character is formed. Birth has fragmented physical oneness between mother and fetus. The offspring and parent must find a new physiological balance, a common link no longer based on direct umbilical connection, but on responsiveness to communicated stimuli.

The infant responds to internal stimuli by crying for satisfaction from without. A sympathetic environment, a mother tuned into her child's needs, answers the call and provides physiological relief. The baby's needs are met. Touch, warmth, food and comfort provide nourishment for the infant and enhance the beginnings of an easy interpersonal rhythm.

The mother too is rewarded in the process. The distress caused by the infant's cry is removed when she understands and responds appropriately. The warm physical contact and gentle tender stimulation she receives when interacting with her baby brings a contented pleasure to her body. They are joined together in a bond of good feeling.

Nursing can provide a time of shared pleasure for each. The child receives the sensual pleasure of sucking, the closeness of skin contact and the release from hunger pains. The mother feels the pleasure of breast stimulation, the relaxation of physical closeness and freedom from painful pressure that might be caused by the accumulation of milk. The formula of their relationship is simple, natural and reciprocal. It is a fair bargain for each.

But the infant's dependencies can be easily denied. If the tension of unmet urgings goes unheeded, the baby moves from longing to agitation, fussing, crying and raging. Rage is the infant's maximum protest of unmet needs. It is diffuse, lacking the subtle communication possibilities that language will later bring.

Rage in the wailing infant is total. It involves the whole organism. If it remains unanswered, the cry for attention weakens and dies, conserving the infant's energy. The baby, its heart cried out, enters a depressed state. Movement is constricted and awareness of the need denied. Direct expression is blocked.

The infant's attempts consistently fail if they are met by a character attitude of withholding or an external environment without enough to offer. A propped bottle falls out of the baby's mouth and cannot be retrieved. A schedule requires "No response now!" even while the child's need grows. A mother confuses meeting a baby's needs with spoiling. The cry is repeated - mother can not hear or is to weak to understand and respond.

The random frustrations caused by fate are reinforced by a systematic way of denying baby when it attempts to stimulate a response. The "good baby" doesn't cry but learns that showing need invites frustration. Better no awareness than the emptiness of being denied.

Through experience, need becomes associated with the chronic denying tensions in the inner tube. The organism grows allergic, hypersensitive so to speak, to its own need system. Fussiness marks eating times. Likes and dislikes are sharp and absolute. Unsuccessful struggles to force eating are frequent. Gluttony alternates with sparse intake, while overall consumption remains low.

The Communicator searches for an interpersonal connection that will be satisfying to relieve tension and answer underlying need. But often, as tense physical areas soften a bit, the contained and denied rage reappears. The potentially satisfying other is driven away before the need can be satisfied. The denying process begins again.

As an infant, supplies were not fully received by the Communicator. Rationed, the baby grows up to be rational. As an adult, attention goes toward the task of getting supplies or understanding what moves the supplier rather than to assimilating what is available. Energies reach for what is wanted with voice, charm, manipulation and protest. Language becomes highly developed in the hope that meaningful communication will lead to a gain of what is needed. It is typically not enough to relieve the rage that blocks the processes of consumption. Demands simply grow more insistent. Spite gets even when the other holds back. The "in-tense" situation grows making it impossible to take in. The dynamic spreads beyond the feeding situation:

> Paul, a Communicator, gently and tenderly asked Georgia to give him a massage. His body hurt. Georgia began to rub his shoulders.
> "A little lower please," said Paul.
> "Your hands are cold," said Paul.

Georgia stopped, rubbed her hands together and began again.

"More toward the middle, deeper, harder," said Paul, a bit of anger coming into his voice.

Frustrated, Georgia moved and pushed harder.

"I'm doing the best I can," she said.

"It's too hard now!" he complained.

Georgia threw up her hands.

"I quit!"

"You always quit!" raged Paul. "I never get anything around here - not even a simple massage."

Paul spent the rest of the day withdrawn and sulking. Still, he felt righteous anger whenever he noted Georgia's pain and confusion.

The infant Communicator grows to adulthood denying its needs for tender comfort and nourishment - unable to easily identify and directly take care of them. If early experience led to holding and denial, the adult continually seeks common bond, community and communication, but has difficulty taking satisfaction in an easy and flowing way.

Life experiences that allow relief to the tense area are sought. Warmth and love can loosen tightness. Raging can get the inner core moving. Complaints, when supported, build to overt outburst, outrage. These behaviors serve to ease inner tube tensions providing temporary release.

The characteristic behaviors of the Communicator are an attempt to solve the problems of the undernourished physical structure. Food, warmth and love are needed for satisfaction A nourishing bond is sought through the application of verbal charm, wit, intelligence, and stimulation of social fairness and equality. The person reaches out for the bond, but because taking-in disturbs the internal holding and leads to the production of rage, the need is often expressed distortedly. The Communicator more typically helps others rather than reaching for meeting. The hope is, "If I do it for them, they should return the favor." But, when help is offered in return, its value is denied, not good enough or not needed.

Recognizing and allowing one's dependency, opening oneself to be given to in times of need, is the only satisfactory solution to the Communicator's dilemma. But along the way to this goal the deprived body will run into the intense feelings of a longing emptiness. These feelings are often too unpleasant to face in everyday life and so are easily lived around.

Holding back needs and denying them satisfaction leads to ideas of being deprived, cheated and treated unfairly. Others are seen to blame for the lack of satisfaction. The situation begun in infancy is replayed in all interpersonal relationships.

For the Communicator it is a small redefinition to project that "Society" is responsible for our not being taken care of properly. It doesn't show enough social concern and isn't attuned to unfairness as the cause of our problems. Real injustices do cause great problems, but the continuing nagging psychic sense of deprivation in the Communicator is not founded in class or social status. It finds its impetus within the body structure and holding patterns that developed early in life.

Righteous indignation and the Communicator's protest can and do stimulate complaint in a way that is beneficial to society. The most strident activists begin their training in early contact with denying mothers and are attuned to deviations in a fair and balanced community by the distortions in their own bodies. In the time when their complaints coincide with society's passing through the Communicator Phase of the Rhythmic Cycle, their voice stimulates movements that initiate improved social responsiveness to those in need.

THERAPY

The solution to the dilemma of the Communicator requires reexperiencing and working with the feelings around needs to see them in their true proportion. Then, learning to take care of one's own well-being becomes possible. Such work results in a change of body structure, an opening of the tensions of the inner tube, and an even deeper responsiveness to energy exchanges between people.

Thomas had been in therapy for a number of years and had made good progress. Tall and thin, his commitment to jogging had provided both the energy and self-discipline to insure continued emotional growth in therapy. He had freed himself from chronic low-grade psychological depression through a regular program of extensive running that overcame the oxygen deficits caused by his constricted breathing.

When he had first came to therapy Thomas's chest showed physical distortions, immobility, and a yellowish color. It was a source of concern. Our work together yielded improvements. His chest had more color and was more alive, though movement remained constricted and the rib cage continued to have little flexibility.

His behavior was true to the Communicator character. Bright and verbal, he wanted to be the favorite client. His charm and wit were delightful. His rebellion was saved for his boss. Despite his intelligence, he had underachieved on the job. His poor performance had been a badge of his rebellious spirit until he realized that his behavior simply prevented feeling fullness as a man.

We had stopped therapy for a while at my suggestion. Intervals allow growth to consolidate. Resistances that seem to be so important often fade with space from the relationship.

During the interval Thomas established a close relationship with a woman. He had had many relationships and often was quite caring but he consistently picked people who did not or could not love back. This time it was different - he was accepted and cared for.

When he returned to therapy we agreed to work further on his chest, the gateway to his heart. It had remained profoundly misformed. The sternum, at the center of the rib cage, was sunken and depressed and seemed to pull in the whole front of his body. It was as if he had sucked in his own ribs rather than sucking in the milk of life.

I worked intensely pushing on the intercostal muscles that held the ribs tight. I massaged the muscles that held the chest high. I had him lie over a breathing bench <(a small stool about two feet high with a round pad on which to rest the back (Lowen, 1977)>. His rib-cage was in a stretched position putting great stress on his holdings.

Suddenly he let go. Deep heavings of the chest and angry, frightened, wailing cries rolled through him. His chest was alive, mobile and open, no longer a solid indented plate but a living vibrant structure.

Release brought two insights. He remembered a feeling of suffocation. He had an awareness of how difficult it was for him to allow anyone to love him - to open and take in. He saw that he guarded himself strongly from wanting another's love because he so feared that it would later be denied him. The heart of the Communicator's dynamics was directly experienced.

THE BUSHMEN

The Bushmen of the Kalahari live in an environment that provides need satisfaction only with great personal effort. The desert is a sparse ungiving home. History indicates the Bushmen were forced there through repeated tribal defeats. The desert offers little to sustain human life, rather, it guarantees periods of deprivation and blocking in the Communicator Phase of the Rhythmic Cycle.

Most Bushmen have a physical structure showing Communicator elements. Their cultural and interpersonal pattern demonstrate its psychology. Their life remains simple. Unlike many other primitive cultures they do not develop complex authority relationships or controlling cultural structures but instead reinforce equality and the common bond. They have no powerful chieftains, complex sacred rites, deep faith in mythic explanations or historically imbued artifacts. The problems that formal systems usually address are handled in simple, non-authoritarian ways.

Bushmen are a communicative people, and use language to maintain a peaceful, harmless interpersonal balance. They are an intelligent people - intelligent in the Western, scientific sense of validating evidence and coming to practical conclusions. In their culture, one sees the dynamics involved in forming a workable community within a setting of deprivation.

Nurturance, the Communicator issue, is the primary concern of the Bushmen. The seasons dictate the ease of its obtainment. At times food is plentiful - gathered by the women and hunted by the men. In winter, though, rainfall diminishes, food becomes difficult to obtain, eating standards drop and hunger is felt. The scarcity of rain means a retreat to more permanent water areas, and limitation on the range of travel allowed to hunt and gather. The problem becomes a crisis during drought. Droughts come regularly.

In some areas of the Kalahari the "probability of drought is about two years in five and, of severe drought, one year in four." (Yellen & Lee, 1976) In other areas the situation is worse and ninety percent of the water is obtained from plants. (Tanaka, 1976) During drought, without dependable water locations for 300 days of the year, migration for food gathering is curtailed. Hunting possibilities are meager.

Severe food problems affect the body structure of the Bushmen. In the desert their height averages around five feet. With better natural conditions, they grow larger, demonstrating that genetic factors are not enough to account for their size. (Tanaka, 1976)

Bushmen are extremely thin. Undernourishment is most apparent in the limbs. They are lanky and wiry. "The muscles on them form firm and well marked cord-like projections" (Schapera, 1930). Their stomachs show different proportions at different times: potbellied when food is abundant; shrunken, leaving flaps of skin, during famine.

Though hunger occurs frequently, nobody starves and infants are almost completely insulated from its overt distresses. Long periods of breastfeeding on demand are customary and insure that the very young eat regularly though their parents' nutritional state may affect the quality of the milk they receive.

Infants are kept in close contact with their mothers, carried on the hip and sleeping in their arms at night. The breast is always available and easily reached. During their early lives interpersonal frustration is kept low. Indulgence is high. (Konner, 1976) This bountiful situation typically lasts until the next child is conceived, sometime after three and up to as much as six years later.

Among Bushmen it is believed that the milk of a pregnant mother belongs to the unborn fetus, so the child is deprived of the nourishment and warm contact of the breast when the mother becomes pregnant. Weaning, based on events outside the child's control, brings a harsh fall from an idyllic, satisfied state. The pain of hunger and loneliness that it brings can cause severe depression and the blocking of the inner tube that imprints the dynamics of the Communicator. Nisa, a Kung Bushwoman, spoke movingly of the situation:

> "I wanted the milk she had in her breasts, and when she nursed him (infant brother) my eyes watched as the milk spilled out. I cried all night, cried and cried, and then dawn broke. Some mornings I just stayed around and my tears fell and I cried and refused food. That was because I saw him nursing. I saw with my eyes the milk spilling out. I thought it was mine." (Shostak, 1976)

As an adult, Nisa herself posited the relationship between this kind of early trauma and later physical patterning. She believed the Bushmen's slight build and short stature came from having been weaned too early and not having been given enough to eat.

For the Bushmen, the trauma of weaning throws the child into demanding supplies from a sparse feeding environment. The result is hunger and a life turnaround that is extreme. Before weaning the children thrive. Well-nourished and with plenty of parental contact, they are bright and active. They develop even faster physically than Western children their age, passing milestones at a relatively early date. (Konner, 1976) Once cut off from the breast they quickly lose their advantage and characteristic signs of Communicator difficulties, a "feast or famine" attitude, disproportionate thinness and potbellies, develop.

The "feast or famine" attitude continues on, coloring adult behavior. When food is available Bushmen have prodigious appetites.

> "Their voracity was almost incredible, and had been commented upon by every traveller who had any experience of them...a single one would eat half a sheep." (Dornan, 1925).

When hunger is great, tastes become secondary. The Bushman's appetite can be triggered by the widest variety of edible substances. Even rotten stench-laden food does not deter their desire. (Dornan, 1923)

Not surprisingly, food images invade their stories and folk tales. They contaminate fantasies about bodily functions as well as social institutions. Oral and sexual concerns, for example, join in the story of the origin of sex. The vagina is associated with the head and eventually with eating.

> "Gara (a God-like figure of Bushmen folklore) tried screwing his wife in the nostrils. Then he tried her ears. Finally, getting nowhere, he tried her nostrils again. He was getting nowhere. His wife looked at him and said, 'Don't you know anything? What do you think you're doing in my nostrils and ears? Can't you see that there's a much better place - here? This is what you eat, you fool.'" (Biesele, 1976)

The beginning of marriage is also associated with food:

> "In the beginning, men and women lived apart and had nothing to do with each other.

Five men went hunting and killed a springbok. Because their fire had gone out they could not cook it. They decided to send one man to borrow some fire from the women, whose fire never went out.

He came upon a woman near the river, gathering grass seeds. She invited him to her village where she would give him fire.

While there, she cooked her seeds into porridge and gave them to the man. He was so pleased that he decided to stay and never returned to his male companions.

The men grew hungry and, not seeing their friend, sent another who met with the same fate." (Biesele, 1976)

The end of the story repeats with each man successively leaving to find a nourishing mate. This Bushman story is a version of "the way to a man's heart is through his stomach." It underlines the importance need satisfaction has as an intense, encompassing concern.

The longing pangs of hunger and loneliness, the feelings of emptiness and agitation as relief is sought, and the frustration and rage when satisfaction is denied required the development of checks and compensations within individuals if the culture was to endure.

Among Bushmen, community processes and the cultural character of the Communicator insure sharing of resources and physical contact to lessen the pain of individual frustration. The community becomes an everpresent mothering source of comfort. The bond between individuals is close. The band eats and sleeps around a common shared campfire. Huts are not separate dwelling places. They are only used to protect from the wind and rain. Family members sleep cuddled, closely together.

Almost all interactions are characterized by proximity and contact. The security and warmth built into the social patterning insures that soft warm comfort is always close at hand. The resulting gentleness and sense of group well-being led one author to call the Bushmen "The Harmless People." (Marshall, 1968)

The easiness that characterizes child-rearing among the Bushmen emphasizes their reluctance to add to nature's frustration and denial. Children and adolescents have no responsibility for adult chores such as hunting and gathering. Nothing is required of them until adulthood, remarkable with the difficulties in acquiring food. The Bushmen's unconscious guiding principle is of community. Little is asked of anyone - each teaches himself and gives to others.

Still, a deep longing sadness growing out of the deprived body of the Communicator remains. It is heard clearly in "the very sad air" (Dornan, 1925) of Bushmen singing.

"We stopped to listen, caught in the net of music which Ekwane had cast into the air, for it was a soft, sad song that he hummed and played, a song in a minor key to wring your heart, to make you think of places far away and make you feel like crying .... ."

It went:

"If you are walking in the veldt, and you remember where a field of melons was growing and you go there and find them but when you taste them they are bitter, so you can't eat them, you leave them, you leave them, that is what this song is about.'" (Marshall, 1976)

The sadness comes from a deeply structured deprivation - of being without. The Bushmen communicate to gain an antidote, the soothing comfort of "being with."

> "Separation and loneliness are unendurable to them. Security and comfort for them lie in their belonging to their group." (Marshall, 1976)

Even one's personal death is viewed against the background of such loneliness.

> "Dasing said: `It is bad to die because when you die you are all alone.'" (Marshall, 1976)

The unbearableness of separation causes status hierarchy to be almost nonexistent. All distance, even that caused by role differentiation, is minimized. Leaders do develop around competencies, but are given no special acclaim or power to accompany their leadership.

The trance dance leader may use his expertise at the ceremony, but gains no special favors for it in other group activities. The hunter with prowess is careful not to achieve too much more than his compatriots, and downplays success or even intentionally fails to achieve in order not to be isolated from the spirit of group equality that a heroic place would bring. An equalizing effect is established among members. (Van Der Post, 1958)

Because enduring status differentials do not develop, the Bushmen's way of relating stays simple, unmarked by elaborate artifacts. Though men and women differ in the division of labor - the men hunting and the women gathering and rearing children - there are no power problems between the sexes. Each is valued for its contribution - a contribution that is seen as naturally defined by sex.

In spiritual matters, relics and sacred connections or lineage that would give power are minimized. Holy reverence seems absent and rituals, though important, do not have an absolute feeling connected with them. The Bushmen's God does not punish, nor is he given the powers of an "Almighty." Though the dead are thought to have influence, they are not a matter of utmost concern, and no elaborate steps are taken to pacify them. Egalitarianism and simplicity are not challenged.

To insure equality of position and protect against undue longing, large presents from outsiders are met with belittling remarks so as not to confer special status. Gifts are given between members to communicate feeling and reinforce sharing. Developing a willingness to give is important when supplies aren't enough. It is taught early in life. "Na." ("Give it to me!") and "I." ("Here take this!") are among the first words that Bushmen children learn.

Giving implies a gift will come in return to maintain the bond between individuals. Property moves around. No one becomes special by amassing things. The most cherished gift only belongs to its owner for a while. Exchange insures the valued prize is held by many. (Marshall, 1976) Through gift-giving and sharing, the group maintains its common emotional balance. The community is not threatened by aberrant acts. Stealing is nonexistent.

Sharing is paramount for Bushmen. Among the hungry, hoarding and the resulting envy would be disastrous. Meat from the hunt must be distributed evenly within the band. Withholding results in mild group censure.

Unlike the Negritos' spoken of earlier, the Bushmen are not an attacked people, not subject to the terror of a violent Nature. No armatarium of creative rituals and great traditions are needed to protect them. Their simple taboos are not associated with grave penalties. No formal courts or banishments are used against infringements. The tendency, as in childrearing, is to indulgence. Trespasses are talked about.

114

Without formal institutions, the burden of maintaining group harmony falls on the development of the Phase of the Rhythmic Cycle the Bushmen are characteristically equipped for communication. Bushmen are expert and frequent Communicators. They are adept with voice, word, story and intellect. They possess a rich musical language and are noted for the oral dexterity required for the percussion sounds that syncopate its rhythms. Variously pitched clicks and pops, part of the spoken word, are nimbly formed and released by the tongue shaping different vacuum cavities in the mouth.

The Bushmen are verbally and conceptually fluid. Folklorist Megan Biesele found most of them were able and willing folklore experts.

> "Their storytelling seems to be a natural outgrowth and perfection of verbal activities they have been practicing all their lives." (Biesele, 1976)

Even the young are adept in storytelling, but for the old it is a favorite pastime, providing the comfort of reminiscence. Many of their tales are enriched with factual knowledge and life experiences.

Other stories, ancestral tales with the Gods as central characters, tend to lightly play out the Bushman's inner rage through the expression of the outrageous. They exemplify how the Dream element is expressed in the Communicator Character. Here "The Gods" are simple folksy characters without any semblance of holy, powerful, or mythic distance. In fact, the situations they are placed in, as in the earlier story of Gara, often arouse the scorn and derision of the listeners.

A central story figure, the God Kauha, is much like the Bushman himself. He epitomizes the Communicator's facile use of wit and quick thinking to suggest and refine options to direct action. If direct means aren't sufficient to attain, and for a tiny hungry people this occurs often, cleverness is required. Kauha tricks and is tricked in return.

The Bushmen, like Kauha, employ their cleverness. In the quest for meat and water they smoke out underground dwellings and hook animals with long probes. They use tiny poisoned arrows on big game which when hit are tracked, sometimes for days, until they fall. They bait traps all over the desert, disguise themselves as animals to get within shooting range, and imitate the cry of the young to attract the mother to within arrow's distance. (Dornan, 1925)

The Bushmen make clever use of the lion as a hunting dog. They let the lion make the kill and eat just enough to take the edge off his hunger. Then they light a fire to drive him away and recover the uneaten portion for themselves. With similar ingenuity, they capture the eye of a giraffe with a "glittering magic stone" to hypnotically draw him into shooting range. (Van Der Post, 1958)

The Bushmen's intelligence is also evident in their fine thought, the refinement of inner communication. Western laymen often view primitive peoples as intellectually inferior. They refer to superstitious practices like those of the Philippine Pygmy whose terror leads to ritual and magical thinking - thinking prior to objective, intellectual processes. However, Jones and Konner (1976) studied the thought processes of Bushmen as they spoke of their hunting strategy and found evidence that contradicts the view of intellectual poverty among primitives.

They found, that while in discussion, the Bushmen carefully sorted out hearsay and interpretation from their voluminous observation of data. They admitted ignorance readily so as to clear the way for acquiring new and useful data. Through logical argument they refined their knowledge, discarding generalizations that didn't fit the data. They took a skeptical approach to what they couldn't verify and expressed their doubts when they felt someone was being gullible or incomplete. They accepted the challenge of others' questioning without distorting defensively.

Jones (1976) concludes that the Kung Bushmen demonstrate the scientist's method of gathering data and making relevant conclusions at a level that surpasses "lay observers and many professionals in Western society."

The Bushmen's intellectual approach is characteristic of the Communicator. Large theories are not formed to control the organization of data, nor is information historically preserved to establish an authoritative body of knowledge.

These lacks are consonant with a personality that does not allow for status or privilege and in general rebels against hierarchic orders of any kind. When controlling superstitious generalizations occur (e.g., a large caterpillar seen only in the rainy season causes malaria) they are easily discarded with new evidence.

The Bushmen's intellect, though developed empirically and conceptually, does not search for the reasons underneath things or wonder about deeper motivations. They are not in-depth analysts, nor do they look into themselves to discover answers and search for hidden meanings. Close decisions are not mulled to define subtle personal preferences. Involved choices are often simply left to chance, determined by the throwing of divining dice.

In-depth thinking demands a more individual approach to life, an inner search. Bushman are not on their own. The individual is not important. Like all Communicators they depend on others and stay psychologically close. Self-absorption would weaken the common bond. Even those with an affinity toward introspective spiritual truths are expected to be group members. They are given little special opportunity to pursue and deepen their individual bent. The character of the culture restricts individual development that might lead to separation.

The logic of language helps the Bushmen master their relationship to the environment. But language also provides the vehicle for social contact and emotional control. Marshall (1976) describes just how central communication is to the Bushmen and how subtly and highly developed it is. The Bushmen, she found, as begets their character are:

> "...the most loquacious people I know... Conversation in a Kung encampment is a constant sound... . The voice and words communicate - criticizing the deviant, remembering events and sharing anxieties about food. Chatter is often punctuated with shrieks and howls of laughter... (because) laughter was an outlet for tension." (Marshall, 1976)

In the Bushmens' "incessant talking", Marshall found fine distinctions were evident between types of communication. Simple "Conversation" were distinguished from a "Talk" during which everyone joins in a disagreement and emotional release increasingly escalates. In such "Talks,":she found:

> "People take sides and express opinions, accusing and denying, or defending persons involved." (Marshall, 1976)

Still even greater energy is expended in a "Shout." A "Shout" is a verbal explosion against a disaster. Here the eruption rages vehemently in volcanic proportions. Marshall calls it:

> "The greatest din I have ever heard humans produce out of themselves." (1976)

Conversation, Talk, and Shout help the Bushmen with the emotions caused by deprivation. Conversation gives an easily accessible reassurance that someone is available to soothe inner agitation. Talk provides a culturally condoned outlet for rage. Shout overcomes feelings of vulnerability and powerlessness.

The Bushmen's culture clearly exemplifies the culture of the Communicator. It answers the experience of lack that is imposed by nature and writes itself into the tensions of their bodies. In overcoming the pain of lack the desire to "be with others" flourishes. A simple social structure assures it. With little hierarchy there is little possibility for social rejection that could destroy the security of common bond, of shared link.

Words provide the Bushmen with a means of simple, balanced connection. They display a verbal ability that is marked by phonetic dexterity as well as conceptual refinement and ready wit.

For the Bushmen words establish the sense of connection and guard against its rupture. They move the rage of unsatisfied longing through vocal rather than physical outlets that would break their bonds. Community provides the psychological sustenance that nature, on the physical level, intermittently denies. The Bushmen society overcomes longing. The Bushman belongs.

ALBERT ELLIS - THE COMMUNICATOR

Words can stimulate or slow the motion of life's energy. The right sentences can identify, permit and encourage excitement. But words, when unconsciously used as a means of intellectual manipulation to control the development or experiencing of feeling, can distort the path of full flowing.

In most contemporary psychotherapies words are only a carrier in the therapeutic process, secondary to fantasies, emotions, release, and action. For Albert Ellis, however, they are primary and of utmost importance. He spends the therapeutic hour in lively rhetoric and argumentative dialogue, trying to change the words the patient tells himself.

Ellis believes words, thoughts and ideas are the cause of neurotic problems. Suffering, he says, is mainly the result of distorted internal philosophies. Correct them, he argues, and neurosis wanes.

Albert Ellis is a student of ancient philosophy. He chose reason to be the guiding principle of his therapeutic system, Rational-Emotive Therapy:

> "The rational therapist believes, in other words, that patients (and other people) literally talk themselves into their neurotic or psychotic states by telling themselves illogical and irrational sentences and ideas, which they previously learned from their parents and their culture, and have internalized and keep ceaselessly and senselessly repeating." (Ellis, 1975)

Emotions, he argues are largely "... a biased, prejudiced kind of thought... ." (Morse). Thoughts it is seen are clearly primary.

With wit and sarcasm, questions and debate, Ellis attempts to engage his client in a Socratic dialogue to reveal the real philosophical system that underlies the patient's disturbed communication with himself.

Ellis summarizes neurotic problems in the "ABC's of Rational-Emotive Therapy." The patient wrongly views an Activating (A) event as causing a negative Consequence (C), for example an unpleasant feeling or a psychosomatic response. This, Ellis argues, is a mistake. It is the missing (B), Beliefs, that are in error. It is the beliefs patients tell themselves that cause and sustain bad consequences.

Clients' troublesome sentences are based on unreasonable assumptions - assumptions that cannot be proven. Therefore Ellis attacks the neurotic ABC's with Dispute (D). He teaches his patients to dispute false assumptions in order to be sane ("or at least, less nutty"). (Robbins, 1975)

Ellis's style is disputational. He parries with the client like a Philadelphia lawyer, protesting inconsistencies, attacking overgeneralization, ridiculing magical thoughts. His voice rises and falls as he emphasizes key words and makes points. Like a hungry bird, his long thin body lunges to the attack when a weakness comes close to the surface:

> "...your behavior is Nutty...stop catastrophizing." (Ellis, 1975)"...all those necessities you feel - you've a case of "must"-urbation not masturba-tion." (Ellis, 1975)

> "...you think you're a worm, you're suffering from worminess." (Ellis, 1975)

Ellis is careful not to attack the person: "The client is only human." (Robbins, 1975) "Nutty thinking," not personhood, is confronted. Wit and humor often soften the blows. In the context of laughter, his aggression is felt as outrageous rather than hostile.

Ellis teaches the client to think like a scientist: avoid overgeneralization and root out "magical inanities." (Robbins, 1975) He demands evidence to support beliefs.

> "You think being unloved is awful? Prove it! What's awful about it?" "Awful" is a catastrophizing statement - something that's 100 percent bad (if not more). Since nothing can be that totally bad, it is wrong to say 'it is awful!' to be unloved. Unpleasant? Yes. Awful? No." (Ellis, 1975)

Ellis claims that it is the belief that it is "awful" that sustains many negative feelings, causes depression and a host of other "ridiculous" behaviors. If one learns to challenge catastrophic sentences, to dispute them regularly when they occur, one can free oneself from their results.

Ellis cajoles, argues, and uses humor in an effort to drive out personal exaggeration - to change the communications that we have with ourselves. He employs interpersonal communication to effect intrapersonal communication.

As a child, Ellis was shy and withdrawn. By his description, his connection with his parents was weak: "A father whose traveling sales job kept him away, and a mother who was extremely self-centered." He learned early that longing brought no useful response and vowed "not to be a baby." (Robbins, 1975) As an adult, he mocks therapies that stimulate the catharsis of tears and rage for encouraging "baby, baby behavior." (Robbins, 1975)

Ellis states that like all infants he too was born "screaming and crying for love." But with his early needs denied by his mother ("My brother and sister had contact with her - I didn't."), he quickly became, in his words, a skeptic and manipulator. (Robbins, 1975)

Left shy and anxious in childhood by a mother who was a "compulsive talker - always telling jokes, a frustrated comedienne," he withdrew into his own thoughts, into a quiet internal dialogue, and played the role of the "good boy" because "it paid off." (Robbins, 1975) At seven he decided his Mother was crazy and after that he never took anything she said seriously. "If she didn't love me - tough shit." (Robbins, 1975)

The "tough shit, sour grapes" reaction he claims as an adult did not come easily. It took solid work and consistent challenge to manage his seemingly overwhelming need for approval and to solve his verbal shyness.

Afraid of being unloved or laughed at, he fought against his number-one irrational idea: "It is a dire necessity for an adult to be loved or approved by almost everyone for almost everything he does." He made up shameful things to do to prove to himself that disapproval was not catastrophic. Later he would ask his clients to similarly challenge themselves. (Robbins, 1975)

His own coming out was aided in his college years by the role he assumed with his male friends. Because he was well read and full of facts he achieved the status of "expert" on sexual matters and became a consultant to his peers. His "expertise" eventually brought him professional reknown as a Sexologist, but his personal approach to sex remained at the time, more intellectual than physical.

For Communicators, words and ideas often take a higher place than action. An early book, "The Folklore of Sex," (1961) was based on reading every major word written on the subject in the years 1950 and 1960. He covered newspapers, magazines, plays, songs, etc., counting and categorizing the times a sexual word, idea or attitude was expressed.

This study of sex, in the style of a folklorist, shows a Communicator's scientific approach. Quantifying the observable, words and opinions, rather than studying what is hidden deeper: feelings, motivations and the course of experience; provided the base of information. The former could be measured, simply handled, without involving the scientifically messy complexities of depth, history or value concerns.

This type of scientific approach is capable of learning only about that which it has developed a technique to study. It lacks the individual's human potential for knowledge and the wisdom of experience. The scientific study of psychology is often criticized as simply proving common sense - what everybody knows.

In denying direct acceptance of common sense, intuitive and personal findings, this approach favors what can be scientifically verified and objectively measured but thereby sacrifices connection with much of the texture and passion of life.

The Rhythmic Cycle of Change

This intellectual, Communicator's approach with what appears at the surface, can lead to the denial of the importance of emotions. At one point, in fact, Ellis argued that there is no need for anyone to feel sustained suffering for more than a minute or two, even during such crises as the divorce or death of a loved one. Reason showed that grief did not change the reality.

Such a view suggests a lack of experience with emotional connection and involvement. Though reasonable as an assumption, the statement: "Suffering isn't logical therefore is needless and should be avoided.", does not appear to be borne out by human experience. This position was later revised.

In his personal life Ellis's needs and energy are completely absorbed in his work. His thoughts about Rational-Emotive Therapy structure his life, lead him to adventures, even provide him with musical expression - "the singing of Rational-Emotive lullabies." (Ellis, 1987)

For Ellis, words are his means of emotional release. His deepest love appears to generate from his own ideas. Aimed in this direction his source of nurturance, the internal dialogue, is never absent, and the pains of unfulfilled longings are circumscribed. He asks for little personal interest or emotional responsiveness from others. He requests only their attention.

Ellis is committed to Rational-Emotive Therapy, working full-time on his projects, letting reason (if not the Communicator Phase of the Rhythmic Cycle) take care of him and guide his life. Reason, for example, tells him not to completely abandon his body for his thoughts. "To live long you had better exercise your body... 15 minutes every day and I hate every minute of it." (Robbins, 1975)

Ellis's commitment seems total. He goes on no vacations and, "except for sex and music" (Ellis, 1988), has no leisure interests. [("That would take away from my Rational-Emotive Therapy." (Robbins, 1975)] His life's goal is to continue his

124

14-hour-a-day, seven-days-a-week regimen of Rational—Emotive expression.

In summary, Ellis relates to life as an idea. He commits himself to observable behaviors and the silent words that they suggest. As is true for the Communicator, disturbed and self-defeating feelings are quickly discharged at their beginning, through words, wit and/or argument. At the level of behavior, Ellis asks that it serve the rule of reason rather than the rule of passion. It makes for a simpler life, one void of emotional tangles.

Ellis contributes to the field of therapy by highlighting the negative and faulty ways we think upon our experience. He shows how thoughts can contribute to and sustain misery. He attacks the magic that accompanies the Dream State and the nonsensical struggles of the Creator State as contaminators of the reasonable idea. The aim, though not poetic, is to provide objectivity.

Still, Rational-Emotive Therapy, as it is practiced, goes beyond sole reliance on cognitive technique. It is behaviorial and emotive in its employment of dramatic and experiential methods, as clients are directed to take their learnings into the world and use them in ways that challenge their erroneous ways.

In his personal style, Ellis emphasizes the traits of the Communicator Phase of the Rhythmic Cycle - a need for attention; a clever, manipulative, objectifying mind; a verbal facility; a sense of outrage, protest and argument; a humorous charm and friendliness; a clear bias toward reason over emotion as well as a simplicity of life style.

Ellis worked his initial unanswered desire for attention into positive contributions around the process of Communication. He moved through the Inspirer Phase of the Rhythmic Cycle by realizing the hopelessness of his own infantile demands, the Solidifier Phase, by working through the shame of his shyness, and the Achiever Phase, by establishing himself, first in the role of a sexologist, then as the leader of a therapeutic school.

The Rhythmic Cycle of Change

Ellis's Rational-Emotive therapy, to which he appears both spouse and father, serves as a personal vehicle to gain a warm verbal connection with others and brings him both fulfillment and completion.

As Ellis reports it, life gains a simplicity, an easiness and an efficiency, once self-defeating thoughts are eliminated, replaced by logical realities. Besides this, little more need be said.

Inspirer

They call him Guru.
He taught them that,
Lifted them to possibilities beyond themselves.
With his strained spirit and his own longing
He called to them to come
But stood above.

They reached higher.
Stretched themselves beyond imagination.
Some found enlightenment, fell away and learned from life.
Others went beyond, in the ever-present possibility of adventure;
Calling him God, truth withered.

THE HOPE

Can a person be bigger than he is, lift himself even above the physical capacity to reach the ground? Energetically, he can. Like a Superman, able to leap tall buildings with a single bound, the Inspirer lifts himself beyond the limits of his own dimensions and encourages others to look up and reach toward him. He breaks through the boundaries and, because he does, he provides hope and the possibility of expanding beyond conditioned limitations.

Inspiration stirs man and excites his being, stimulates him to break out of the confines of daily patterns. It provides a magnetism that attracts and enlivens, arousing the inner fire. Like a wind on not-yet-dead coals, it momentarily uplifts the flame.

Inspiration fires a surplus of energy that can contagiously ignite others. It moves to hyperbole, stimulates grandeur, awakens genius, provides hope and possibility to carry one away from the tribulations and chains of limitation, to live a life that's more than a life.

The Evangelist shouts:

> "So much is possible. Believe! Give yourself to the glory, let your spirit be more than you are. Come - I'll show you the way. Move upward and beyond. Salvation lies in the upper reaches."

THE CHARACTER OF THE INSPIRER

The Inspirer moves beyond limits and stimulates others to do so, stimulates them to enter into an experience of adventure, prior to discipline, order or containment by the learned patterns within which energy customarily flows. Oblivious to the chains of life, the Inspirer rises above them. Loving to attract, his character draws people toward him; they depend on him for buoyancy in their climb to the heights.

The relationship is two-way. The Inspirer needs others for substance, weight and anchor. Their methodical work provides underpinning and support for his flights. Boss, politician, evangelist and guru, attractive positions for the Inspirer, require others to modulate their charismatic movements, prevent their energies from too great excess, and carry and extend their magnetism into the world.

Absolute positions attract the Inspirer. Without them he longs for focus, is in danger of whirling out of control and falling into personal confusion, uncertainty and despair. The busying activity that he stimulates and stands upon needs to find some point of stability. With it he can stay upright through his quick changes and moves. Without it to provide a focus, he is apt to stumble, and fall into confusion.

To monitor and keep balance in his position, to avoid a precipitous fall, the Inspirer develops sensitive antennae that feel out external threats to the stability of support. This sensitivity to external threats is matched by a developed sense of options. A quick mind and fast footwork redirect to a new path at a moment's notice.

Every new possibility provides opportunity for further excitement and adventure, hides the ego from the mundane and stirs energy to heady action removed from earthly concerns. In the quieter moments when a residue of restlessness still prevents full relaxation, the Inspirer's own instability can become haunting.

At best, the Inspirer deftly handles the myriad stimuli, bringing into control and focus the confusing, constantly changing patterns he ignites. With sharp perception, the way is wended toward the heights. Others follow the path he blazes, encouraging and rekindling the fire. Though the way may vary, the intensity is always great. He blows the air that ignites spark into flame and then hopes for regulation to appear from somewhere to maximize the potential to produce a good, steady fire.

At worst, the Inspirer burns maniacally out of control, soaring wildly and quickly extinguishing; a flash fire in danger of igniting others into a raging and destructive holocaust that decimates everything in its path, leaving nothing but ash and desolation. His fears may mount to paranoiac proportions if those under him seek to break his charismatic grasp and the cult that supports him threatens to slip away. He is like Humpty Dumpty close to the great fall. He fears he won't be put back together again and so his legs stumble to keep up with his momentum.

THE DEVELOPMENT OF THE INSPIRER

The heady excitement of the Inspirer, his sense of adventure and need for stability express the developmental situation of the growing child as he leaves the Communicator phase of the Rhythmic Cycle between the ages of 8 and 24 months. This is when he learns the upright position and makes his first self-propelled adventure into the world.

Seeing others, the child rises to his feet. It is not a natural event, no instinct controls the appearance of this move to upright locomotion. We are better built for crawling. Without the example of the human community we might simply remain on all fours like feral children lost in the woods and raised by animals. Standing, perhaps, might be noted as Humanity's first great inspiration.

For the maturing baby, the journey starts with a headlong thrust and is marked by numerous tumbles to the ground. He falls forward, feet scurrying to keep up with head. Parents offer a hand as he reaches upward for support.

Soon, in this new upright position he is better able to move toward that which intrigues. He begins with a precarious balance, uncertainly toddles toward the goal. Shortly, with improved coordination, he picks up speed and range and becomes the "run-about baby" (Stone, 1968), flying after a direction with an adult chasing close behind. Chaos threatens the household.

With burgeoning curiosity, the child impulsively grasps for everything that fascinates. The toddler moves to obtain what has caught his attention. When he arrives at his chosen place, he is captured - tasting, touching, turning and manipulating the prize until

130

he has played out the possibilities of his impulses or is distracted by a new, more interesting object that seems to demand exploration.

Speech, too, becomes a fascination. Questions and words bring response. He plays with language to gain attention, express feelings, and catch hold of others. Verbal facility expands rapidly. The child's statements are a great "Yes!" to life. Everything has a name, every question potentially brings a response.

The change that is occurring in the living rhythm between parent and child is profound. The parents' activity level increases to match the impulsive acting-out of the boundless child. Often a step behind, they watch for the threat of danger, scurry to keep up and even to be a bit ahead, to provide a protected arena so the child can safely enjoy the adventure in his spirit.

It is a time when the parental principles of both fathering and mothering are important. Though the child may find these principles embodied in persons other than the biological parents and in adults of either sex, they must be found for successful development through the Inspirer Phase of the Rhythmic Cycle.

Fathering spells mothering, giving rest from the constant demands of vigorous care while protecting the emotional sensitivities and acceptance of the nurturing role. Its strength and mobility are assets stimulating and teaching the child in the play of the adventure, while its personal boundaries, an outgrowth of heavier muscular dynamics, provide energetic containment for the toddler's brisk energy.

The youngster who, until this time has been so strongly attached to the safety and nourishment of mothering, reaches out and up to make contact with the father figure who can safely help him go farther.

If parenting figures are not able to meet the requirements of this stage, the child's range of movement becomes laden with confusion. Parents who form the Inspirer character may overstimulate the natural excitement of adventure, unconsciously using its promise to excite, lift and awaken their own feelings, to charge up the life in their own bodies. To a bored or mildly depressed parent, the child's excitement can become overly important and tacitly encourage freedom from even the safety of beneficial boundaries.

> Margarita would constantly interrupt the group's process whenever things grew quiet. A joke or inappropriate remark would break the mood. At times she was truely funny, at other times disruptive. Her interruptions would inevitably grow annoying and destructive to the mood.
>
> Her spontaneous inspirations, no matter how great their brilliance, stopped the group's development toward deeper feeling and further work. She would physically duck when a verbal attack in the form of a barb or complaint was proffered by others in an attempt to check her.
>
> Through her own work, she saw that she had behaved with her parents in a way that was similar to what she was now doing with the group. She had been her parent's joy, functioning to surprise and upend them when they were down.
>
> As a child she had the freedom to do "bad" things, to play the part of the lovable imp, and had learned to prepare for the chastisement that followed when she went too far and her behavior became too devilish. As an adult, this continued pattern of "going too far" had led to the destruction of her marriage and the emotional health of her child.

When things grow dull, excitement alleviates low spirits. The child offers the chase, the adventure of reaching out. But allowed to go too far, the youngster passes the limits of safety, goes beyond the range of the adult's capacity to protect and contain. What ensues is apt to exaggerate the development of Inspirer characteristics. When the threat of a dangerous situation is perceived, for example, the adult may release their feeling of rising panic with a threatening yell. Shocked by the sound, the child's movements are stopped in the startled posture of respiratory inspiration; breathing holds as the diaphragm tenses and the reaching freezes.

The overstepping of a boundary followed by a harsh, threat-laden limitation is the pattern for the parent-child relationship in this phase of the Rhythmic Cycle. The characterological structure of the Inspirer, with its issues of adventure and limits, its confused thoughts and panicky threatened feelings, is physically set in the body.

ENERGY DYNAMICS

The posture of the adult Inspirer shows similarities to the child's appearance during the Toddler Stage. The adult remains top-heavy; a large head and full torso are paired with arms and legs that function without a balanced connection to the trunk. The tensions originally introduced to the body cut off full flow of movement to the limbs leaving them long and thin, remnants of the Communicator Phase that preceded. (Robbins, 1977)

Although strong impulses develop, the legs cannot support the impulsive drives nor keep the balance to ensure contact with the ground. The Inspirer tends to be off center, up in the air, needing extra support for reassurance against the panic of falling. With chest lifted and spirits high, inspiration is a true physical reality. The fall brings expiration and collapse and, with it, the danger of holding in the opposite down position, a place of depletion and depression.

The Rhythmic Cycle of Change

The reader can experience the Inspirer's high energy position by pumping up the chest with sharp, rapid breaths and then, holding it inflated, breathing in the inspired position. Uplifting the chest gives a hyper feeling of extra energy. Continued breathing in this way allows for a physical and psychic lift, a sense of hope and possibility. Light-headedness, a bit of drunkenness, is apt to ensue.

Inspiration inspires, but organization of the myriad of impulses must follow. Impulsive release is usually too disorganized and unfocused to build into anything meaningful; a confused response typically misses the target. A sudden letting-go of the high position often leads to a panicky release. The bubble bursts and brings a profound drop of energy that ends in feelings of hopelessness.

The toddler, too, lives through the physical dynamics of the Inspirer Phase of the Rhythmic Cycle as he learns to walk. He moves to his feet unsteadily, with an upward lift of his chest and a top-heavy forward movement. His hands are held out and high for support and balance. He almost lunges forward, his legs running quickly to catch up and prevent him from falling.

Only gradually does the child learn to control his limbs, the toddle maturing to a walk as the center of movement drops down from the diaphragm to the middle of the abdomen in response to this new upright relationship to gravity. Through time and practice, the toddler grows more solid. The top-heavy approach gives way to balanced centered movement. The leg muscles connect the trunk to the ground, and the arms, no longer needed for balance, are free to contact and explore the surroundings.

In the Inspirer character, this physical transition to coordinated down-to-earth walking was only partial. Under stress; impulsivity, unsteadiness and upward-lifting, markers of the Inspirer stage of development, become evident in the adult's body and behavior.

People with an Inspirer Character, like toddlers need to drop down and develop balance. When able to do this they bring meaningful possibility down to earth. Then movements excite and delight without running the danger of either irresponsibly carrying others away or, more immediately, causing their own selves to be carried away by excess.

Noel, an Inspirer, was in therapy for over a year. The relationship of his distorted energy rhythm to his life difficulties had become evident to him. But within he still carried statements from the past. Internal shouts he directed att himself limited his mobility and his ability to personally establish fluidity.and integrity.

The dynamics of his body were those of the Inspirer — big top, long lanky arms and legs. Problems in coordination were marked whenever the pelvic area needed to participate in a movement. To work toward body unity, he was asked to lie on his stomach, grab his ankles and lift himself, forming an arch along his backside.

In previous work he had prepared him to attempt such a move. He had the flexibility, but the coordination required for this exercise was a new challenge. It demanded a smooth muscular interaction and an energy reach from lower back through the hips and buttocks to the upper legs.

Initial attempts were floundering and clumsy. His breath held. He rushed and then collapsed with a series of rapid, short grunts. Trying, and again failing, his frustration mounted. His chest inflated and his face grew red. Coordination worsened.

Noel needed focus, but suggestions seemed to compound the problem. Asked what he was thinking, he said that he was repeatedly screaming to himself, "What the fuck do you think you're trying to do?" While his body fought to move toward the goal, his inner words were shouting at him; limiting his movements, confusing his efforts and arousing panic.

As he took time to think of his past he remembered many messages like the one he was telling himself. They had seemed to come from everyone. Now he saw the threatening limiter was within.

More relaxed, he started again. Slowly and purposefully, now able to use suggestions, what had looked and felt impossible began to take shape and then was mastered. His muscles worked together in a harmony that delighted him. He had come a step closer to self-coordination and fuller bodily integrity.

THE JEWISH MYSTICAL COMMUNITY

There have been times when a group of people have been brought so low, so hurt and weakened as to be almost destroyed. Unable to raise themselves, sunk in despair, they look up for an answer, an inspiration to lift them, to strengthen their life force and reestablish in them the value of living.

Throughout history the Jewish people have been subjected, captured and oppressed only to be brought up again, revitalized and moved closer toward their redeemer. Reaching toward God, they have found an answer that maintained them through suffering and adversity and lifted their spirits toward redemption.

The length of Jewish history and the physical range of its cultural spread has allowed many developments. One of the fullest arose from repeated encounters with the despair that attended a suffering that seemed without option. At these times the promise of the Messiah, the Savior, gave strength to endure and renewed the hope that an answer would come. Created out of a Biblical Dream consciousness, the communication of Inspiration's hope provided relief from the totality of oppression.

A promised Messiah gave strength to endure, a Messiah-at-hand gave joy and exaltation, but when a Messiah-proved-false it led inevitably to disarray and confusion.

In the mid-1700's the Jewish condition was ripe for the development of the rhythmic phase of Inspiration and a leader to rise and uplift. Two historical tragedies set the background for despair. One had taken place a hundred years previously when Mid-European Jewry was brutally ravished. The Cossacks swept down massacring 100,000 Jews, while destroying 300 communities. Emptiness and despair prevailed in the psychological void that was established.

From the experience of this void a new dream emerged into public consciousnes. Its seeds lay in yet an earlier period of devastation, the Jewish expulsion from Spain in 1492. Its source was the visions of the great Kabbalist, mystic and ascetic, Issac Luria.

Luria was a Dreamer, withdrawn from the everyday and at home in the "other" reality. "He ... dwelt perpetually in this mysterious world, and his visionary gaze caught glimpses of psychical life in all that surrounded him. ..." (Scholem, 1972) From what Luria saw he spawned a mythos that was to greatly influence what was to come over a century later in Mid-European Jewry. Luria's visions remain alive, a living reality to this day in the Jewish mystical community of Chassidism.

The Rhythmic Cycle of Change

A new mythos gains acceptance if it broadens human meaningfulness by more fully answering the needs and encompassing the process of a time. Luria's vision gave further breadth to the Biblical story of Creation. It arose from a question, "If God is everywhere how is there space for the creation of the world?" The answer came in a vision.

Luria saw God as withdrawing into Himself in order to leave a primordial space which could contain what was to come. In a moment of great instability God then proceeded to emanate Himself into the volatile vacuum created by his withdrawal.

God's intense energy slowly, carefully reached into the emptiness of space. But the movement was neither slow nor careful enough. The result was explosion - holocaust. Chaos reigned. Sparks flamed and flew, breaking from the source, scattering near and far.

The bits of scattered fire, it was said, gradually cooled. Around each, a crusty shell formed that contained a spark of the Divine. These crusts account for the material dark aspects of the world. Captured within each, remains the spark of holiness, removed from divine perfection only by the thickness and imperfections of the outer shell. Man's task is to free and reunite these holy sparks thereby perfecting the world, returning it toward the Divine.

A Mystic, like Luria, is rarely able to rationalize, codify and carry his own vision to the people, nor does he develop a method. His character moves him too soon to his next vision. Luria was connected to others who wrote down the products of his inner life. The dream was remembered by a mystical few for over a hundred years until the time was ready for it to serve as inspiration to the next generation of despair.

In the mid-1600s, after the Cossack massacre, Luria's vision was delivered to the masses of the people by a self-proclaimed Messiah, Sabbatai Zevi. An Inspirer, his personality suffered both depression and manic elation yet his personal mania was to be tried as an antidote for the despair of the times. A far from perfect vessel, Zevi's capacity to inspire was often left unchecked by the rules of reality.

> "It is said of Sabbatai Zevi that for fifteen years he has been bowed down by the following affliction. He is pursued by a sense of depression which leaves him no quiet moment and does not even permit him to read, without his being able to say what is the nature of the sadness which has come upon him. Thus he endures it until the depression departs from the spirit, when he returns with great joy to his studies." (Scholem, 1972)

Zevi's depressions could go on to manic excesses in which he would engage in acts that involved "demonic and erotic" flauntings of moral limitations. Then as his "enlightenment" faded he was "like a normal man and regretted the strange things he had done for he no longer understood their reason as he had understood it when he committed them." (Scholem, 1972)

In moments of elation Zevi called himself "Messiah" but in calmer moments even he couldn't take this seriously. His outrageous behaviors and claims might simply have been judged as madness, by himself and the community, if they hadn't been elevated in importance by another.

Zevi was distressed by his emotional difficulties and personal excesses. In a healthy period he sought the advice of a young Illumined, Nathan of Gaza. Unknown to Zevi, Nathan during a period of intense fasting and prayer had himself fallen into the Dream State and had come to believe he heard God's words claim Sabbatai Zevi was in truth, the Messiah.

Zevi came to consult Nathan, "In order to find peace for his soul." - "He came as a patient to a Doctor of the soul." (Scholem, 1972) Nathan, however, acting from his own dreams, convinced Zevi that his claims and actions were not the ravings of a madman but indeed, the true words of the Savior. (Scholem, 1972)

Nathan went further. He became the announcer of God's (Zevi's) Presence, interpreter of "His" acts, and theologian of "His" messianic movement. He provided words and reasons that communicated with the masses. He forged a link between Zevi's mad acts and God's holy purposes.

With Nathan's supportive interpretations, Zevi's mania now served to stimulate others to also see him as the Messiah; as He who had come to break the shells, uplift the sparks and fix the world, fulfilling the Lurian Mythos.

Zevi's mania approached ecstasy. His fire fascinated and enthused those who witnessed it. Like many Inspirers he seemed free from the rules. He openly desecrated the sacred, speaking and acting against the Holy Books. Desperate for inspiration to lift them from the despair of the times the people overlooked the depressive aspects of his pathology.

For two years Zevi's messianic movement grew in power and scope as Jews hastened to follow the light and inspiration of this charismatic leader, but the situation rapidly darkened when the "Messiah" was captured by the Turks. The Turkish Sultan gave Zevi a choice of converting to Islam or being put to death. He chose conversion.

Though some rationalized his decision as simply an example of the Messiah's freedom from earthly rules, for most the act was catyclismic. They felt betrayed and fell away. The life stirrings that he had aroused among the main body of the community quickly died. Sweet hope turned to bitter disappointment. The spiritual loss of a Messiah-turned-false rekindled and deepened the lingering mood of depression caused by the Cossack massacres. The people fell again into dismay, confusion and hopelessness.

Could it have been different? To consider what might have occurred if a historical legendary figure like Zevi had been able to be a modern therapeutic client rather than having been under the influence of a misguided Illumined may appear far-fetched, but the impulse for such consideration is in the spirit of this chapter. The boldness of the Inspirer encourages the adventure.

Value lies in understanding the psychological dynamics that evolve into the legendary role that such characters play. It is also good to contrast the dark side of the Inspirer with the magnificence of its positive aspects, which for the Jews became manifest within the century through the personality, legend and influence of Israel ben Eliezer, The Baal Shem Tov, Master of the Good Name, founder of Chassidism.

Zevi, motivated by a mixture of pain and fascination, would probably have been attracted to the work of one of the more famous therapeutic practitioners. Participation with greatness is heady stuff. Beginning the process with such a person in itself would provide a temporary uplift. He might even have begun personal work with the hope of becoming a therapist himself.

Zevi's therapist would have to avoid the trap that caught Nathan. Rather than support acting-out, he would need to diffuse it, to bring Zevi into contact with the excesses of his conduct.

Nathan's support had given a false sense of reality to Zevi's claims. In therapeutic terms, Nathan made a major counter-transference error. His own dream became contaminated with and acted out through the dream of his client's. The therapist would have to be on his toes not to be inspired to do the same.

The Inspirer does stir hopes. Perhaps Zevi would offer new clients or helpful connections. If the therapist unconsciously supports the Inspirer's maneuvers to exaggerate his and the therapist's importance, objective therapeutic capacity, as had happened with Nathan, could easily be lost.

The therapeutic work would proceed through two phases: first making Zevi aware of the physical dynamics that occasion his Inspirer orientation, then helping him incorporate discipline and self-control to gain the containment of the Solidifier Phase of the Rhythmic Cycle.

Observing his own body during periods of elation, Zevi could see the uplifted inspired chest and the red blustery face that serves to avoid feelings of threat and control by threatening and intimidating others. He would note that the expanded chest serves to oxygenate the body, causing the hyper-excitement that leads to manic elation. When Zevi could see this happen and consciously experience the confusion and panic it causes, a process of change could begin.

In depressed moments the opposite stance would be worked with - the collapsed sunken chest could be experienced as hopelessly unavailable for even the normal inspirational phase of the breath. Without this there is lack of energy and a psycho-physiological dullness.

Therapists know that these processes are easier to understand than experience and change. For the Inspirer, every awareness threatens a change in the habitual way of being and such threat stimulates those very defensive processes that need to be modified.

Experiencing in the safety of the therapeutic setting allows exploration without threat of external attack. Physical techniques with the body could be used to demonstrate Zevi's processes to him. When the chest is inflated, therapeutic pressure in the area of the diaphragm could induce a sudden dropping of the expanded chest. With it would come the sensation and release of panic.

In the opposite case, the depressed chest, held in the deflated position, could be mobilized by having the patient lie down while the therapist used his hands to apply a gentle bouncing to the tightly contracted rib cage. As holding let go, the resultant freer breathing would bring a lightening in mood.

With repetition, an ever-increasing realization of the relationship of mood and body block would develop. The need to again and again let down and take one step at a time during panicky moments would be emphasized. Through consistent conscious work, grandiosity could gradually give way to the stability of the matter-of-fact.

The nature of the relationship of held inspiration to the stimuli of daily life, those specific stimuli that for Zevi arouse unconscious feelings of threat and confusion, would need to be explored. It would be expected that these triggers would be found to involve personal limits and particular social rules that were areas of concern in the client's own life history.

Over time as the body musculature became freer more energy would enter the pelvic area. Confusion about the feelings and sensations this arouses could be expected to become stronger. Intense pressure might again build to act out impulses through the sexual and pornographic excesses Zevi had previously used to release these feelings.

The impulses would be talked about and placed in the context of what was best for the total being. The client would be asked to contain himself and use his diaphragm to breathe fully so that sexual pulsation could grow into solid clear drives - feelings that could provide a clear inner reality on which to base appropriate release rather than triggering maniacal actions that renew feelings of threat and a return to depressive controls.

Slowly, limits would become an almost natural unconscious process and Zevi would gain in stability. Personal importance would still be a concern, but its limits in relationship to the importance of others would be appreciated. He would find himself less caught in acting-out.

The Rhythmic Cycle of Change

As his self-knowledge increased, humility about Zevi's personal place in the world would develop. Overblown feelings of inspiration would give way to realistic rather then grandiose hopes. Depression would soften into a sadness that would serve both to make Zevi aware of his own impotence in things that are impossible and free him from having to respond to the demand to save others.

The process would not be easy - despair and depression would have to be lived through; losses and limitations understood and accepted. There could be no promising of success and the danger of acting-out would arise at each threatening challenge.

With patience and perseverance, the task of growing into a fuller way of functioning could be achieved. Impulses would mature and be expressed in satisfying ways. Inappropriate excess would subside into healthy experience. Mood swings would be less intense, of shorter duration and consciously managed. As the rhythm of Zevi's breath expanded and contracted in a more balanced way, he would move from the heightened airiness of being God toward the solidness of being man.

From a position of increased well-being, he might still choose to lead but with awareness and control of his Inspirer characteristics he would be able to manage their expression to keep balance. His neurotic traits could be transformed into skills that relate both to others and to natural law. They could now be a means to gain centered pleasure for himself as well as used as a continuing asset for others.

Through successful therapy, Zevi would have opened the energy flow through the Rhythmic Cycle. Exploring the concerns of the Inspirer would lead to the work of the Solidifier period, work to attain limits and gain a self-center. In the Achiever phase, he would develop a positive means of self-expression that would bring a fuller relating and an end to formal therapy.

Within his historical time, a healthier Zevi might have changed the Jews' place on the Rhythmic Cycle. Indeed, as a disturbed Messiah he provided only a temporary respite. His passing left the people again without hope. Despair and confusion were even more intensified by the blow of his conversion. The preconditions for a new Inspirer remained.

The life of Rabbi Israel ben Eliezer, several decades later, provided a new and wholer answer for the problems of the times, an uplift from despair through a participation in joy; a taste of and a way to paradise, a fuller life.

Unlike Zevi, Rabbi Israel worked through the critical problems of the Inspirer to free his energy and evolve a fuller, more complete personality. He became known to his people as the Baal Shem Tov, Master of the Good Name. He used his power to effect a "strengthening and consolidating influence on the soul-center of his fellow men, which enabled this center to regenerate the body and the whole of life ... ." (Buber, 1972)

Many in those times were called "Masters of the Name". They used magic and their own wisdom to promise succor and healing to individuals. They were said to know a name of God and to be able to invoke it for the benefit of man. Some helped, others were charlatans. Only the Baal Shem Tov was able to win the people's confidence by the goodness of his being and the solidity of his teaching. They added "Tov", "Good", to his name, to distinguish his level from that of the others.

The Baal Shem Tov did not proclaim himself "Messiah" but encompassed a wholeness that participated in holiness. He offered not salvation but inspiration. Each could find the way for themself He provided the means to help.

The Baal Shem Tov founded a tradition of orthodox Jewish mystical communities that continues today. His presence and life-force uplifted weakened souls infusing them with exalted joy. He, like Zevi, brought the mystical vision of Luria to the common man. A master too at stimulating the ecstatic, he, however, provided a continuing antidote for the despair of the times.

The Rhythmic Cycle of Change

Where Sabbatai Zevi's personal inspiration was incomplete and led to mania and depression, the Baal Shem Tov's was full. The Baal Shem taught it was possible to bond every aspect of God's creation to joy - joy, the antidote of despair. He welded his energy to life-truths, providing a continual and safe inspiration; an inspiration that recognized the divine spark in each as well as, what was so conspicuously absent in Zevi's leaderhip, the attendant personal responsibility to develop and control the inner burning in order to participate in and magnify the good and the Godly.

Through the Baal Shem Tov's teaching, the leader could help, encourage, inspire and point the way, but the individual had to take charge of developing his own soul, and effect his own destiny.

Through the Baal Shem Tov, the Lurian vision of holiness-in-all was brought to the people and could be utilized by them. It did not call for great intellectual ability nor ascetic sacrifices. It provided a way — a way of prayer, a way of dance, a way to see the totality of God's presence everywhere. It unleashed a tidal wave of primitive enthusiasm and energy. From it a rich new culture was established and a healing of spirit attained.

The Baal Shem Tov taught his followers (Chassidim or Pious Ones as they came to be called) that God's presence was in everything and could be reached not only through study, which traditional formal Judaism advocated, but also through deep intent, focused attention, cleaving to the holy in all things.

Since it was believed that through the holy sparks God infused everything, there was constant cause for celebration and joy. The dourness of the time was brightened. The burden of life became a source of song. The Chassidim were taught to allow their spirits to soar in fervent prayer. Each could participate directly, had a crucial role to play, in the "uplifting of the sparks".

The effect was a revitalization of the community. An outburst of story, song and dance infused hope and inspiration in all.

An unlearned boy prayed the only way he
knew how, leaping back and forth across a stream.
The gates of Heaven immediately opened.

Niggunim, melodies without words, carried
the soul-song of the community on high.

It was even heard that a Rabbi laughed during
prayers and fiddlers danced on rooftops.

The details of the Baal Shem Tov's life are surrounded by a
legendary surplus provided by the love, faith and inspiration of
those who talk of him. Reality and legend intertwine to illustrate
and delineate in mythic proportions the character of the Inspirer.
Born in poverty, an orphan by five, his father gave him a deathbed
blessing that permitted the freedom from earthly limitations that is
common to all Inspirers.

"Before you were born it was made known to
me that God would always be with you, for within
you there lives one of the innocent souls of Heaven.
Go fearless through your life on earth, do not be
afraid of man and do not fear the enemy, for the
highest power is in you.". (Levin, 1966)

Young Israel, with no one to ground him and, with such a
charge unafraid, went on to cross the limits. The license he took led
to trouble. Sent to school by the community, who assumed
responsibility for his care, he quickly became a noted truant,
running to the woods rather than to his studies.

The community despaired of "ever making an upright and
honest man of him." (Minkin, 1955) The rule of attendance was
relaxed. He was given the job of leading the younger children to
school. In this too, legend shows he soon went out of bounds.

Once, it is said, Israel took the children a circuitous route, through the woods and close to a werewolf, the Evil Spirit incarnate. Frightened, the screaming children scattered about and were lost in all directions. When the children were finally found and Israel's role evident, his position was taken from him.

Remembering his father's words Israel went, unintimidated, to each parent reassuring and persuading them to allow him another opportunity to lead their children. Listening to his words, their hearts softened and he reassumed his responsibility.

The Evil Spirit appeared again. This time Israel, wielding a strong stick, vanquished it. As its body lay on the ground Israel reached into it and for a moment held the werewolf's dark pulsing heart in his hand. He was in a position to destroy it, and evil, forever.

Staring deeply into its blackness, Israel saw that profound suffering and incredible pain lay at its very center. Filled with enormous pity and compassion he returned the heart to the still quivering body that lay on the ground before him. In so doing evil was allowed to continue its life in this world.

There was little public hint given of Israel's compassion or his capacities as he grew. As a young adult he was a simple Synagogue custodian. But alone at night, he educated himself, taking out the Holy Books and studying the mystical treatises of Kabbala. Soon he felt the barriers to his soul, the limits of his life that were constricting him and he set out to realize himself. His character pressed for a more expanded role in life's tapestry.

"He wanted to be free, as free as he saw the
birds, flowers and trees in his childhood haunts. He
dreamt of the new life in which he would be bound
by no authority except the commanding voice which
already made itself felt in his heart." (Minkin, 1955)

He began to teach children, manifesting a warmth and
excitement that inspired his young charges.

"The little he knew he breathed into their very
souls, as it were, and they became transformed as
though touched by a mysterious hand." (Minkin,
1955).

His fame spread. Soon people came for counsel when there
was legal disputation. His judgments, fair and honest, were
delivered in a manner that even satisfied the losing party.

The father of the learned and celebrated Rabbi of Brody was
so inspired with a judgment rendered on his behalf that he betrothed
his daughter, the famed Rabbi of Brody's sister, to Israel in
marriage. Israel, knowing his ignorance and poor station might not
allow acceptance into such a learned and successful household,
made the father promise the betrothal agreement would be kept
secret.

Upon the father's death, Israel, contract in hand, arrived at
the home of the Rabbi of Brody. Seeing the poor shabbily dressed
peasant and fearing the dishonor that would be brought to his
household, the Rabbi attempted to convince his sister not to marry.
But she stayed true to her father's word and the two were wed.

The Rabbi tried to help Israel, his new brother-in-law, gain
responsibility, but his efforts repeatedly failed. Even a job as
coachman proved too difficult. Israel, in character, almost killed his

passengers by driving over the road's edge, beyond the limit into the ditch.

The Rabbi, despairing, sent the couple away to avoid further embarrassment. The two settled in a hut near the mountains. Israel spent his days away from home immersing himself in the surrounding nature returning home only to celebrate the Sabbath.

It is said that for seven years, in this way, he gathered the wisdom of nature's law. At night he studied Holy Books and learned the substance of the Torah. Grounded in both the laws of nature and the Biblical laws of the Jewish spirit, he now had forged an anchor for his restless, limitless Inspirer ways. He evolved an ability to contain his impulses and carry them into the Solidifying Phase of the Rhythmic Cycle. Here they were worked into a more mature and stable stance.

The attention of the local peasantry was attracted to him through the rapture and intensity of his prayers. His forest flights into ecstasy were magnetic. People began to come to him for wisdom and healing in greater and greater numbers. His way and method grew stronger.

Now near 40, he felt the need to extend his influence to his fellow Jews. Traveling through Mid-Eastern Europe, covering new ground, he attracted hundreds, then thousands of followers who developed communities devoted to his teachings. At first it was his simple approach and ability to heal that appealed to them. He lived as other magic men did, giving amulets and using the superstitions of the people to heal their ills.

The educated often call such men charlatans, men of excess who prey on the ignorance of the common people. But Israel was different. He combined his charisma with a love and devotion that aroused a deep confidence within the masses. He was "The Baal Shem Tov." Legends about his work spread. The waves of enthusiasm rippling through the masses drew the attention of the most learned Rabbis - the establishment of Jewry.

The focus of the Baal Shem Tov's work now shifted. From the healing of neurotic personalities that were the manifestation of sick souls, he developed a more general psychology and philosophy that stressed a positive outlook on the meaning of life. He moved from healer of the body to healer of the spirit, from the uplifting of the individual to the uplifting of the community. In a way, the community had raised him, now he was to raise them.

The Baal Shem's reach began to encroach on the place of the most powerful of religious leaders. His influence moved into the Synagogues. He rivaled the Rabbis themselves and was tested, criticized and scorned. The most prominent Rabbi of the time "officially" excommunicated him.

It was to no avail as many of the learned found the Baal Shem Tov genuine, a true leader who expanded the faith by breathing life and vigor into religious practice. They joined him. The sparks were gathering.

To further his purposes he took up residence in Medziboz, a city with a long proud Jewish tradition. No longer disregarding the boundaries he settled right on them. Medziboz lay on the crossroads, the borders of Poland, Ukrania and Lithuania. There, more came and fell under the influence of his work.

His practice emphasized and manifested concepts of joyous worship and service, reaching toward totality through the act of prayer. He taught others to do the same. In this way he gave more than personality to the people. He went beyond being a cult figure demanding focus solely on himself. Beyond inspiration, he gave method.

The method emphasized three aspects of prayer: concentrated focus, cleaving to God, and spreading the light everywhere to uplift the mundane to the holy. These practices carried the Chassidim beyond the everyday to an ongoing ecstatic experience of God's unity.

The Rhythmic Cycle of Change

The experience of The Baal Shem's way is physiologically based, available to everyone though inhibitions and controls stand in its way. For the Chassid it begins with a focus, an intention toward contact with that which is holy and then it builds into an intense involvement through cleaving. Cleaving involves spiritually reaching and clinging to the Divine with all one's might.

When the effort given to focusing and cleaving pours over the point of physical limit, the tension collapses. Letting-go takes over. Release, relief and renewal occur. Energy expands throughout the previously overextended muscles. A feeling of joy, love and happiness occurs as blood pumped from the heart rushes upward and out in exaltation:

> "As the Chassidim stand praying their song together they sway and rock back and forth. The chant strengthens in enthusiasm, inspired by example of the Rebbe upon whom their attention is riveted. The effort grows more intense, louder, more ecstatic, ever increasing as it strives to reach the level of ...the highest sort of prayer - one that not only moves the soul but sets all the limbs of the body astir, as it is written, `All my bones shall say Lord, who is like unto Thee?'." (Minkin, 1955)

The Chassidic prayer has similarity to the charismatic rites mentioned previously (see Creator Section). Here, too, chanting and rhythm built inner movement to and beyond the limits of physical control. But the primitive involves his whole body, ending with a fall to the ground and reflexive spasming: the Chassid sustaining the upward reach of his prayer remains on his feet, heaven-bound. His is a religion and a culture in which the ultimate point of Inspiration is uplift.

The Chassid's ecstatic spirit is to continue. He is not to go fully over the edge, not to fall. The tradition of the Baal Shem Tov requires him to modulate his experience so as to bring it down into connection with the community and thereby spread the holy light so that the sparks of the soul may be united and strengthened. The flame aroused within the individual is to be used to imbue life with holy purpose in the performance of acts that reach to others.

The Baal Shem Tov and his way succeeded in providing the antidote to despair. His life is an example of the Inspirer character successfully lived. Ironically, throughout his own personal history boundlessness had caused him personal difficulty in meeting the community as an equal. Yet he was able to gain his place by being above others: a teacher with students, a master with followers, a Rebbe with Chassidim, a Saint reached for by man while he reached for God.

The physical dynamics of this Inspirer's upward thrust remains until today, embedded in legends. The Baal Shem's body is described again and again in scenes where it is rising, like the infant moving toward and into upright locomotion. He moves with "uplifted arms," a foot raised "to climb from mountain peak to mountain peak" (they move to support him), He "jump<s> in leaps and bounds of ecstasy." (Buber, 1972)

The Baal Shem's charisma inspired and attracted. He was able to move on beyond it along the Rhythmic Cycle, by gaining support and solidity through an understanding of both the law of God as written in the Holy Books and the law of Nature as experienced for seven years in the woods.

His capacity for limitlessness came to allow him to reach and attain union with many. Focused concentration contained his impulses, contact with others provided balance. The child and young man who couldn't or wouldn't learn, became capable of leading in his own way - the way of Inspiration.

A Chassid asked the Baal Shem Tov:

"Why, at times when reaching for God, does one feel a sense of interruption and remoteness?"

The Baal Shem answered:

"A father teaching his child to walk stands in front of him, hands held outward to reassure him he cannot fall. Encouraged, the child, reaching, moves forward. As he comes closer, the father moves further away to stimulate greater effort. He does so repeatedly until the child learns." (Buber, 1972)

The outward reach of the Baal Shem Tov, toddler grown big, encouraged an entire community brought low by devastation, confusion and despair to reach up and move forward.

"Perhaps nowhere in history has a man taken such a long stride forward and carried almost a whole people with him." (Minkin, 1955)

JACOB LEVY MORENO - THE INSPIRER

Jacob Levy Moreno was in his 70's when I met him in 1966. He had the body of an Inspirer. A huge head and upper torso was supported by thin legs. The dominancy of his upper frame, exaggerated by excess weight, gave him an overpowering appearance. His toddling unbalanced gait was noticeable. The upward thrust of his energy was marked.

At the time, I was studying Psychodrama at the Moreno Institute. During the day, Moreno's wife, Zerka, ran sessions, evaluated work and helped gain mastery of the method. At night Moreno himself held forth, asking questions, reminiscing about his life, explaining his theories. His language was often flattering and flamboyant. He would call one student "great!" and another "genius!" He would tell of people who had taken his ideas and given him little credit. He would aggrandize himself, mentioning with an exaggerated aura of importance the rewards and fame he had achieved: the popularity of his work, his nomination for the Nobel prize, his influence on John Barrymore, Peter Lorre, and Martin Buber. He'd go on to spin legends about his life and the therapeutic practices he had spawned.

On some nights he lacked energy and the room grew lifeless. The students felt the pain of being members of a captive audience at a dull performance. On other occasions he was charged, dynamic and brilliant, his charisma exciting everyone around him.

Once, while reading a poem from what he considered his most important book, The Words of the Father (Anonymous, 1941), his excitement grew mammoth, his vibration overpowering. Charismatic vitality filled the room. Each listener was magnetically pulled toward him, suspended on chair's edge.

Moreno was more than unusual, gave more than charisma. There have been two major trends in psychotherapy, the analytic and the active. Sigmund Freud dominated the analytic mode of treatment. Jacob Levy Moreno has been the seminal mind of the methods of action. While Freud has been properly recognized as the father of modern treatment, Moreno has hardly been appreciated.

Though his work began in 1915, it was not until the 1960's that action and group methods boomed in popularity. Then, everyone seemed to use Moreno's methods. Few credited his contribution. Eric Berne, author of Games People Play and creator of Transactional Analysis, suggested all therapists suffered from

The Rhythmic Cycle of Change

"The Moreno Problem." (Berne, 1972) Whatever techniques they developed were likely to have been previously invented and written about by Moreno, the Father of Action Methods. In the boundless `60's though, paternity was rarely to be noted.

It had been Moreno who, as early as four decades before, coined such to-become-common phrases as "group psychotherapy," "encounter," "sensitivity training" and "here and now." It was Moreno who developed instruments to analyze the structure of groups through a strategy called "Sociometrics."

It was Moreno who, out of a central interest in spontaneity, created and developed the method of Psychodrama with its rich technical storehouse of action techniques and concepts such as warm-up, role playing, role-reversal, empty chair, mirroring, auxiliary ego, double, sharing and others.

Through Psychodrama, Moreno emphasized acting-out. He encouraged people to dramatically express their experiences and vivify their imaginations by replaying life's events, memories, plans, hopes and dreams. The setting was the stage; the props, a table and a chair or two; the actors, members of the therapeutic group; and the Director, a therapist trained as a Psychodramatic facilitator.

The protagonist, with the director's help, would describe the scene he wished to explore, something remembered or imagined. He would pick others to play out the different roles that were involved, give them clues as to how the parts should be performed. Then through the spontanaety of those on stage the play would unfold anew. The director could and often, for therapeutic purposes, did suggest scenes or different ways of playing crucial parts.

In a Psychodrama, bound emotions could be dramatically discharged, impulses could be acted upon. Life's challenges could be rehearsed. Traumatic milestones could be emotionally relived with the chance for new therapeutically designed outcomes to be experienced, outcomes that provided for better, more life-affirming support than reality had given.

No impulse or image proved too small or too large for the pretending of the stage. Every concern and possibility could be explored in the safety of the Psychodramatic setting. Each moment could be lived in its reality and magnified so that its "surplus reality" (those things that are not said or lived out) could be brought into the open and explored. On the stage, life could be seen in an atmosphere that was even bigger, even grander than the real.

Moreno, too, was bigger than life. A fantastic personality, an Inspirer, he lived his own Psychodrama directly, in a grand, if at times grandiose way. His genius lay in a readiness to move the impulsive feeling and quick idea to the "here and now," allowing it to develop into a new action technique. He emphasized the moment and the setting for spontaneous action. Uninhibited, he would try out what popped into his awareness. Certainly in doing so he could be oblivious to limits, but for him it was all right that his boundlessness could reach megalomaniacal proportions:

> "I wanted to show that here is a man who has all the signs of paranoia and megalomania, exhibitionism, and social maladjustment and who can still be fairly well-controlled and healthy, and indeed, of apparently greater productivity by acting them out than if he would have tried to constrain and resolve his symptoms." (Moreno, 1971)

For Moreno, life itself was his stage. He acted out his problems "in situ." As a therapy, however, acting-out in life tends to be inefficient and at times damaging. It allows for a free expression of pathology that frequently leads to unnecessary wounds to both self and others. Control is absent.

The Rhythmic Cycle of Change

It is likely that Moreno's aggrandizement diminished the credit he got for his work. Others were reluctant to respect or credit him because he would discount their efforts. Paternity, he claimed with good cause, was his. It was easy for others to discount and dispense the primacy of his claims by laughingly noting the grandiosity of his expression and asking, "Why take him seriously?"

But Moreno was a true Inspirer. He dipped into the visionary and creatively communicated his sources in a fashion that emphasized the grandness of his character. His life highlights and summarizes the process and development of the energetic flow of his character: impulse, uplift, boundlessness, grandiosity, acting-out and charisma. His history and bodily pattern fall into the Inspirer Phase of the Rhythmic Cycle.

The relationship of Moreno's parents was a difficult one. Like many wealthy Jews of the time, his mother was educated under Catholic auspices. Her successful brothers, fearing she might be converted, arranged a marriage to his father, Morenu Levy, when she was 15.

The brothers came to regret their choice. Twice his wife's age, from a Spanish rather than a Middle-European tradition, customs and lifestyles differed. A restless traveler and adventurer, an inconsistent source of support, he was away for months, sometimes years at a time. Financial responsibility repeatedly fell to the brothers, who denigrated him as head of the household and respected male figure. (Robbins 1970)

Still, Jacob was the first born boy in a Jewish home, a special position. In the tradition, a boy was desired as a carrier of the name and a vehicle of blessings. His acts could bring his parents closer to paradise. Intelligence too was a great boon. Jacob's precociousness was evident in both his early speech and mental development. (Robbins, 1970) His mother adored him, "Indeed if anything, he may have felt too much mothered by her and it may have helped to push him into the world at an early age... ." (Moreno, Z. 1983)

Jacob walked early too, but around the age of one his legs, dynamically important in the Inspirer, required special care. (Robbins, 1970)

By four years of age the fantastic side of Moreno's personality, his striving toward the heights and an unawareness of limits was concretely manifest. As he told it, he led his playmates in a game he invented, a game he called "God." (Robbins, 1970)

In the game the upper reaches of Heaven were created through a tower seven chairs high, built upon a large table. The structure was held together by the protective arms of the "angels" (his playmates). Jacob ascended. He, of course, was God, boundless father-figure.

The play proceeded until an angel challenged "God" to fly. "I will!" was his response. Perched on his heavenly throne, he spread his wings. A moment later he crashed to the ground and broke his arm. (Robbins, 1970)

The reality of this fall, the betrayal of his underpinnings, didn't limit Moreno's God-playing. Rather it was the beginning of what he called "The Therapy of the Fallen Gods." (Robbins, 1970) God-playing became "a red line" that ran throughout his life. (Robbins, 1970)

Jacob's energy pattern was set toward the heights. He would overrun boundaries and act-out the impossible. A lifted expanded chest and an enlarged head insured his upward movement. His legs were thin, weak and undernourished. He wasn't grounded on earth. Motor and mental quickness dared the forces of physical and psychological gravity.

When Moreno was twelve, a second important God-playing venture occurred. He encountered and was impressed by a statue of Christ. He vowed then that he would not be like this "Son of God" - to be the son was not enough. He would rise higher.

Moreno's adolescence was not easy. After a long absence his father rejoined the family in an attempt to re-establish his marriage. He found work in Germany and moved his wife and children away from Vienna.

Germany was difficult. The harshness of the culture, its constrictiveness and practicality were painful to Moreno's expansive character. He decided to leave home and returned by himself to Vienna. There, at the age of thirteen, he attended school and supported himself by tutoring young children. (Robbins, 1970)

Moreno did not thrive during this period. Though he successfully supported himself, he failed to maintain his status as a student and ran into trouble with the professor he lived with. As might be expected from his character, under the stress of separation from his family he had difficulty "playing the game." He dropped out of school, spending his time instead wandering through the Viennese Gardens. (Robbins, 1970)

It was two years later, with her marriage ended, that Jacob's mother returned to Vienna and her son. She found him strange and eccentric. He would occasionally come for dinner bundled in numerous shirts, as if he were physically and symbolically covering a depleted chest. (Robbins, 1970) He was lost to her, physically and emotionally separated. His inflation had been punctured, his inspiration was gone.

Feeling himself too much for his mother to understand, he found acceptance elsewhere. He played with the young in the gardens of Vienna, telling stories while sitting high above them on the limbs of a tree. The children were fascinated by this story-teller. Soon even their parents began to listen to his legends.

In these gardens, "The Kingdom of the Children" was born. (Robbins, 1970) Moreno was the leader. With the children's acceptance he found fresh support for his inspirations. He made up a game, "Choose Your Parents." Each child could pick new parents, whoever they might desire. It may have expressed a hidden inner wish of his own.

The form of the game eventually developed into one of the first scientific instruments of Sociology. The question of who wished to be with whom became the cornerstone of Moreno's sociometric investigations which measured the structure of social groups. The technique spawned such a volume of significant research and theory that the journal "Sociometry," devoted to publication of findings related to this method, became an official publication of the American Sociological Association.

The "Choose Your Parents" game can be seen as an acting out of Moreno's psychic concern of the time. Who would raise him? He felt:

> "I don't belong to the family, but to the cosmos...the family was inferior to me and my cause. It was the beginning of my association with God. The idea of playing God and encouraging others isolated me from the world but gave me a feeling of exquisite satisfaction that I was doing something extraordinary." (Robbins, 1970)

God-playing had come to take the place of absent parents. Moreno's eccentricities now were consciously placed within its framework. He had a cause, an "idee fixe." He studied philosophies and concepts related to God. His acting-out grew more audacious.

Marching onto the stage of a professional theater, Moreno stopped a performance of the play "Thus Spake Zarathustra" and exhorted the leading actor to speak his own words rather than the dead lines of another man's creation. Only "real" people, he argued, were entitled to present themselves. "Substitution was a prostitution." (Robbins, 1970)

With tensions building toward the first World War, Moreno, in a protest ahead of his time, ran nude through the streets of Vienna. He wished to demonstrate the truth of an old fairy tale. He, like the Austrian Emperor the people were following, had no clothes. Such acting-out was too far from the mainstream; too impulsive, unrefined and unacceptable. Moreno, as he tells it, spent a night in jail. (Robbins, 1970)

Gradually Moreno developed a more socially adapted, less fantastic, expression for his God-concerns. He reasoned that if God had a role to play on earth it would be as a healer, and so he entered medical school.

The period of World War I brought great despair. Death and needless destruction were everywhere. Moreno felt the mood acutely. It tapped the profound question of his character, a question he felt belonged to everyman:

> "Was man of no importance?"
> (Moreno, 1961)

He meditated:

> "Am I nothing or am I God... ? If there is nothing else except a dreamlike passing into nothing, at least we can protest against an unreasonable fate, an unpardonable sin, a mistake of the cosmos to have thrown us out here into the desert of this planet, perceiving, feeling, thinking without any chance or hope to become something which really matters."
> (Moreno, 1961)

Then on one exceptional day "in those days of deep loss of faith" (Moreno, 1961), a new inspiration answered his despair in a profoundly mystical moment.

"... I suddenly felt reborn. ....I began then to hear voices ... a voice which reaches all being ... one who gives us hope, who gives our life a direction." (Moreno, 1961)

The voice stimulated a frenzy of excitement and movement. Without the patience to sit and write the words down he rushed to the top room of the house and in red pencil wrote the words he heard upon the walls. Then, done, he collapsed exhausted onto the floor. (Moreno, 1971)

In this period of despair, Moreno had struggled to find his way out, to create an answer to the existential question "Am I nothing?" Through the channel of communication a voice reached him. Inspired, he flew to the high point of the house and feverishly wrote all that he had heard on the walls. His work done, he collapsed.

Moreno had followed a Rhythmic Cycle that peaked and exploded in the Inspiration Phase of his character and then feverishly worked itself down through his scribblings on the wall.

When he woke he searched to grasp what had happened to him. He read the words he wrote. They began, "I am the Father." He wondered, "Who was this `I'?" "Where did these words come from?" They were not his words, though he had formed them. These were not the words of the remote God called "He" in the Old Testament, nor the words of the closer God called "Thou" in the New Testament, but the words of an "I" - an "I" God. (Moreno, 1961) God, and Moreno, had used the same word, the word "I" to speak what came.

In the terms of the Rhythmic Cycle, Moreno felt he hadn't personally achieved these writings. They had not come from an integrated conscious personal center with which he could identify. The words, as is the case with the mystical aspect of the Dream Phase, were experienced as cosmic, not a result of his unique personhood. Yet they had directly come from him and were spoken out from the word "I." What could it mean? He concluded, "I am God." (Moreno, 1961)

Moreno took his realization of this new expression of God, the "I-God," and held fast to it. As God, the limitless nature of his Inspirer character could go no higher, no farther. He had reached the edge of being, the limit of existence. He judged the Creator God of the Old Testament too remote to be of help. He sensed the soft acceptance of Jesus as a person of love, but found the concept of God the Son as insufficient. He reasoned that God, like himself, was a spontaneous creative actor.

Now, with this view, "God-as-Himself" could provide an additional element of continuity and control to the acting-out nature of his being. He saw that he could and indeed must be responsible for himself as well as for others. He had heard the words of the Father within and strove to live the role without.

Moreno saw that as God acted as a teacher, he too had to act this way. His name had been Jacob Levy. He now added "Moreno." "Moreno", a variant of his father's given name "Morenu," meant, in Hebrew, "our teacher."

Through the acting out of his new relationship with the God within, and through the taking of a new name, Moreno achieved a rapprochement with an absent part of his personality, the father-figure. From it he grew more limited and more grounded. It offered a constant point of stability and a way to begin to develop much needed Solidifier aspects in his personality.

"God-the-spontaneous-actor" became the model for his work and a method of healing through action developed. God acted out His potential, expressed Himself in the moment. Man could do the same. Each man could be God and know the importance of spontaneity, "being inspired only by the present and not by the past, using the past only as a vehicle." (Robbins 1970)

With experience, Moreno's personal God interpretation was modified, became more social and gained in meaning. In his 30's, he realized all men thought they were God. It was a turn of mind that reflected an ordering and acculturation of impulses, brought him even closer to earth, deepening the process of the Solidifier Phase. Not quite so special, his license more limited, he found he related better to others as he responded to their Godly expression. (Robbins, 1970)

> "The universe is not just a jungle and a bundle of wild forces. But it is basically infinite creativity. .... We are all bound together by the principle of all-inclusiveness. ... We all have to assume responsibility for all things - there is no limited, partial responsibility. ... Everything belongs to me and I belong to everybody. ... Billions of partners, invisible hands, arms stretched one to touch the other - all being responsible for what happens in this world and all being able through this responsibility to be Gods." (Moreno, 1961)

As God, Moreno had published his books anonymously. Surely, he reasoned, God had no individual's name. With his growing sense of personal responsibility his books were republished under his authorship. They were his achievement. His accountability became publicly visible. Owning his personality, he was able to marry and have a family - acts that he had once thought lay outside the Godly realm.

Moreno's God-concept was inspired by experiencing the creative, spontaneous healing fount. As such it included little of the everyday mundane side of totality - its earthy, solid, at times even boring lawfulness. Others were needed to help firm his ideas and work. His work took form as an evolved and integrated whole, embodying both theory and method, as his wives (he was married twice) and students filled in loose areas.

Moreno's eccentricity had to yield to the necessities that advancing his work demanded. "Without it (his work, R.R.) I'm not sure what trouble I would have had." (Robbins, 1970) Still with his colleagues and peers his relationships remained difficult.

Even today full appreciation of the jewels that his work contained has not yet occurred. The patrimony of his contribution suffered neglect from the more illustrious people that he influenced. Perhaps most notable in this regard was Fritz Perls, who practiced Psychodramatic methods under the umbrella of his own therapeutic approach, Gestalt Therapy.

Perls too was an Inspirer. The late 60's was a time for inspiration. "Doing one's thing," as Perls called it, became the slogan of the day. After regularly attending Moreno's public psychodrama sessions for over a year-and-a-half, Perls brought the techniques of forty years of psychodramatic development to the attention of the public-at-large. He used many psychodramatic methods in his popular work at Esalen Institue during the '60's, but gave no credit to Moreno. Most who saw his therapy believed that Perls himself had developed Psychodrama.

At an American Psychological Association meeting Perls attended a session at which Moreno was presenting. Moreno sought to encounter Perls about the confusion about Psychodrama's patrimony. From the dais he had his opportunity, "Fritz, who is the father of Psychodrama?" Perls, in an action gesture, bowed low before him. (Moreno, 1971)

The physical structure of the Inspirer was evident in Moreno to the end. He leaned heavily on his wife Zerka who solidified his work, taught his students, republished his articles. A gifted woman in her own right, her character was built around the solid practical strength that he lacked. When she lost her right arm to cancer, he responded to the stress with a weight explosion. As he grew huge, his legs grew correspondingly unsteady. Zerka's role as supporter expanded.

Clutching to the God concept had helped him learn to stand alone and develop. But Moreno never fully came to terms with limitations and always had difficulties checking his impulses for his own well-being. A man of greatness, a man of genius, he appeared to remain lacking in the inner sureness and confident position that comes from solid fulfillment.

In a way, his boundlessness put him beyond the reach of even his own methods and techniques, methods and techniques that were so helpful to others. He rationalized that God could have no therapist giving direction. He was unwilling to directly rely on the support on his own method for his own therapeutic development. Not once over the course of his life did he take the role of patient in a Psychodrama.

At the time of our interviews, Moreno's therapeutic work had gained far greater acceptance in Europe and Latin America than in the United States, where the difficulties of his personality were more directly experienced. There appeared to be some pain mixed in with the great pride he felt when he spoke of the occasion of his then recent reception of an honorary Doctoral degree from the University of Vienna. He spoke with special relish of the moment when the speaker announced that the University had failed to honor Freud in his lifetime but would not make the same error with Moreno.

Time will provide distance from Moreno's eccentricities. Moreno himself knew this and hoped others would gain a full degree of recognition and respect for his work, recognition that he felt he was unable to fully achieve. (Robbins, 1970)

To the end Moreno maintained his association with the fantastic part of his personality, his role as God-player, the ultimate expression of his character. He was in his mid-70's when he was asked if anything had been added since he first played the part of the

Deity. He paused a long moment and then with chest swelling pronounced:

> "Nothing has changed. I am still God!"

(Robbins, 1970)

JACQUI LEE SCHIFF - THE INSPIRER

Jacqui Lee Schiff treats schizophrenics. Skilled therapists, including her mentor, Eric Berne, the author of "Games People Play" and founder of Transactional Analysis, witnessed her work and verified her success. Undaunted by the "impossible" case, she has reached out to bring people back from the other side, to reality and sane productive lives.

Both Schiff's personal story and her psychotherapeutic approach are exceptional. Already at age three their threads appeared to interweave and foreshadow what was to come. It was then she dreamt of having 100 children of her own, saw herself marching them to the grocery store, with the bigger ones taking care of the little ones. It was organized, without confusion or problem.

Dream grew to reality. In "One Hundred Children Generate a Lot of TA" (Schiff, 1977), Schiff tells of treating 100 schizophrenic patients, replacing the sick parental voices they incorporated in their past with new healthy parental messages of her own. She called the method "Reparenting."

Through the process of Reparenting, concepts and methods for "curing" the difficult, often called "unsolvable" problems of schizophrenics were developed. Through her, psychotic adults found a new mother and a chance to grow up again, this time in a climate that was caring, clear and hopeful, and which led to an independent responsible healthy life.

Schiff's extraordinary way of working grew out of her background, her history and her body. When she was born her mother was only 15, her father 16. Concerned she not be raised by these "too young" parents, her grandparents agreed to share the responsibility of childrearing. The result was a variety, a virtual community of caretakers.

Her real parents, as parents, were lost to her. Over the years Schiff's father made only several contacts. The relationship with her mother was also intermittent and strongly colored by the judgments of her maternal grandparents. They saw Schiff's mother as a negative, a dangerous lesson in irresponsibility. Schiff internalized their attitude. She viewed her mother as a failure, a constant threat who might take unjust advantage of even the slightest loyalty and interest. Schiff did her best to avoid her.

Until she was four, Schiff spent weekdays with her father's parents. They were middle-class and proper. Grandmother was a no-nonsense woman. Her home was quiet, efficient, emotionally cool. The matter-of-fact nature of Schiff's earliest memories of this period reflect the emotionally cool tone in the house. Their main theme, food, indicates the dynamics of the Communicator Phase of the Rhythmic Cycle. Inspirer dynamics, it will be seen, came from somewhere else.

> "I remember sending an invitation to a friend to come over for a little tea party. Refreshments were set out in advance. The girl stayed to the appointed time and then left." (Robbins, 1979)

Once, Grandmother found a chicken who laid double-yolked eggs:

> "I didn't like eggs but was motivated to eat them to find out if the egg in front of me was of the double-yolked kind." (Robbins, 1979)

The Rhythmic Cycle of Change

The loss of her natural mother and the emotionally sparse environment of her paternal grandparents' home reinforced the formation of Communicator characteristics. As a young child Schiff was extremely thin. She talked precociously, was clever and bright, developed in reason and logic. At three she first suffered a disease that affected the covering of her bones and resulted in periods of multiple breakage at times throughout her life. She carried on nevertheless, as if her bones weren't broken, learning to compensate for her physical deficiencies, denying a life of fragility.

The environment and energy in the home of Schiff's other set of caretakers, her maternal grandparents, provided a background of stimulation that went beyond the Communicator Phase of the Rhythmic Cycle and carried her into the Inspirer Phase. Until she was four she visited them on weekends. Then her mother gained custody and there was a shift in caretaking emphasis. She moved into the home of her mother's parents permanently, though many days were still spent in the home of her father's parents.

The new home, in a large and extended Scandinavian family, was energetic and alive. This was an immigrant family full of activity and life drama. As many as 17 would be present for dinner. The only girl in a house full of boys, she got a lot of attention. Schiff was special. The others were large and she, small and skinny, became known as the "runt." The boys went so far as to suggest she not have children because they would all grow up to be midgets. Inside she fought back, reinforcing her early parental dream with the firm decision to have lots of children.

The family's exuberance and her place of specialness provided the energetic thrust for the development of Inspirer dynamics that occurred soon after her mother married and she gained a stepfather. Though she continued to live with her grandparents, this new male figure had his influence. She was five when he married her mother and adopted her.

He was:

>"...a big, strong, very masculine man of Icelandic extraction who was a juvenile officer and later became the Chief of Police in the community...

>He gave me the message: 'You're a damned smart kid. You can do anything you want to do! My father's belief in my being able to do unusual things gave me the confidence to try to treat patients whom other therapists considered untreatable.'" (Schiff, 1970)

"A damn smart kid. You can do anything you want to do!", an inspirational message, one with no limits. It became a theme that was reinforced and acted out through her life.

Schiff's intellectual ability furthered her sense of exceptionality. She alone in the household showed superior intelligence. She was studied by a Stanford University project on gifted children. Schiff was different from the others, a budding literate in a house of little literacy.

Her intelligence brought special treatment from the town librarian. She was allowed to take out five books a week - three chosen by the librarian, two by Schiff. By age 10 she had read all of Shakespeare and many of the classics. She had also dropped out of school.

Schiff hadn't been an easy child to teach, preferring to read and do her own thing rather than participate in class. Early in grade school she decided, "Since they couldn't provide a proper education for me I should be left to educate myself." As a result she stopped attending classes regularly and only took semester exams. Intermittently they provided tutoring. This was agreeable to her grandparents who held education in low esteem anyway. Schiff was unfettered, free to do what she wanted.

Physically, she expressed her upward direction. Though she still suffered numerous broken bones she loved to climb trees and became a skilled tumbler. By adolescence she was a proficient mountain climber, a member of the mountain rescue team.

Work, with all its limits and constrictions, was important and enjoyed in her family. All helped and contributed. Schiff did her share too by helping to take care of the other children. Goals were given and she learned to develop some control and suppress her impulsivity to accomplish ends. When control faltered, she found a clever violation or manipulation was tolerated and even appreciated in the family. (Robbins, 1979)

When Schiff reached adolescence, her mother left her stepfather to run off with his best friend. In response to her stepfather's request, she moved in. She immediately appreciated her new place in the home. Between 2-3 years later, though, her mother returned. Schiff's position displaced, she ran away. A young adolescent, she was on her own, responsible for herself.

Schiff spent a year with broken bones, in a children's hospital. There she got some additional schooling. She worked fields as a migrant and got involved in the teen-age excesses of the day, drugs, drinking and cars.

Eventually she returned to high school and did well in an honors program. The staff assisted her in applying to college. She cooperated, feeling she had to move beyond the educational and cultural limitations of her family.

At home she got no support. The family was threatened about the possibility that Schiff would be exposed to "intellectuals," a threat reinforced by the McCarthyism of the time. Even her stepfather was no help. When she told him her plans he grew furious and slapped her. He had given her the idea she could do anything. Now she was going too far. (Robbins, 1979)

In college and in character, Schiff "attended classes at random without bothering to work toward a degree." (Robbins, 1979) She was soon married and a mother.

Tragedy struck when her three-month-old daughter died of lung collapse. She thought of herself as a mother without a baby. The stress brought impulsive urges into consciousness. She wanted to snatch infants off the streets and nurse them. The intensity and urgency of these irrational impulses threatened and confused her. She didn't know if she could contain them. (Robbins, 1979)

A long deep depression stifled both impulses and confusion. Finally her paternal grandmother, in her no-nonsense way, shared that she too had lost a child, that many mothers had. It was part of life and she had to move on. The talk freed Schiff to continue.

Schiff and her husband had three more children before he responded to severe vision problems with a desire to withdraw and, as she saw it, live off his family's money. This threat of passivity was anathema to her. With the Inspirer's urge to move on and impulses pressing for action, passivity was difficult to bear. The marriage became intolerable and she proceeded with a divorce.

By this time Schiff was actively involved in social welfare work and a participant in the weekly seminars in Transactional Analysis (T.A.) being held with Eric Berne. (Schiff, 1970) Through her intelligence she quickly established her familiar special place. Though untrained, with little experience and holding no advanced degree, Schiff, as might be expected, had no compunction about contradicting and challenging the concepts of the older, more experienced and established professionals.

One argument that occurred in the seminars became the keystone for Schiff's future work. Transactional Analysis thinks of personality as made up of three ego states: Parent, Adult and Child. The Parent state is the part of us that provides both nurturing and judgmental statements about how to be. It is learned from messages received from parent figures. The Adult state is objective and reality-based. It makes intelligent observation, free of values and emotions. Its interest is in facts. The Child state grows out of the expression of emotions and has two parts, the Natural and the Adapted Child.

The Natural Child expresses needs, wants and emotions freely and playfully. The second part, the Adapted Child, distorts feelings in response to parent's expectations and pressures. Its behavior is bent into modes of action that satisfy parental requirements. When these requirements are pathological, they result in the child behaving in grossly unnatural and sick ways.

In the seminars Schiff attended, it was believed the Parent aspect of personality was fixed in the mature person. She argued against this, reasoning that since the Parent ego was a learned response developed in childhood, it could be replaced with new learning. Schiff believed new parent models could be found. Furthermore they could be internalized.

Not accepting the limitation of an immutable Parent ego state led to a new conceptual approach for working with schizophrenics. In time, Schiff would prove her point by changing the Parent state in the dynamics of her "children."

The Transactional Analysis meetings provided a professional orientation in working with people. Schiff's skills sharpened. She found herself more and more helpful to people. To legitimize her professional interests she entered a school of Social Work. While there she met and married Moe Schiff, a fellow student.

In Schiff's first book, <u>All My Children</u>, written with professional author Beth Day (Schiff, 1970), her relationship with her husband was presented as a "true love" story. In interview, however, she portrayed the marriage more matter-of-factly, as one of convenience. (Robbins, 1979) She gained a father for her three children while she offered her husband, who very much wanted children, a chance to be an instant parent. Neither knew how boundless this "parenting" arrangement would become.

When a mother's helper the Schiffs employed became severely disturbed, schizophrenia became a living reality in their home. Schiff tried to be warm and helpful but was unsuccessful at playing out the mother role as the girl desired. The girl left:

> "... not well, disappointed and angry at my withholding." (Schiff, 1972).

The experience fascinated Schiff but its end left her incomplete. She wanted to do more. Her husband's Social Work position involved contact with young schizophrenics. They agreed to take in a paranoid adolescent and soon the house was filled with disturbed youngsters. The task of "curing" schizophrenics, a task that reason would argue seemed to promise only failure, became an irresistible possibility.

A new treatment approach, designed to do the impossible, was gradually honed through experiences of success and failure. The work developed into two major treatment phases, de-energizing the Parent ego state and redeveloping the Child ego state.

The initial step encouraged transference. The Schiffs at first "played" the part of the child's parents, then crossing the limit they went even further. They psychologically displaced the real natural parents and assumed a level of responsibility far surpassing the boundaries of the conventional therapist's role. Eventually the program even went so far as to lead Jacqui Schiff to legally adopt seven of the children.

Schiff's aim was to change the Parent ego by taking energy away from disturbed Parental messages that had been learned as a child. She found these messages terrifyingly irrational and monstrously hostile. By appealing to the objective Adult ego, she could show the children how their old Parental messages did not work in practice.

Schiff's Communicator characteristics were well developed. Like Ellis, the Rational-Emotive therapist, she could argue the "children" out of the insanity of their irrational ideas and then teach them to think in ways that strengthened the Adult aspect of their personality.

She provided new Parental messages, clear helpful rules to replace the disturbed state. The work wasn't easy. The old messages, though distorted, provided a measure of containment for destructive impulses. Without them violent acting out could and did occur. (Schiff, 1970)

Living in a home in a normal community with very sick young people brought problems. But because of her own character, Schiff was personally prepared and willing to tolerate the impulsive, limitless and destructive behavior of her "children" until the new controls she was giving began to be effective. (Schiff, 1970)

As the children progressed they became more reasonable and relaxed. Nevertheless they would still often regress, acting in infantile destructive ways inappropriate to solving the problems that faced them. She began to follow their lead, allowing the regressions to be acted out within the home, and learned that the distorted Adapted Child state had to relive infantile periods to learn appropriate responses that hadn't developed normally in childhood. From a healthier base, emotions could mature.

The first step in treatment had been to change the Parent ego. The second step, now seen, was to allow the "children" to fully regress. Life became a continuous psychodrama in situ. Early life scenes were acted out. "Children" were raised again; fed with baby bottles, toilet trained, etc..

With the addition of this second phase of treatment many of the children made astounding gains. They were able to succeed in school, hold jobs, function on the "outside." Eric Berne saw and said, "She cures schizophrenics."

The development and techniques of Schiff's therapeutic approach violated the boundaries of traditional practice and everyday mores. The children's unconventional ways and her unusual methods threatened her with controversy in both the communities where she lived and eventually in professional circles. Her therapeutic approach played out some of the liabilities of her character, but in the process, she did what many thought impossible and she provided theories, ideas and methods so that others could do the same.

Schiff physically manifests the character of the Inspirer. Her thin limbs are set off by the largeness of her head and trunk. Though small as a child, her frame grew in adolescence as she moved herself away from her family and strove to make it on her own.

In adulthood she gained extra weight when she separated from her husband. (Robbins, 1979) Alone, she felt threatened by her charges' potential for murderous acting out. Weight for the Inspirer, as has been noted, can give a look of strength, exaggerating the appearance of power and providing unconscious psychological relief from feelings of threat. To get a more realistic feeling of safety took even more. Schiff obtained a large guard dog to sleep with and protect her at night.

Schiff's large size added to her capacity for charisma. Schizophrenics could easily fall into transference with her; she offered an "earth-mother" appearance and the promise of a cure that stimulated directly the Dreamer capacities of those caught in the schizophrenic process. Her work developed to make good on what she inspired.

The giving that Schiff provided was not one-way. Her "children" came to provide the structure and support that she, as an Inspirer, needed. She credits them for "Parenting" her when she neglected or rebelled against routines that she needed to follow. They checked to insure she took required medication for her physical condition. They helped to limit an admitted tendency toward grandiosity. (Robbins, 1979)

Besides this, "the children" were active in developing Schiff's therapeutic ideas, even assisted her in writing her major theoretical book, The Cathexis Reader (Schiff, 1975). When a threatening suggestion was made that her theories must be written or that they might be stolen, Schiff reacted by organizing her staff and several of her "children." In just one weekend The Cathexis Reader, an outline of her theory and work, was produced.

Schiff's work, unique and attested to by others as successful, still lacks a connection and solid attachment to the mainstream of mental health. Many professionals have never heard of it. Her treatment procedures to some extent are outside the boundaries of professional practice and, representing a new way, have brought considerable difficulties. Only a special person could live at home with the threat of the disturbed behavior of acting-out Psychotics. Few would go so far as to take full parental charge of a number of schizophrenic adults.

Even her own colleagues in Transactional Analysis seem to have found her ways and personality too far-out. After a long period of bitter dispute that involved them in questions of her professionalism, she chose to leave the country and continue her work in India. Milton Erickson, prominent for his work in hypnotherapy and familiar with her work, suggested that her critics should be criticized. (Rogers, 1979) Schiff, he said, had gone where others hadn't, putting her own self and totality on the line.

Schiff has not yet achieved the position that the results of her work appear to warrant. The place of honor that the Achievement Phase of the Rhythmic Cycle brings is yet to be attained. The establishment's failure to see, evaluate, and implement the successful attributes of her work, to adapt its methods to the structure of care currently available, appears a tragic loss of a potentially life-healing method that offers significant promise to the many whose problems appear the most hopeless.

> This week a young man and his family were referred to me. He had been suffering schizophrenic episodes over the past two years. In a psychiatric consultation they had been told to give up hope. It was predicted to them that he would remain psychotic, take drugs, and be in and out of mental hospitals all his life.
> I suggested he enter a program that works with Reparenting to rehabilitate schizophrenics. Though the financial resources were available, by now the emotional ones were gone. In despair they responded: "Everyone knows schizophrenics can't be helped."

SUMMARY

Jacqui Lee Schiff, Jacob Levy Moreno and the Baal Shem Tov all grandly rose to play out the special role organized in their bodies and personalities at an early age. Each suffered vivid losses with absent father-figures who couldn't be steady forces for them. Each had a sense of limitlessness and a capacity to disregard the cultural norms that led them into difficulty with the established rules. Each had in some way been designated and treated as a special person. They all left school early and were on their own by their early teens. Each emphasized responsibility in others and each had the strong steady support of a close or a number of close followers who shored up the development of their inspirational work.

Each reached upwards and functioned in a role above others, inspiring them to move from life's lower depths, to raise the level of their lives and become more than what they were. They all could be powerfully charismatic and each had difficulties with the establishment while forging what appeared as a completely new path. All of their contributions were in a way incredible.

For Jacqui Lee Schiff and for Jacob Moreno the physical dynamics of the Inspirer, the toddler grown big, is evident in appearance. For the Baal Shem Tov appearance is lost in history but his legends consistently contain themes of bodily upwardness.

Each of us can inspire. The flux of our life forces expands and rises naturally with every strong inhalation we take. With it there is a buildup of charge and hope, a rise in excitement and potential that can lead to going beyond ourselves to new levels. In the Rhythmic Cycle of Development the Phase of Inspiration is followed naturally by an energized plateau that confronts us with the containing boundaries that shape and form our energy into something solid.

For the Inspirer, the reach seems boundless, as early in life those who might have been there to teach the containment of energy and impulse were absent. For others, a significant adult teaches the ways of limit. Rules allow energy to cohere. A solid dependable reality develops. A new responsible dimension of the personal and interpersonal is shaped. The pattern of the Solidifier becomes set.

Solidifier

Dray horse.
Plodding clomp,
One foot and another
Marching along the deep worn way.

Head hung down,
Tired captured bones bent over.
Never set to pasture
You carry the load and hold the burden.

If you could be set free
The strength of your heart and steadfastness of your way would
Powerfully flow through your hard-earned stature.

THE METHOD

Slow and steady, holding ground; Resisting when pushed; plodding when forced, the concrete person becomes the foundation and rock. Evolving slowly, steadily, there are no surprises. Grit and determination insure methodical movement. Wound up and set off, the outcome is predictable and determined.

The Rhythmic Cycle of Change

Never straying from the outward course, the pressurized, robot-like form secretly moves inside to develop inner riches while holding fast to the external path. Others slowly come to know the consistency and stability. Adversity doesn't shake this one, rather engenders admiration for dutiful dogged containment. Methodically, without grace, the job gets done.

A whining tone or quiet procrastination are the only hints of the bitter suffering of inner complaint. Sitting still and holding in is the utmost expression of defiance. Life is met without motion. What is, is. It takes the strongest of stimuli to release feeling. Even waves of outer excitement can be insufficient to move one from the fundamentals.

The Solidifier is a fundamental person. A heavy, earthbound presence brings steadiness and calm to the environment. Order and practicality are the base of life. Care is manifest in reliable concern during troubled times and in the dulling of personal potential for the service of others.

Masters of containment, Solidifiers give strength and boundary to the visions and goals of others while hiding their own dreams, hopes and desires in fear of humiliation and disdain. In serving, they suppress a secret attitude of superiority. The servant, after all, provides the foundation for advance. There is strength in the ability to hold on, methodically to get the job done, resisting all distraction. A quiet inner pride grows as the effort is maintained while others are dissolving under life's pressures. "When the going gets tough the tough get going."

Holding, though a strength, necessitates freedom's sacrifice. Imprisoned feelings, both negative and positive, build to full proportions behind walls of containment. Neither modified nor freshened through interactions with reality, distortions grow grotesque. In periods of assured acceptance or overwhelming stimuli, the containing forces give way and powerful emotional currents explode. Unrefined, the bad and the good burst into the open.

> When she was good
> She was very, very good
> And when she was bad
> She was horrid!

PHYSICAL DYNAMICS

The Solidifier's encasement is evident in their muscle-bound appearance. Inner motions moving to release are stifled by outer muscles holding back. Stagnation is evident in dull, at times even brownish, skin tone. Movement against barrier is hard work. Progress is slow. Constant contraction thickens muscles. Their weight alone bogs down locomotion.

> Tom was solidly built, six feet, 235 pounds. I asked him to hit the bed as hard as he could. He slowly moved to the task, in character, steadfastly maintaining that he wasn't angry.
>
> Tom's huge squared body, thick legs, massive chest and arms, all suggested he could smash through the bed. He arched back, came forward and down, but his muscle-bound movement was stifled and slow. The force on the mattress was negligible. A 95 pounder could hit harder.
>
> Asked how he had done at this task, Tom replied he had hit very hard. He was completely misled by the strong muscular effort that he had felt in his body. His strength had been used to check rather than drive his movement. No emotion or force could ride out on it. He had to learn to release

resisting muscles to allow full movement and feeling
in order to make an impact.

Inspiration's impulses are checked by the clod-like weightiness of the Solidifier's skeletal muscles and their tendency to work against the self's expression. Pressure builds as the excitement aroused in the viscera is blocked from release. Bodily movement is gross, held, lacks play.

The posture of the Solidifier's thick contracted body ranges in degree, from one squashed like a a gremlin to one held steadfastly erect against the pull of a contracting musculature.

The more developed squared-off erect person shoulders responsibility. A dutiful soldier he follows the route and procedures set by the commander. The heavy body sits solidly on the ground, thick legs planted in place. Outer pushes and inner urges are stubbornly resisted. Change is slower than slow.

The overloaded squashed person gives way under the heaviness of contraction. Spinal extension is not strong enough to hold the body erect against the pressure. At times this Solidifier functions nearer to the earlier Inspirer Phase of the Rhythmic Cycle with impulsive release. Puffiness in the chest allows some escape of emotions through the voice, leaking a stream of impulses. The positive in such cases is apt to come out in a maudlin exhibitionism. The negative exudes in whine, complaint and general unpleasantness.

Gene was short and stocky, a surface layer of baby fat added to his thickened musculature and an everpresent fixed smile resulted in the squatty appearance of a kewpie doll. A therapist, he served the poor, "society's downtrodden."

In the days of welfare fraud and Medicaid review, his financial success with this clientele courted trouble. His practice was being examined for irregularities. Investigators, he complained, were using him to show their zeal and gain publicity to deter others. The difficulty of the situation was too much for him. He couldn't mobilize any aggression as the governmental reaper threatened to break him and destroy his practice.

Through therapeutic work the physical encasement of his chest gave way. His voice could no longer be fully contained. He complained, belittled, and whined about the unfair abuse to which he was being subjected. This release, little as it was, allowed narrow escape from the fuller depression that had come from restricted respiration.

Regressing to the Inspirer phase of the Rhythmic Cycle, Gene experienced intense panic. We worked together on his body, relaxing his diaphragm, belly and legs to decrease the pressure in his upper body so he could use this energy to feel the wholeness of fuller flow.

As he increasingly mobilized his energy, excitement rippled through him, loosening thick muscle tensions. Distorted negativity transformed into a realistic anger toward what was happening to him. He decided that rather than maintain the Solidifier's solution of "standing still for it," he would fight back.

A month later he had a lawyer and his pride. He felt good and alive, in charge of his own life. The excitement of the challenge he faced provided real growth, moving him past the Solidifier phase of the Rhythmic Cycle, beyond his neurotic stuck-point.

The Rhythmic Cycle of Change

DEVELOPMENT OF THE SOLIDIFIER

The boundless adventurousness accompanying the Inspirers' rise to their feet gives way to stability as they master movements that give better balance, a firmer relationship to the earth and solid physical and psychological boundaries. Able to hold a stable position, the child becomes "workable" and is shaped to behave.

"Behave" describes the terms of the Solidifier Phase. The word has two parts, "be" and "have". They outline opposing forces. "Be" indicates the flowing capacity, the potential for movement and moment-by-moment change. "Have" means "to hold in possession" or "in one's use, service or affection" as well as "to be compelled or forced to." (Merriam - Webster, 1974) The whole word, "behave," means "to bear, comport or conduct oneself in a particular and especially proper way." (Merriam - Webster, 1974) Thus when one behaves, the potential for free movement and change become placed in the service of that which is defined by an outside definition of proper.

In the Solidifier Phase of the Rhythmic Cycle the vitality, the very being of the person is checked to gain proper behavior. The issue is who will be in possession. Will the child be allowed to discover the rules, directed and guided to follow them, his essence being the initial impetus for containment and behavior, or will he be forced by an overbearing adult who impresses the rules into the body as self-destructive muscular barriers that fix and routinize behavior?

For the healthiest development, the child must be guided to express his own individual and self-directed way, naturally becoming aware of the social reactions his behavior evokes. He learns through the consequences of his own behavior.

As the child approaches the age of two, the Solidifying stage, cultural shaping as well as social testing becomes possible. The parent directs, the child objects. Defiance and negativity occur.

The child is capable of negating with a loud clear "no," reinforced at times with "impossible" behavior.

> Two-and-a-half-year-old Judy did not want
> to go home. Her mother demanded she get ready.
> Judy sat down. Defiantly - she removed her clothes.

At best, parents, during this time of the "Terrible Twos," will find humor in the child's spunkiness and impossibility, treat it as a phase in the development of self-assertion and individuality while firmly holding to what matters. The child will learn the rules through imitation, communication, trial and error, gentle pressure, firmness and guidance. New habits and capacities for constructive containment will develop that are useful in both forming and regulating the self in a way that allows coming to terms with the social world.

At worst, parents burdened by duty, obligation and authority are shamed by the negativity that is part of the normal growth of the child. They move to break the child. The child responds by powerfully fighting for freedom. When parental suppression, ridicule or shaming becomes too strong, the defeated child uses the capacity to contain in order to protect against the adult's negative response. They tensely hold in, binding the musculature to shield off the attack of the other and avoid their own unacceptable spontaneous expressions.

The Solidifier's parent disciplines with an overbearing presence that bends and shapes behavior to desired patterns. "Correct" behavior is provoked through prodding and pushing. Deviance is punished by shame and blame. Expectancies are based on exaggeration of the "good" and "bad" categories of social acceptability.

The child learns to mind, to follow the "mind" of another. With outward negativity suppressed, individual inclination is curbed, freedom and independence are weakened. Emotions grow distorted by exaggerated compliance, duty and responsibility.

Responsibility becomes a burden when duty demands routine without satisfaction, life without freedom. With liberation the burdensome task becomes something else.

> Harry whined diffusely about his work. His complaints were useless. They had no emotional power and brought no relief. Body work loosened his chest and throat. He began to cry and his tone changed. He poignantly spoke of how after college, the army, and 10 years of marriage he was still living with his very neurotic mother, working in a "nowhere" job as a parole officer three blocks from his childhood home. He hadn't moved far.

> For a moment his lack of movement seemed lamentable to him but suddenly a breakthrough of energy brought good feeling and moved him along on the course of the Rhythmic Cycle. A genuine smile brightened his face as he said, "Sometimes I get really excited about it, it becomes like a mission. I identify with the people I work with, parolees whom I help to keep out of jail."

> The muscular imprisonment of Harry's body visibly eased as he thought of his mission. We talked of the need to relax his own self-imposed jail, his large thick muscles, as the way to freedom. Over time, as he made these necessary changes he gained in personal freedom and chose to make some liberating changes in his life.

Duty and responsibility reach masochistic proportions with the breaking of the will. Needs, desires and natural responses decrease in value to the extent "required" behavior is forced. Loyalty goes to the power that checks. Respecting the outer force that molds, the child looks to it to reinforce containment.

Routines, controls and expectancies are formed into habits in this time of socialization. Psychoanalysts have focused, perhaps too exclusively focused, on toilet-training as the crucial context of parent-child interaction during this period. It is true that at this age maturation of the anal sphincters allows the child to regulate elimination, but with the generally greater muscular control that is developing, the training ground extends further to eating, dress and general comportment. The culture's basic forms of behaviors can be impressed.

Through socialization the "self" develops. A constellation of ideas regarding personal experiences is formed. Self-evaluation as "good" or "bad" becomes possible. The child remembers the approvals and disapprovals of behaviors. Initially the child does not separate their self from their acts, and esteem is based on the reactions received from others. The self-concept that develops in this way can become an important, if unnatural, determiner and regulator of behavior throughout life.

THERAPY

Unlocking the body requires finding the key to the trap. Solidifiers learn discipline and strong control as necessary ends in themselves. They bend under the load of unneeded extra effort. Their normal assertion signals muscles to act in a contrary way to block urges. The result is an in-and-out physical battle in which desires for assertion are turned inward by the heavy restraint of the large muscles. Self-retribution bends negative aggression around toward the self, the only target allowed. An increase in effort tends only to result in an increase in self-wounding.

> Margaret, a Solidifier, was charged with energy. Deep breathing, from jogging in place, temporarily brought color and tone to her usually lifeless grey skin. Her heavy thighs and thick muscles were active. Excitedly, she moved to strike the bed. As she came close to contact she pushed to make an extra-good effort.
>
> The extra push interfered. Her forearms bound and her wrists collapsed. As she hit, her hands were painfully bent backwards. By forcing beyond the free flow of her assertiveness, she hurt herself. Self-inflicted punishment stopped her aggression in just three blows.

The Solidifier is split between inner and outer. Sensitive feelings consciously develop but the possibility of using them to move in life is blocked by the immobility of the body's exterior. The inner being cries for freedom while the outer surfaces hold fast. The song of life develops in silence. Pride is chained to restraint, expression to humiliation.

The Solidifier hides. Afraid of social judgment he is reluctant to risk it. As a child he feared parental negativity; as an adult he fears condemnation by peers and self. Energy-bound, he is stuck, rooted to one place. He can't open to action until the capacity for freedom and the courage to move develops within his own internal urgings.

Unfettering requires the freedom to express and assert the inner experience in an environment of acceptance. The acceptance of the therapist builds self-acceptance. This allows development of personal authority and strengthens the courage necessary to project one's own experience into life without being stopped by fear of neurotic shame.

Expression, with therapy, gradually moves from the banal and grotesque toward the profound and clear. As it does, the heavy, thick physical armor loosens and stretches. The body changes and becomes more permeable. The silent suffering of a heavy heart gives way to poignantly tender sadness and the powerful thunder of strong focused negation. The person is no longer held slave by oppressive feelings of shame and humiliation. The self can be expressed while the individual remains in possession of a clear conception of reality, a well-developed emotional intensity and personal integrity that brings admiration.

CULTURE AND SOLIDITY

Cultures are passed on in the Solidifier period. This is the time of socialization when the child is asked to contain himself and establish firm boundaries. Some cultures, such as those of Continental Europe, emphasize the containing, solidifying process itself to characterize their cultural form while others, like America in the early and mid-`70s, pass through it as a Rhythmic Cycle develops.

Continental Europe is made up of a number of relatively small clearly delineated countries. Each advances and protects its own culture. In some, such as Belgium and Switzerland, different languages within the country further delineate cultural sub-groups. The pot holds but doesn't melt.

Between these closely lying Nations the natural limits of geographical boundaries are emphasized by border patrols and checkpoints to control all who pass. A history of erupting wars and power struggles serves to add further firmness to national loyalties that reinforce the barriers between peoples.

The Rhythmic Cycle of Change

In working with psychotherapists of these countries, one is struck with the intensity and pervasiveness of in-group feelings of nationhood. A favorite pastime is to collect opinions about the national character of other countries. This inevitably leads to shaming derogatory judgments, "You know the Germans (or French, Belgians, Italians etc.) they're so... ." Such "You know ..." and "They're so ..." statements, psychologically re-emphasize the physical boundaries separating cultures.

Citizens within each country are pressured to maintain their own cultural form. In some countries, language guardians insure foreign influences don't effect changes in speech. Cultural watchdogs present and patrol the old, now classic, creative works their societies have spawned. National cuisines are protected. Recipes are kept secret, handed down from generation to generation. Each country's works of high art are revered and maintained, supported by the society as a national treasure in their possession.

The bodies of the people generally reflect the importance of barriers to these nations. They tend to show the Solidifier's dynamics, solid and thick, steadfast and earthbound. The physical and cultural boundaries are imprinted early and seen in the contained behavior of the children. Things don't move quickly, but do function steadily and reliably.

The therapists I teach are in a program they label "Formation," a Solidifier's word that suggests they are to be molded. They feel the weight of their cultures and complain of the slowness of change. They often call their countries moribund but then go on to suggest their own superiority and the refinement of their ways.

At times they use their cultural attitude to defend themselves against emotional risk. Statements like, "The Germans do it this way;" "We French behave like... ;" and "It is not the Flemish way" all indicate national roles that are reinforced through group pressure and prohibitions and then used to regulate behavior.

In the early stages of a therapy workshop in Holland there was considerable resistance to expressing any human problems. Ralph smiled as he told me, "You simply don't understand the Dutch. Haven't you heard of the "Happy Hollanders"? The appellation fits their social behavior - pleasant, cooperative, on the surface easy and without problems.

With a few day's work, the cultural resistance faded and the truth of their life stories brought the "Happy Hollanders" into therapeutic contact with deep human pain emanating from very real universally known human tragedies.

Europeans try to characterize America just as they do their neighbors. Their judgments in this case is often drawn from films and newspaper accounts. America, with its hegemony of peoples and geography, is reduced to stereotypes drawn from the observation of politicians and businessmen. Those who have visited the States repeatedly but futilely contradict the one-dimensionality of their compatriots' visions.

America is hard to characterize because it is constantly changing. It swings along the Rhythmic Cycle at times in integrated fashion, at times with difficulty. It moved through the Solidifier period during the 1970's.

The defeat of Lyndon Johnson ended the Inspirational energies of the excited '60's. Nixon suppressed. He refused to hear or recognize appeals. Protest was no longer acknowledged. Vice-President Agnew labeled much of the country masochistic. A quiet conservative shift contained, then redistributed power. "Big Daddy" government and the "War on Poverty" were disassembled. Federal money was pipelined to the community. The hard-working Solidifiers, the "Silent Majority," could solve their own problems.

The wild were contained. Nixon and his stolid aides, Haldeman and Ehrlichman, "listed" the unacceptable. With the use of "dirty tricks" the most extensive presidential victory to date was amassed.

Success and popularity opened Nixon. For the first time he publicly revealed his political philosophy. He even was reported to have danced at his inauguration and went to a Broadway show. Home free, the President appeared to act out of character - he was enjoying himself.

The revelation of Watergate ended this openness. The President stubbornly defended himself against attack. With twisted morality, he held on to a claim of innocence for the underhandedness he brought to the Presidency, but he couldn't cover the grotesquely contrived negative undercurrents at the base of his position. Claiming honor, he was mocked, "kicked around" once more. Shame and humiliation encompassed his person, his office and his country.

Nixon chose Gerald Ford to replace Vice-president Spiro Agnew who himself had gone through a period of bad behavior. If Nixon had Solidifier traits, Ford was a Solidifier character. From bedrock middle America, the football-playing lineman was a solid citizen, hard worker, a plodder perhaps, but in everyone's opinion a "Good Joe." Impeachment proceedings against Nixon pushed Ford to the Presidency, an office for which he, as befits his character, had never openly striven.

Ford moved to cover the shame his countrymen felt. He buried the Watergate issue by pardoning the ex-President. Some wondered if it was part of a deal given Nixon so he would step down, but there was no outcry. Containment and shame wore heavy. The politics of the country seemed oppressive.

In 1976 Ford's re-election campaign reflected his lackluster personality. The nation, nearing the end of the Solidifier stage of the Rhythmic Cycle, rejected him. They chose the gentle Southern grace of Jimmy Carter to replace the dull and plodding bulwark, Gerald Ford. Ford had done his job. The end of the Solidifier period seemed near. New advancements and achievements were sought.

CARL ROGERS

The two physical characteristics of the Solidifier, soft sensitive interior and steady slow-moving exterior, resulted in two very different expressions in the work of Carl Rogers. One expression, the tender-hearted, bulwarked his caring emotional concern and was manifest in his work as a therapist. The other, the hard-headed, underlay his tough steady building of a scientific position. It was a division that could bring him pleasure. He stated:

"I thoroughly enjoy the complete immersion in a highly subjective relationship which is the heart of psychotherapy. I thoroughly enjoy the hard-headed precision of the scientist and the elegance of any truly great research... I feel myself fortunate in having these two sharply different selves. I like both of them and they are both a real part of me." (Rogers, 1967)

Rogers delineated what he viewed as the qualities necessary in the therapeutic relationship for healthy growth of the self-concept. He saw three qualities as primary: empathy, genuineness, and unconditional positive regard. In the method he developed, clients are not led, behavior is not interpreted, things to do or ways to go are not suggested. Direction is left in possession of the client.

Rogers let clients freely be where they were at. As a therapist he attempted to accept all that was presented. He worked to understand the client's position by identifying similar reactions in himself. Then, reflecting and communicating his understanding, he non-judgmentally rephrased what he heard. When this approach was maintained, he found, change took place without the client needing to undergo any personal submission.

Rogers' therapeutic effort called on the Solidifier's developed capacity to serve rather than control, to follow rather than to lead. Witnessing him at work in a film of his method (Shostrom, 1965) one sees the slow, steady development of a caring grasp of a person's life situation. There are no interpretations, argumentative encounters, leading questions or calls for actions. Advice is absent. Every therapuetic statement closely relates to the client's utterances.

When the client's meaning is elusive Rogers asks for clarifications or he repeats what he doesn't understand until the client responds in a way that allows the confusion to be resolved. He genuinely admits his own misunderstandings, endeavoring to stay with the client until the working connection toward which he aims is reestablished:

> "With amazing sensitivity, Rogers could stay right with a person's feelings, whatever they were, through all forms of defensiveness and hostility and fear. He followed every turn, every subtlety, and always let the person set the pace and the direction. And while there were many aimless, plodding hours, there were also many breakthroughs of insight and emotionality." (Farson, 1975)

"Out of a number of very down-to-earth steps" (Rogers, 1975), he developed his hypotheses:

> "...that the individual has within himself vast resources for self- understanding, for altering his self-concept, his attitudes, and his self-directed behavior - and that these resources can be tapped if

only a definable climate of facilitative psychological attitudes can be provided." (Rogers, 1975)

Through a "pedestrian approach:"

"... he built a base for what was to become psychology's largest area of interest, the normal person and his or her potential for growth and creativity." (Farson, 1975)

Unlike most clinicians, the base Rogers built carried the weight of formally tested observations. He was the first to provide detailed recorded transcripts of his sessions, revealing both mistakes and successes. He initiated his own research and stimulated others to test his concepts and hypotheses. He clearly differentiated ideas that were avenues for new and further study from those that were confirmed by experimental work.

No other therapeutic theorist so exposed their approaches and procedures to others. None were so publicly rigorous in their attempts to specify concepts in clear operational ways, test their predictions, allow open observation of what they did in sessions; nor did others delineate the consequences they expected along with the results they obtained.

Rogers did what had to be done in a workmanship-like fashion. The result was a solid, logically consistent, scientifically organized theory of personal growth, an outline of the conditions for its occurrence and a body of confirming scientifically respectable research.

The character of both Rogers' therapeutic and scientific work grew out of his personal determination to find ways to be open and free - "psychologically free and self-responsible." (Rogers, 1967) Like most Solidifiers he had been molded in "a greatly suppressive family atmosphere." (Rogers, 1967)

Rogers' parents "were highly practical and `down-to-earth' individuals", both raised on farms. (Rogers, 1967) Exercising strong, fundamental religious convictions, their Midwest home life was a successful witness to the Protestant Ethic. They devoted:

> "...a great deal of time and energy to creating
> a family life which would "hold" the children in the
> way in which they should go. They were masters of
> the art of subtle and loving control." (Rogers, 1967)

Though father had a college education, home tended to be anti-intellectual. Hard work was the cure-all for difficulties. To "have your nose in a book ... except perhaps in the evening, was not a good, practical or hardworking thing", but nevertheless, as a youngster, Carl read. (Rogers, 1967)

Rogers' reading was a concern to his parents. It often caused him to be guilty of missing his chores. But as a diversion from the suppressive moral rigor of the household it was passive enough to be allowed:

> "I was buried in books and anything was
> grist for my mill. If there was nothing else, I read the
> encyclopedia or even the dictionary." (Rogers, 1967)

Rogers' parents sheltered him during grade school because they were "concerned about the temptations and evils of suburban and city life." (Rogers, 1967) To avoid exposing their children to high school temptations, the family moved to a farm at the beginning of Carl's teenage years. Extensive chores occupied him before and after school:

> "It was understood by all that we did not
> dance, play cards, attend movies, smoke, drink, or
> show any sexual interest." (Rogers, 1967)

Cut off from normal adolescent socializing, he felt different and alone. Family life was all there was. Its intense steady pressure stifled expression. He developed an ulcer. Half his siblings suffered the same malady.

By the time Rogers left for college he was shy, uncertain about his worth, and uncomfortable with his aloneness, but he was also intellectually adept and capable of long hard work.

In his third year of school, to his surprise, he was selected by a religious organization to represent them at a student conference in China. The trip was the beginning of his unfettering. It began with a six-month voyage.

During this time Rogers underwent a quiet transformation. Exposure to foreign students and ideas brought intellectual stretching beyond the firm barriers his parents had inculcated. He kept a journal of his experiences and reactions and sent a copy home:

> "I ... kept pouring out on paper all my new feelings and ideas and thoughts with no notion of the consternation that this was causing in my family. By the time their reactions caught up with me, the rift in outlook was fully established. I had been able freely, and with no sense of defiance or guilt, to think my own thoughts, come to my own conclusions, and to take the stands I believed in. This process had achieved a real direction and assurance which never after wavered, before I had any inkling that it constituted rebellion from home."
> (Rogers, 1967)

Rogers found himself through self-expression in a non-pressured setting. The "self," overly bound in the Solidifying Phase of the Rhythmic Cycle, opened and changed in the free, undirected atmosphere he found at sea. He would, in his way, provide a similar safe setting to allow non-directed self-exploration for others through the therapuetic technique he was to develop.

Even with a process for, and a commitment to, his own development, it still took time to grow in confidence toward his own self. He wrote:

> "I am sensitive to any judgment which I think is a competent judgment, can readily be made to feel that I and my thoughts are worthless and inadequate, and could very easily have been crushed by even the ordinary experiences of academic and professional life in my earlier years. By the time I was forty, I was beginning to have a confidence in myself which would not have been easily beaten down but, before that, negative judgments from competent people would almost certainly have destroyed me." (Rogers, 1967)

The confident strength Rogers came to feel is evident in the film series "Three Approaches to Psychotherapy" (Shostrom, 1965), a series which also provides opportunity for comparison between the character and techniques of Ellis, the Communicator; Perls, the Inspirer; and Rogers, the Solidifier. Each conducts a session with the same patient, Gloria. Ellis communicates with her through thought and reason. Perls excites and inspires her to cross a personal limit and act out anger. Rogers' dogged efforts to understand and stay with her touches her heart.

Rogers' slow deliberate style is evident in the therapeutic session with Gloria. The Solidifier's body build and characteristics of postural containment, physical steadiness and constraint are all apparent. He wastes no words. His movements are well-defined. He works towards a climactic point of intense contact. Once arriving, Rogers' voice noticeably loosens as inner excitement vibrates through his exterior. The client visibly responds with loving appreciation to both his measured concern and their emotional meeting.

The competitive possibilities of comparing the three therapists - Ellis, Perls, and Rogers - are not overlooked by the filmmaker. In response to questioning, Gloria states she is most fascinated with Perls and would most want to work further with him. He seemed the winner. Years later in his quiet understated Solidifier way, Rogers mentions something that suggests the unexciting tortoise may have caught up. He revealed that over the stretch of time Gloria continued to maintain contact with him. They carried on a long correspondence.

The more overt expression of Rogers' competitive side required movement to the Achiever Phase of the Rhythmic Cycle, beyond the effort and constraining judgments of the Solidifier Stage to the challenge and rewards of greater assertion. To achieve it fully required the loosening of his steadfast attitude toward passive resistance which, he had learned, could gain his way:

> "I discovered early in my life that I could successfully gain my way by waiting it out, being patient, containing myself. Often others would slowly come around to where I was." (Robbins, 1975)

Rogers was proud of his role in non-directively battling the psychiatric profession for the rights of psychologists. At the time, Medicine strove to dominate the practice of clinical psychologists. Rogers, having provided a unique respected therapeutic approach stemming directly from the field of Psychology, without overtly seeming to intend it, became a figurehead in a slow but successful fight to gain professional parity for himself and his colleagues.

The Rhythmic Cycle of Change

Rogers was also drawn into a kind of combat, philosophical combat, in the field of Psychology itself. His views, though not formulated for such purpose, stood against the extreme behavioristic position of B. F. Skinner.

Rogers' emphasis on freedom brought his scientific view into direct theoretical competition with the determinism of Skinner. He didn't like Skinner's emphasis on manipulation, and saw it as a threat to individual self-development. They presented their positions in a series of debates. (Evans, 1975)

The debates highlighted the philosophical differences between the Communicator and Solidifier positions. Skinner believed an organism's behavior was totally determined by outer events. Man, like a hungry infant, was empty, neither freedom nor feelings were relevant. Such an organism was simple, rationally understandable, fully explainable by a few rules of environmental conditioning.

Skinner's was a Communicator's position expressing the emptiness and lack of feelings that result from the personal experiences of holding in the inner tube and the resulting concern with outer stimuli.

The position of Rogers, the Solidifier, reflected his dynamics: tough outer shell, sensitive inner being thriving in a safe self-determined atmosphere. He carefully built his argument on the fact that what Science studied and controlled was the result of and emenated from free subjective inner choice: hard science served inner decision.

Rogers said the inner man, though it was not outwardly apparent, was the motivator and the controller. Control did not result from outer stimuli as Skinner claimed. Therefore, he concluded, responsible decisions and respecting the internal rights of others could and should be required in scientific endeavors.

Though Rogers' expression in battling the Psychiatric field on behalf of Psychologists, as well as in debating Skinner for the cause of personal responsibility, exhibited a certain degree of personal confidence, it was still somewhat circumscript, weighted down by his Solidifier Style. He was proud he could fight and characterized his behavior simply as what might be expected from someone who grew up with a house full of brothers. But the fights of siblings are really not the training ground for the hard powerful challenges for positions which occur in the Achiever Phase of the Rhythmic Cycle. Something in his expression was missing.

In his 70's Rogers was the key speaker at a meeting of the Eastern Region for Humanistic Psychology. The conference theme was education (1975). Rogers was recognized for having carried non-directive principles into the classroom and allowing students to come up with both means and content for their own self-directed learning. He was to lead the final summary session.

The audience was large and excited after a day of intense workshops. High expectations for his presentation were a pressure of the kind that didn't help his Solidifier's defenses against expression:

> "I ... am absolutely at my worst if I am expected to be a 'leading figure' or an exciting person. ... I simply 'clam up' and seem to be the dullest person around." (Rogers, 1967)

Through his stiff posture, Rogers' halting voice clumsily expressed his inner concern. He gave a slow uninspired matter-of-fact reading of a prepared paper. Then the microphones were opened to the audience.

> He commented on and supported statements recognizing education's growing concern with feelings. He grew somewhat more alive as he shared a recent realization that for him, it was time for

another phase of growth. It would be a step further along energy's course, into the body dynamics of the gap that occurs at the end of a Rhythmic Cycle. He saw it as involving movement towards: "... more respect ... for the wisdom of the organism, or intuition, or the functioning of the inner spirit, or the natural flow of our lives." (Rogers, 1975)

The words were satisfying but the halting way of delivering his musings lacked conviction. They did not appear to have grown out of the strength and potency of the Achievement Phase. In his presentation, these had been absent.

In absolute terms, of course, it would be impossible to say Rogers hadn't achieved. He had been the central figure in Clinical Psychology for decades. He had been President of the American Psychological Association, Humanist of the Year and won the Distinguished Contribution Award of the American Pastoral Counselors Association.

Rogers had received the Professional Achievement Award from the American Board of Professional Psychology, and the first Distinguished Professional Contribution Award from the American Psychological Association. A similar award had previously been given him for his scientific contribution. He held honorary Ph.D.'s from a number of institutions.

Still, all this had not been done with the drive and thrust of the Achiever in evidence. In fact he was often both surprised and overtaken by his rewards. (Kirschenbaum, 1979) At times, it was suggested, he was naive about his position and how things worked. (Kirschenbaum, 1979) The aggression, power, force and knowing of the Achiever phase was lacking.

Rogers was well into his 70's when he wrote <u>Carl Rogers on Personal Power</u> (1977). The book's subject, style and content reflected a real change. Here, at last, Achiever dynamics showed

through. The "Introduction" set the background and identified the
source of his change:

> "Some months ago a strange thing happened
> to me. I think it was the nearest I have ever come to
> having a psychic experience. I was intent on some
> work I was doing at my desk, when suddenly there
> flashed into my mind a complete sentence, `I walk
> softly through life.' I was puzzled by the intrusion,
> but since it had nothing to do with the work at hand I
> shrugged it off. A bit later the peculiar nature of this
> 'flash' struck me... .
>
> All sorts of associations crowded in. As a
> boy I'd read hundreds of books about frontiersman
> and Indians, men who could glide noiselessly
> through the forest without stepping on a dead twig or
> disturbing the foliage. No one knew their
> whereabouts until they had reached their destination
> and accomplished their purpose, whether they were
> on an errand of mercy or a warlike mission. I
> realized my professional life had had that same
> quality.
>
> When I was told early in my career that it was
> absolutely impossible for a psychologist to carry on
> psychotherapy, because this was the province of the
> psychiatrist, I made no attempt to meet the issue
> head-on. Instead, I first used the term treatment
> interviews to describe what we were doing. Later
> the label counseling seemed more acceptable. Only
> after years of experience, and the amassing of a
> considerable body of research by me and my
> colleagues, did I openly speak of the fact - by then

obvious - that we were doing psychotherapy... ."
(Rogers, 1977)

Rogers goes on to describe what appears to be a personal turning point from the dynamics of the Solidifier to those of the Achiever. It occurred in response to a questioner who asked, "What were the politics of the client-centered approach?" His reply that there were no politics in client-centered therapy was "greeted with a loud guffaw." (Rogers, 1977)

These events were the start of Rogers' political education in the meaning and role of power:

> "The more I thought and read, and the more I sensed the present-day concern with power and control, the more new facets I experienced in my relationships in therapy, in intensive groups, in families, and among friends. Gradually I realized my experience ran parallel to the old story of the uneducated man and his first exposure to a course in literature. "You know," he told his friends later, "I've found out I've been speaking prose all my life and never knew it." In similar vein I could now say "I've been practicing and teaching politics all my professional life and never realized it fully until now." (Rogers, 1977)

Carl Rogers On Personal Power (1977) presents Rogers strongest, most forceful statement of his therapuetic position. He martials powerful arguments for non-directive principles from research, practice and case reports. He juxtaposes his beliefs with those who might be his opponents ie; Freud, EST, etc. He makes positive, even inspiring statements of what individuals and organization can accomplish, then goes on to report, unabashedly, incidences of success.

Through the pages one hears a new voice from Rogers, a voice of personal authority. Polemic in nature, the book clearly aims to advance a personal position while still holding true to non-directive person-centered principles. The reader is not told what to do, but strongly told what can be done and the means to do it.

The Los Angeles Times quote on the book's cover called the work "Challenging and life-enhancing ... the sum of Rogers' philosophy." It is, for sure, a clear example of the life and work of a Solidifier expressed through the energetic thrust present in the Achiever Phase of the Rhythmic Cycle. For Carl Rogers the work stands as a real change and fully attests to his belief that:

"There is in every organism, including man, an underlying flow of movement toward constructive fulfillment of its inherent possibilities, a natural tendency toward growth. It can be thwarted but not destroyed without destroying the whole organism." (Rogers, 1977)

Achiever

Drive on champion.
Hurtle on.
Drive to the summit,
A further view - a new challenge.

Others emulate.

THE ACTION

From the base of containment gained during the Solidifier Phase of development, a new coordination grows. A capacity for graceful integrated functioning ripens. Subtle nuances of expression become available to change, modify and mature the body's balance in response to external reality. The Achiever, a winner, the star on center stage, rides the power of charged energy, checking it lightly to maintain control and direction. He or she is the embodiment of accomplishment and success.

Achievers are a pleasure to watch. Their awesome level of high power, their own position and subtle grace, invite emulation, impel identification. Their focus and assertion express a clear individuality and a well-defined position. The Achiever is a picture of personal fulfillment.

The Rhythmic Cycle of Change

The Achiever's glow of success invites challenge by the stronger, courting by the weaker as they too desire to share in the perquisites of power. The glorious show encourages others to move towards perfection, more complete answers, more accomplished movements, more graceful style. As these others strengthen their position, as they come closer to their goal, their competitive urge to gain the dominant place increases.

There is room at the top for only one. Reacting to the challenge of those who might displace him, the Achiever assumes and elaborates the trappings of power. Appearance and behavior give notice of strength, and express the continuing desire to extend the scope of status.

To do so, energy is maneuvered, fashioned into its most powerful form and then put into action. Opponents are warded off and conquered. The pains of battle and a willingness to strike, even to eliminate others when necessary, are accepted. Compassion, sensitivity and an awareness of a common humanity become secondary.

The Achiever's goal, the aim to be in the strong invulnerable position, the position of glory, grows naturally out of the body's instinctual desire for full pleasure in release. Everybody loves a winner. Their attraction attracts. They arouse strong feelings in others, feelings that excite, pull, and stimulate response.

This is all natural to the Achiever Phase of the Rhythmic Cycle, part of the courtship dance that expresses sexual potencies. The desire is to be chosen and loved, loved fully and intimately. It is something that all, some place in their being, know.

But Achievers, when caught in their character, are apt to get waylaid and lose contact with the natural meaning and expression of their behavior. Position becomes the end in itself. The fulfillment of instinctual drive is sacrificed to insure a continual outward appearance of success.

To obtain the goal, the need for full physical gratification, at times must be conquered by the desire for position, the body's instincts and drives subjugated to the demands of the challenge. The athlete plays through pain. The campaigner endures grueling hours on the campaign trail. The entrepreneur overcomes spontaneous feelings of empathy in removing excess employees. Nature's end-perspective, at best only temporarily, is sacrificed to the individual's goal.

Challenge alone however can become the full definer of behavior, searched for because it stimulates the excitement necessary to stay strong, keep trim and be out there. Success or failure then determines the bottom-line value of experience.

The character of the Achiever fears the possibility of failure and loss. There is little glory, little attraction in defeat. Losers are quickly forgotten. The task of staying at the top is not easy.

Even while roses are gathered, others wait in envy to profit from the hero, to conquer him and embody his position. The King risks overthrow from rivals. To insure the "place in the sun" is maintained, the body's natural energetic thrust can become transformed into an endless series of moves alternating between those that fend-off and those that attract courtship.

To really move in and through the Achiever Phase of the Rhythmic Cycle involves the courage to take the risk. But when an individual is caught in the unconscious character strivings of the Achiever position their posture of continuing pride and unyielding confidence can lead nowhere. Risks are avoided so that the posture is maintained, little true success occurs. The position is a stance, rather than an indicator of real advance toward the aim.

The Achiever, in character, strives to cover losses, failing to learn from them while continuing a pseudo-display of confidence and the nobility of the posture. Loss is buried from conscious awareness by the outer emanation of a false pride. Emotions are repressed. Intimacy with others, with its innate truthfulness, is forsaken.

More tragically, the Achiever when caught in character, may come to stand against any possible surrender to Nature's course. Yet it is only through surrender that one is returned to their humble place in the totality of things. For the caught Achiever, ego, "I," stands supreme as it strives to fight off the inevitable fall that a full release of energy brings and thereby avoids the climactic moment of the Rhythmic Cycle.

Climax is avoided because it would bring an end to the energy charge and cause a fall to the gap. The end of the Rhythmic Cycle with its epigram of truth and meaning, is anathema for the Achiever. The dreams of the body that uncover the well of eternal truths and burst the seeds of new beginnings are kept distant.

This tragic aspect of the Achiever provided the driving tension behind the stories of ancient heroes. Dazzled by the power of the position they occupied and the string of outer challenges that they faced, they universally could not see or accept their human fate or their own personal flaw. Even when confronted with truth by oracles and soothsayers, consulted to gain vision and learn meanings, they could not comprehend the truths they heard. The messages were of no help.

Out of touch with their inner wisdom, again and again the distortions and hubris of their Achiever Character tragically led them to strive to overcome destiny.

Alexander the Great, hero of ancient Greece and conqueror of nations, confronted the Emperor of India. Vulnerable, the Emperor saw his forces faced certain defeat. In weakness, it was apparent; much is superfluous for life. To avoid meaningless suffering and destruction he offered to surrender all his nation's wealth and power.

Alexander, appreciating the graciousness of the Emperor's offer, was moved. He embraced his adversary, momentarily meeting him in common humanity, but then, in a quick reassertion of character, he went on to revive the aura of challenge by casting the other in the role of competitor:

> "Do you think ... your kind words and courteous behavior will bring you off without a contest? No, you shall not escape so. I shall contend and do battle with you so far, that how obliging soever you are, you shall not have the better of me." (Plutarch, 1972)

The ensuing battle destroyed many and much. Another victory was attained, an opponent laid low.

For Alexander every victory led only to another battle. His succession of successes left no respite. Without the quietness that comes in periods of peace and renewal, a living wisdom remained distant. Ego pushed the end away.

By his early 30's the troops that advanced him gave out. Refusing to go on, even for further glory and victory, they returned instead to less heroic more satisfying living. Alexander, now unable to fend off his inner life with outer challenges, was overtaken by a roll of nightmares and painful fantasies. Repressed dream forces broke through. They signaled personal destruction and a macabre quick death. The finish came rapidly. The true challenger had been within.

Alexander's life shows that when locked in the Achiever Phase, victory brings little fulfillment. Rather, it only furthers the movement that leads to more activity, more battle. The humbling vulnerability of exhaustion is constantly checked by striving to drive against the urge to discharge, against the urge to rest that expresses the body's weakness. Ever glorifying the ego, the hero dies but once.

The Achiever strives to keep in command at the top of the Rhythmic Curve, the position of glory and power. The strength, commitment, and capacity to stay, awakens admiration. Grace and beauty suggest life can be lead with ease. The workings of the character, however, can come to belie the living out of the humanness of experience if its issues are not resolved.

ENERGY DYNAMICS

To keep the aura of success, the Achiever patterns energy into a posture, a consistent stylish form that expresses excitement. The form gives an ongoing appearance, an identity that resists the demands and pressures of change and hides the separations and disjunctions, the pain, the ugliness, the weakness that is part of the life of every body.

The maturity of Achiever's bodies, the coordination and strength of their large muscles, allows them to express themselves easily and attractively in the world. The whole frame of the body is harmoniously involved. The body extends and flexes to move in a coordinated harmonious way.

The strong straight posture of the Achiever proudly and consistently shows an appearance of high energy charge. The energetic tone is vibrant. A bright-eyed expression highlights aliveness and mobility. Good-looking, the body exhibits balance, harmony, power and ease both in rest and in action.

Life for the Achiever, however, isn't as easy as it appears to be. A nearly continual holding in the belly and lower back is used to control against potentially overpowering energetic movements that would discharge excitement and bring pleasurable release to both the heart and the genitals. In this way the ego's dominance as well as the noble physical stature is assured.

The center held firm, the form of the body is directed by the development of an appearance that models coordinated posture. Public lapses aren't allowed. The stance and play of the outer musculature reacts against disruptive outside incursions as well as against upsetting inner movements and emotions to maintain standing and express the chosen identification.

The Achiever is capable of a refined display of an ideal, one that attracts and encourages ideal-(idol)-ization. Their bodily movements, when challenged, may take two forms of expression, either boldly assertive - hard and direct, or receptively arousing - yielding and subtle.

It will be seen later that these two expressions are the basis for gender identification. For now, in terms of energy dynamics, it can be said that bold expression meets challenge strongly. It uses the large muscles involved in the direct driving of the body to displace what is in the way. Receptive expression differs in using aggression subtly, flirtatiously inciting and seducing the other off balance and out of position. In either case the result is apt to be a winner to someone else's loss.

The setting was an International Workshop of the Bioenergetic Institute. We were studying the physical energy flow of the Achiever. <The Rigid Character in Bio-energetic terms. (Lowen, 1975)> I asked two women of this character, one from France and one from England, to stand and walk inside the circle formed by the group.

The group was immediately captured by their beauty. The Frenchwoman, tall and blond, graceful and rhythmic, slowly, entrancingly seemed to let her body pour from one side to the other as she glided across the floor. Her pouring flow was an aphrodisiac, arousing a yearning desire in those who watched.

The dark-haired Englishwoman in her finely tailored clothes was equally captivating. Strong and handsome, sure and confident, she moved with a bold force. Her proud head, the slight uplift of her face, gave a statuesque picture of feminine assurance and pride.

There was silence when they ended their circling. The group had not simply seen two people walk but had been audience to a glamorous display of movement, a display of the physical capacities of the Achiever. Unconsciously, the two had divided the physical distance between them in perfect halves, each owned a section of center stage.

It had, however, been unnatural, not two people simply walking but rather a show, a fashion show of sorts, at once lovely and pleasurable to watch, but then, for those watching, it became anxiously disconcerting as they grew acutely aware of their own awkwardness.

Between them, the walkers had competed and reached a standoff. The watchers were left with vague feelings of gracelessness and inadequacy.

For the Achiever, giving in to the natural seems dangerous, it flies in the face of the fear that a possible moment of vulnerability might be engendered by an uncontrolled and/or weak position. Aggression, whether bold or flirtatious, maintains alertness. A high energy level provides the defense. Body and ego remain battle-ready, ready to offer proofs of strength and competence to avoid the chance of deep hurt and defeat that is always possible in any competitive encounter.

The Achiever's high charge is very close to instability yet it is avoided. They operate at or near the peak of bodily coordination. With an increase in stress their ego musters all its versatility to keep body cohesion. A conscious display of power or a deflection of energy through quick and subtle movement keeps things just below the breaking point.

Each of us to some extent knows the fear of vulnerability. The Achiever, so attached to his or her position, fights its urgency, not admitting its fullness into experience. Yet the body longs for the completion and the pleasure that can only come in vulnerable moments.

Surely vulnerability can lead to the physical disorganization and anxiety, exposure, pain and heartbreak of defeat, but it can also lead to the fullest pleasures of love, the excitement of climax, and life's deepest, most meaningful generative moments.

With a refusal to let go to the totality of release, the Achiever is ripe for the anxiety of a partial coming apart. The defense against this is recommitment to the stance. The forces of nature are opposed in a match where true success would be to allow the position to be taken by larger currents. Avoiding this, the Achiever continually looks for goals and safe victories where energy release can be partial and ego-approved. Exposure in the spontaneous catharsis of full release is prevented.

With such tactics, situations of full intimacy are avoided. In its extreme, the fall to a full loving connection with another is impossible. To keep the stance of the character in place, heart and genitals are unconsciously separated by a blockage in energetic flow. In body terms, the pelvis is put in a physical position, locked forward or backwards or blocked by a narrowing of the abdominal region.

The result of this blockage is that energy flow is stopped from moving freely between the heart and the genitals. The ego now is forced into a choice, to identify with the energy on one or the other side of the block. The two areas cannot be united through natural flow. If the ego chooses to identify with the side of the genitals, the heart is left cold. Tender loving feelings and compassion are weakened. If energy is blocked on the side of the heart, the genital area and its reach for meeting is cut off. In either case the individual, when caught in these dynamics, has difficulty responding in an integrated way that is feelingfully connected to the rest of the body and to another human being.

For some locked in the Achiever character, the feelings of the heart are narcissistically diverted to the physical surfaces of their own personality, its productions and accomplishments. They love too much their own positions.

For others, sexuality, stimulation on the lower side of the block, becomes the energetic outlet. There is a search for people who will serve as objects, without demanding feelingful and enduring connection, to insure a controlled, safe, uninvolving release.

In both cases, narcissistic self-love or object oriented sexuality, the risk that others might attain a more powerful position is avoided. The posture of invulnerability is sustained.

Which ever side of the block is identified with, there is fear of a deep full loving sexuality which would overcome physical stance and ego's strength. What could be worse for the Achiever than the time after full release? The recovering body, moving slowly and heavily, is then so vulnerable. A quick partial release and return to strength, or a non-participating frigidity serve to avoid the danger.

DEVELOPMENT OF THE ACHIEVER

Between the ages of three and five, the primary Achiever Phase of the Rhythmic Cycle, there is a marked maturation in the body. Containment no longer suffices to absorb energy. Muscles strive to move strongly, seek the pleasure of intimacy, and the experience and joys of release. A potent new source of sexually charged energy heightens the general level of excitement and provides a powerful impetus to movement.

The child's high body charge is given into activity. Already at this young age movements can become patterned to express talent, success, beauty, strength, drive, grace, whatever the environment teaches is of value.

The skills attained become attractive moves in the courtship dance of life, their aims: enjoyment for their own sake, fulfillment of the desire for meeting and the conclusion of release. The child, at this first, "mature" end of a Rhythmic Cycle of physical growth, appears a "little man" or "little woman", capable of complex gender identities, competitive moves and developed sexual behaviors.

Adults who have difficulties satisfying their own desires for a loving sexuality can prove unable to accept the naturalness and innocence of the child's affectionate sexual assertions. Rather it introduces a source of tension into family dynamics.

Parents who can't get together in a loving, sexual way may become rivals. Their battles interfere with the identification process. The child is left unable to bring the lessons the two models offer harmoniously together in their own consciousness. The result is either a penchant for inner conflict about which model will dominate or the rigid acceptance of one side while the other is just as rigidly rejected.

Unfulfilled adults may increase the problems by using the child's natural drive to achieve in an attempt to resolve their own frustrations. This is done by directing the child's energy into behavior and positions they feel will assist in advancing their own competitive position.

The child in this case learns to achieve what the adult wants. The adult, by identifying with the child's successes gains a vicarious feeling of affirmation. The parent's potency and excitement are thus aroused without having to assume the difficulties, responsibilities and consequences for the risks of performance. These are given over to the child.

What is the mechanism by which this diversion of energy into adult purposes takes place? The healthy child's body moves freely into the Achiever Phase of the Rhythmic Cycle with little coercion to maintain a pose or to wear a mask. Tension releases without interference from a dominating outer reality. Inner drives spontaneously interact with outer situations to determine position. Play runs its course.

As the child develops, he or she succeeds in vicariously joining with adults by entering into grownup roles; Mommy, Daddy, soldier, builder, cook, doctor, nurse - whatever has positive valence and gives the promise of pleasure. In the process the child develops the capacity to identify, to participate in something more than their self.

The parent of the Achiever however, disturbs the naturalness of play, seeking out ways to capitalize on it for their own victory. The adult may identify with the child's future promise and forces a rehearsal attitude that seduces or coreces child's play into a command performance. Adult goals displace the natural play of the child's expressions.

When the child enters play for its own sake, play has its own full energetic rhythm and ends with its own feelings of satisfaction. Forced performance, however, hooks play to a more distant and elusive reward, the adult's love that comes with achievement. The requirement to perform, to act "per form", carries with it anxiety about uncertain conclusions. Failure to please, brings the punishment of rejection and pain.

Even success eventually brings hurt. A parent's promise of love, upon completion of desired performance, must eventually be betrayed. Real love, like any emotion, can't be produced at will.

Instead, shows of love are offered as reward, shows that appreciate only winning behaviors and lack a genuine commitment to the person behind the performance.

At other times what adults give as love is apt to be simply a reflection of their own narcissism. The child is appreciated as a successful product, an extension of the adult's self. The adult's commitment in such a case comes from ego and at the bottom line is designed to reward and advance their own position. It is a bitter moment when their show of love is seen by the child as a fraud.

The child's performance even if successful never truly suffices for the parent. Parents who attempt to make up for their own lack of accomplishment and intimacy through the movements and accomplishments of their child are inevitably left incomplete.

For the child playing out a parent's desire that has been forced on them there is no way to gain real fulfillment. Failure brings angry adult response, success empty victory. Each is only the prelude to a demand for more performance. The truth, when finally noted, is fraught with disillusionment, bitterness and pain.

The natural urge to complete the Rhythmic Cycle moves one toward contact with others. In meeting, a moderating of excitement leads to the final surge of energy that breaks the rigidities of posture and position. For the adult left locked in the Achiever Phase at an early age, hard experience taught that the desire for such union and release can be dangerous.

Desire is a powerful and at times dangerous motivation. The components of the word itself, "de"-"sire", remove the sire, suggests competition, combat and displacement. Indeed flooded with "de"-"sire", the child doesn't feel the realities that separate full meeting between parent and child. He or she moves toward direct physical contact from instinct, instinct that at this age has a clear and arousing sexual component striving to remove any obstacle in the way.

Freud used the Greek tragedy <u>Oedipus Rex</u> to dramatically illustrate the dynamic of desire in action. Oedipus removes his frustrating Father (killing him) and fulfills his desire with his Mother (marrying and conceiving with her).

In Oedipus, the desire dynamic is placed in dramatic context. Freud called it representative of everyone's childhood situation, but this has clearly been magnified in its reality terms, imbued with literary license.

Though children hardly know what murder and sexual intercourse are, they do experientially know, from bodily urges and lived experiences, the positions that arouse pleasurable feelings of release as well as the combative actions necessary to ward off frustrating obstacles.

> Three-year-old Donna tells her Mother: "When Daddy comes home I'm going to give him a whole bunch of kisses."
> Her Mother responds: "That will be nice, Daddy loves your kisses."
> Donna retorts: "I know he does. He likes them a lot better than yours."

.....

> A male student of child development entered the Nursery School and began talking quietly to the woman he was to assist. All the children noticed his position but only the boys began to buzz. Jealous feelings of rivalry stirred. Their position was being usurped.
> Conversation with the teacher over, the student began to move about the room. He was quickly challenged by several of the boys who were

still aroused by his behavior. They began bantering with him in growing excitement.

Soon one gave a slight, almost accidental hit. It was a test. The student, wanting the boys' acceptance, didn't respond. In a rush, the boys drove forward for the kill overwhelming him with a flurry of fists.

The teacher moved to the rescue, related to the boys and reestablished contact with them through her position of authority. The boys, assured by the power of her presence, immediately eased.

Adults fixed in the Achiever Phase find it hard to move from the posturing of position to the point of meeting and release. They dare not pass on through battle and courtship because this might lead to letting go of the form. Loss of the "strong" position, it is projected, would be seen by others as a defeat, an invitation to put-down, embarrassment and hurt.

So the Achiever remains constantly charged, questing for pleasure, challenging adversaries, searching for applause. Always progressing, never arriving, the action continues. Intimacy and end, the true answer to their bodily desire, is avoided.

Emotionally, their unexpressed love doesn't move farther than the outward surfaces of the body. Power, image, success, status and accomplishment are valued as supreme. The attempt is even made (and through the cover of assertiveness often successfully) to present flaws as attributes in order to stimulate the desires of others.

Everyone moves in the Achiever Phase. It is within this phase that one learns to court; develop gender, character and personal identifications; and take on the regalia, the persona, with which life's challenges are met. (Robbins, 1980)

With health one moves beyond the battles, victories and defeats of this period to surrender to a participation in an existence that is larger than individual ego. The Achiever Character, though, wounded in this phase of the Rhythmic Cycle, continues to live the problems of this period intensely until its unconscious dynamics are seen and worked through.

GENDER PRINCIPLES AND ACHIEVER STYLE

Two major gender principles underlie the bodily expression of energy in the Achievement Phase of the Rhythmic Cycle. The Masculine Principle manifests assertive thrusting strength, the Feminine Principle, yielding enticing flexibility.

These two Achiever Styles, with their sexually related undertones, are powerful ways of moving that can strongly influence the movement of others. Each, in a somewhat caricatured way, is seen in the development of sexual subcultures such as in Gay communities, Macho societies and the gender sub-groups of many primitive tribes.

Their sharply delineated styles can also be seen in two major forms of oriental combat. Kung Fu demonstrates the masculine power of thrust and its explosive conquering force, while Tai Chi involves a slow-motion feminine gentle yielding that stimulates an attacker to disastrous over-extension and loss.

Both are combat strategies that can end in devastating climax. Both seek to control drive and emphasize timing and balance. One appears the height of aggressivity, the other the epitome of receptive invitation.

More often the Achiever style and its functioning are less overtly delineated, playing out their shaping potentials in less obvious ways through the individual behavior of persons adept at this phase of the Rhythmic Cycle..

Individual differences in aggressive thrust and enticing invitation, the masculine and feminine gender styles, can be seen in the Presidential identities of Jimmy Carter and Ronald Reagan. Both are Achievers. Both rode to power when America was moving within the Achievement Phase of the Rhythmic Cycle.

They served in an Achiever's period; when Rocky and Rambo thrilled Americans with their victories, Dallas's power intrigues swept prime time, and soap opera love triangles recaptured the country's afternoons. Morning and evenings were spent jogging, weightlifting, and in aerobic dancing, making Americans fit and strong while promising each participant aid in the battle against their own individual rendezvous with death.

Both Carter and Reagan were successes outside of politics and each overcame seemingly impossible odds to achieve the Presidency, doing it with Achiever ease. Carter was a virtual unknown before beginning his successful campaign. Reagan was identified with an extremely unpopular political movement. Both campaigned against governmental fetters which they saw as suppressing something dear to their character, the quest to compete.

Jimmy Carter's personality seemed to promise to get the country moving again after Ford's prosaic stand-still Solidifier's style. Carter exuded a quiet and appealing Southern disposition that soothed and comforted. He encouraged feelings of well-being, emphasized personal honesty and portrayed a comfortable ability to relate to the average man. Having no notable identification with any political establishment, he promised an easy kind of non-political, non-power oriented leadership.

Carter was a family man, taught Sunday school, and even campaigned right from the homes of the voters. He stood for decency, fair play and human rights. He was as American as Mom's apple pie. In many ways, like Mom, he displayed the Feminine Principle in life. His style and grace were receptive, gentle and inviting. He appeared an approachable man, accepting, trustworthy, willing to soothe and nurture. He was quietly appealing.

The crowning achievement of Carter's Presidency was the peace he brought about between Israel and Egypt. Israel's Prime Minister Begin, generally holding a tough position in regard to the conflict, credited the President's continued subtle efforts for bringing the desired result. Begin's stubborn resistance finally yielded when Jimmy Carter offered him autographed pictures to take home to his grandchildren.

The gentle feelings this gesture aroused softened Begin. An appeal to feminine concerns, home and children, melted his militancy, eased the way for him to yield his tough position and move toward peace. It was a soft tender moment, a receptive feminine moment that Carter used to win the day.

Carter was at ease with the feminine in himself but he showed difficulty when he had to act according to the Masculine Principle, to be direct and forceful. Indeed he was often accused of "waffling" from side to side on issues, changing his mind from day to day. His open and honest expression of feelings of weakness in confronting the difficult issues of the day only seemed to express ineptness when boldness was called for. His lack of thrust in the face of tough challenges aroused disturbing feelings of impotence in the body politic.

The Iranian hostage crisis magnified the limitations of too great a reliance on the Feminine Principle in Carter's personal style. He was completely committed to the lives of the captured. Life being the highest priority in the feminine, for days Carter's only tactic seemed to be a yielding one. It left him waiting it out with no sign of a big stick.

When Carter waffled from this waiting tack, aggressively trying a rescue attempt, sending planes to Iran, the plan and the planes never got off the ground. The bungled thrust only seemed another example of Carter's impotence when directly and violently confronted.

Near the eve of the election, Iran, threatened with the possibility of Ronald Reagan as a new, aggressive, more potent adversary, one seemingly less committed to American lives than to American position and pride, took the initiative and announced they would release the hostages. With this, the emotional reaction in America was profound. A Nation's total exhaustion signaled the end of the Rhythmic Cycle that involved the Iranian crisis.

Within days the public's relief turned to anger. There was no patience left for the incumbent President. They disliked the feelings of weakness and impotence that blanketed the country and made America vulnerable in the eyes of the world. Voters fell away from Jimmy Carter.

Carter's wife Rosalind, with her more masculine orientation, pushed her husband to take off the gloves. She strove to win voters back, attacked Reagan directly, called him evil. It was too late and of no avail. What had been an extremely close election contest rapidly reversed in the half-week before the election. The result: Reagan by a landslide.

Carter's yielding approach, his real achievement in gaining the hostages' safe release, this time brought him no glory. Rather it loosened an avalanche that buried him in defeat.

Reagan, with an aggressive masculine style, lost no time capitalizing on his electoral victory. He called it a mandate for his policies, ignoring the central contribution of the country's temporarily unstabilized emotions. He too, like Carter, had an attractive charm but he followed a different principle and moved with a thrust to action. When the way was clear, he boldly laid out his goals. It was most important to act. A bullet in his body couldn't slow him. The powerful forward pace of his program was an antithesis to the gentle passive yielding the country had been used to in the Carter administration.

The Rhythmic Cycle of Change

Reagan had no difficulty striving for "tough guy" policies even when they caused hardship and difficulty for others. The poor and weak were to lose benefits to balance the budget. Their numbers grew and the homeless appeared on the big city streets.

The strong and powerful were to gain new perogatives with the promise that their increased accomplishments would `trickle down' to fill the gulf left by government withdrawal from the "bleeding heart" programs of social concern that had developed over the previous 40 years.

Reagan had plans and he aggressively pursued them. Initially, they seemed centered around a balanced budget but that goal was belied by an increase in military spending. Reagan, following the Masculine Principles of thrust and strength, was committed to strengthening America's muscle and surpassing that of the Soviet Union. Foreign policy was marked by a confident aggressive stance.

The conciliatory, peace-producing and human rights posture of Carter was quickly forgotten as America led the world into an atmosphere of bold aggressive confrontation. The way to peace, it was said, was through strength.

Reagan confronted everywhere. He attacked the news media when they gave as much time to an out-of-work citizen as they did to him. He supported a high interest rate and a strong dollar as poorer nations rapidly grew poorer. He took credit for success in the battle against inflation, making no note that the economy had begun improving in the latter days of the Carter administration. He proposed the Star Wars program to dominate space and dictate the means of peace.

When Reagan's programs showed signs of failure, the confidence he portrayed never wavered. He drew "a line in the dirt", challenging others to forward something better. If they responded, he used his position to advance himself further by attacking their efforts. His Achiever capacities of warmth, friendliness and smoothness lead him to be called the "Teflon President". Criticism slid off his no-stick quality.

Reagan was a winner, liked by the public. His aggressive style had maneuvered them away from feelings of uncertainty and generated a widely welcomed sense of strength and well-being even as hard times increased for many. A Time magazine cover story portrayed him as King.

By the time of his reelection campaign Reagan had led a marked change in the nation's psychology. His first term had been marked by a string of legislative successes that left his fundamental Conservatism entrenched. Even the youth, so typically rebellious and liberal in their views, had come to identify with him.

Shortly into Reagan's second term the announcement came that doctors had removed a second cancer from his body ("Just a little cancer, nothing much."). Strangely, this closely coincided with a new political campaign, a complete reversal of Reagan's position. He communciated with the Russians about disarmament.

Reagan had previously cast Russia in the role of absolute untrustworthy enemy, used them to symbolize the Arch-Competitor in order to get passage of his military programs and build the country's might. Perhaps his reversal was an attempt to win a high place in history ("... attempting to do what eight Presidents before had tried and failed at."). However, it should also be considered that his move toward peace was influenced by the suggestion of his own dying, a bow towards the reality of weakness brought home to him by the events taking place within his body.

Initial negotiations with the Russians were accompanied by a continued aggressive stance toward Communist-leaning Nicaragua. The inconsistancy in attitude toward the Communist enemies seemed to pose no real problem for either Reagan or those who were loyal to him.

Reagan had become "The Great Communicator", but not as one operating from the Communicator Phase of the Rhythmic Cycle.

There was no attention to need, detail, logic or ideas. There was no raging protest here, no relating to fundamental human needs.

Reagan was an Achiever who called upon commoncuiator capacities for Achiever ends. He used word, style and smoothness to communicate well being, strength and pride. He used communication to engender mood, a mood which would allow him to advance his position. He could and did smooth over any hints of tension that might arise from his inconsistancy towards the communists.

With all his communicative capacities, Reagan quickly followed his Achiever instinct for position and grew silent with the Irangate disclosures. His kind of communication couldn't bridge the public's disbelief that the Iranians, with their intense anti-Americanism, had been provided with American support and the funds gained had been funneled around congressional advice and consent into the Contra battle against Nicaragua. The thrust, for a time, was laid low.

Still, when Reagan suffered diplomatic defeat as Central American countries moved to to gain a peace in Nicaragua, and political defeat when his nominee for Supreme Court judge was rejected, his personal aggression seemed to revive and for a time he fought back aggressively, saving face by moving his policy forward with yet another Contra support bill.

Then in a climactic two weeks, with his wife undergoing an operation for breast cancer, the mounting of an attack on Iranian positions, the stock market spasming to its biggest one-day loss in history, the threat of arms negotiations with the Russians yielding little and the death of his mother-in-law, the fortune of the times clearly moved away from the man.

The weakening of Ronald Reagan's true position, his political position, foreshadowed the predictable end of a period. A Rhythmic Cycle that had begun with John Kennedy's visions of restoring America's clear position of power in the world was drawing to a close. Under Reagan's leadership, with America, at least for a time, now clearly in command as the world's most powerful nation, the dream had been fulfilled. Things were moving on.

As if on cue, Mike Dukakis and George Bush led their ways toward the Presidency. Each lacked the charm, smoothness, charisma and style of the Achiever Phase. Each through the experience of their own character seem to be bringing America to a new period, a time of quiet non-excitement — a return to the gap and the beginning of a new Rhythmic Cycle.

THERAPY

Society's gender roles are based on natural physical differences between assertion and yielding. They highlight biological differences. Male hormones allow accretion of muscle tissue through exercise and cause male bodies in general to be heavier and more forceful.

A looser musculature, mammary glands and a fleshier pelvis give greater softness, flexibility and receptive appeal to a woman's body. Though the rule is certainly far from absolute, where men are generally stronger, women are generally more emotionally facile.

Societal exaggeration of the different identities based on these principles limits the natural possibility for an individual to develop and coordinate both the masculine and feminine in everyday life. The changes in sexual definition in Western society over the last two decades has brought an increased acceptability for each sex to display attributes that had been exclusively assigned to the other. Western society has come to condone women's aggression and men's emotion.

It is during the Achiever Phase that the child's specific sexual feelings and behaviors develop their expressive style. A gender identification is shaped with a personal position that summarizes the chosen sexual role. The form chosen develops through experiences:

> Chris called himself a homosexual. An adolescent, he suffered the pains of an effeminate style among "the guys" who were busy developing what he called their "macho" stance.
>
> Chris was an Achiever with a strong desire to be a successful person. In school he hated the isolation his identity brought but covered a sense of not belonging with an attitude of contemptuous superiority.
>
> Outside of school he found others who shared his identification. He loved them for their acceptance, but hated them too for the social compromise he had to make to be with them. The stress affected his performance in school and motivated him to therapy.
>
> Chris traced his effeminate behavior to childhood experiences. By chance, only girls several years older were available for playmates.
>
> He vividly remembered the frequent childhood cruelty of a cousin who would taunt him with her doll. She would hold it out for him, but as he reached would pull it away mocking, "You're just a boy. You can't play with it." Unknowing, he accepted her statements. They hurt deeply. For the moment he took them literally.
>
> Chris thwarted his frustration in order to keep contact with his cousin and remained very much a victim to her teasing. His jealousy and envy grew. He remembered wanting to be like her, to have her position with its perogatives.

When he entered nursery school he had his chance. The doll corner became his favorite place. There he could accomplish what had been stopped at home. While the other boys played with blocks he joined the girls to fulfill his desire to be one of them.

His feminine identification had begun. In grade school it was strengthened by name-calling that labeled him and led to his rejection. He fought back with feelings of superiority and expressions of contempt. In early adolescence his effeminate postures made him an easy mark for an older homosexual. He was initiated into "the society."

Chris's musculature expressed his effeminacy. Thick rounded thighs and soft blubber around the waist gave a womanly appearance. With therapeutic work and emotional release their form, however, very quickly changed, giving evidence that his sexual identification had modified his body and the changes were reversible.

As his masculinity showed through, Chris appeared healthier and stronger. A pale yellowish skin tone increasingly showed life and color. School performance improved with the freeing of his energy.

A girl at school began to relate closely to him. He took it as a clear sign affirming his masculinity so he was profoundly stunned when he learned that she had long been interested in him but also considered herself a homosexual.

It was a traumatic experience. Chris couldn't so easily change the way he was seen by her or the other students and his homosexual identity seemed to him to be the real basis for her caring.

The Rhythmic Cycle of Change

The hurt struck deeply at Chris's emerging desire for maleness. He painfully felt the need for the closeness and protection of his homosexual friends. They were his "team." A promising male liaison seduced him away from his decision to work in therapy.

Chris left aware that his identification was a result of an early choice. A choice made at a time when its implications could hardly be understood and which could not now be changed without living through the loss of something that brought him a sense of belonging.

He chose not to go through the feelings of isolation and rejection that would occur in changing a role that had provided a way to relate to others, one that he was familiar with and others had come to expect.

For Chris, his body identity, the naturalness of his physical form and movement, were distorted by an evolving identification with a sexual role, a role that led to rejection by the larger culture.

To achieve fullest well-being requires that identifications be released in their time so that a true body response can be expressed when called for. When this happens, a subtle alternation and blending, rather than a sharp divorce, occurs between the masculine thrusting principle and the feminine yielding principle. Their differences become part of a larger unity.

This unity can best be seen in the full sexual act, which when done with bodily freedom involves both thrust and reception. When two move together in an integrated natural rhythm the result is a coming together, a merging in union and a time of fulfillment.

VIRGINIA SATIR - THE ACHIEVER

Virginia Satir was interviewed at a convention in New York where she was to give a major presentation. She had just learned of a friend's death, her sixth close loss within a half-year.

At the start of our session Satir, in tears, wondered "What's real in life?" She was considering stopping a teaching schedule that recently brought her from Czechoslovakia and had yet within the year to carry her to Egypt, Puerto Rico, Nigeria, South Africa, Argentina, Brazil and Poland. She said:

"Somewhere I have to take a break."

But immediately went on:

"I have some films to make, books to write, a network to care for." (Robbins, 1979)

Virginia Satir is an Achiever with high energy level and commitment to successful action. Her strong interest in families and her active personality led to a central role in the development and spread of Family Therapy.

Working therapeutically with whole families was a major therapeutic development of the revolutionary 1960's. Until then, largely under the influence of Psychoanalysis, therapists had taboos about breaking the sanctity of the one-to-one session. When an interaction between people was troubled each was seen individually.

Family Therapy brought the interactions between people into treatment. Changing the focus from individuals stimulated new concepts and techniques. Communication, power, organization and problem-solving could be directly explored.

Satir's book, Conjoint Family Therapy (1964), outlined the concerns and techniques of this new approach and stimulated the development of a large body of theory and methodology. One of the first major works in the field, it quickly became a classic and established her as a dominant figure in the field of family treatment.

A later book, <u>Peoplemaking</u> (1972), expressed Satir's Achiever emphasis. Dealing with the "how" of behavioral change, it suggested means by which families could change things. The approach followed a pragmatic principle: "If the goal isn't reached, change the method." The language Satir used was the language of production. She spoke of "blueprints" and "maps" designed to "engineer" change. The aim was to get things accomplished.

Satir provided more than just her writing. Her dynamic personal and teaching style drew many to her interests. An energetic and attractive performer, she remains a highlight at conventions. Humor, charisma, a Huck Finn bubbling "can do" energy, along with her powerfully displayed therapeutic mastery make her a delight to watch, a star performer.

Her aura of success is encompassing. Even criticisms appear as backwards compliments. Some tell her of their discouragement in becoming successful therapists. They despair of reproducing her personality and attribute her therapeutic acumen to her unique individuality rather than to a skill they can acquire. They complain she is "too good."

It is like that for those with an Achiever character. The pull for others to identify with them is strong. But such identification lacks the effectiveness that results from working to develop complex skills for oneself. It can cut short a development that would better proceed slowly by passing through all the phases of learning necessary to gain mastery. The quick but shallow learnings that occur through identifications are not organic to the learner's own being. When put into practice they lack breadth and depth.

A more substantive way of passing along her approach is offered in the Process Community that she has established. She sees it "as the forerunner to a University for Being More Fully Human." (Satir, 1987) In the Community, the factors underlying her work are "teased out and taught so they can be successfully used by others." (Satir, 1987) Here Satir, following her positive approach, differs from most mainstream therapists in her emphasis on health:

> "It is like looking at a field. Some see the weeds and spend their time in pulling them. My approach is to plant more seed and in the process the space for weeds lessens so that they are driven out." (Satir, 1979)

Satir's own development in studying families has a long and full history. It sprouted from a childhood desire to investigate what went on in the bedroom of her parents. She was an outsider trying to glimpse the primal scene. At five the goal was set. She then decided:

> ".. when I grew up I'd be a childrens' detective on parents." (Satir, 1972)

Satir's choice was established within the context of her own family's interaction. Her task of "investigating parents for the welfare of children" was a creative means to deal with the identity conflicts formed within her by the rivalries between her mother and father.

The relationship between Satir's parents was characterized by the power battles that are often in the background of Achiever characters. These fights, each battling for the dominant central position, interfere with healthy gender identification. In the atmosphere of hostility the child may search for safety by emulating the power figure of the moment rather than moving to the rhythms of their own biological unfolding. Innocent childhood possibilities of pleasurable sexual feelings, ones free from adult conflicts, are subverted.

Satir attributes her parents' conflicts as stemming from the rejection of their own sexual nature:

"My father was a handsome man but never felt it. My mother was a beautiful red-headed woman who didn't accept that either." (Robbins, 1979)

Her parent's sexual energies were transmuted into attack and resulted in almost continuing conflict between them. They battled to rule, each advancing the identifications to which they were loyal. Along the way they lost sight of the natural course of things. As will be seen, it almost cost them their child's life.

The playing of the game `Who's on Top' and the message "Sexual behavior was wrong." (Robbins, 1979) powerfully disrupted the natural course of Satir's growth during the Achiever Phase of development. Absent was the example of wholesome courting that resulted in loving meeting. Absent too, was the safety and togetherness that would allow for the gathering of positive experiences of physical intimacy.

A climactic period in Satir's development occurred when she was five, the critical time in the formation of the Achiever Character. It was then that Satir fell ill and her sickness became the center of a profound, long-enduring parental conflict.

Satir's mother was a Christian Scientist with an absolute position against medical care. Father didn't take her views seriously. As their child's sickness grew, debate over principle became an acute practical concern. They battled as to whether Virginia should be seen by a doctor.

After three weeks of hostile parental exchange, Satir was in desperate physical condition. Her father finally stopped the fighting and acted. He drove 19 miles to the nearest doctor and carried his daughter, by then comatose, into the office. Her stopped pulse was revived. She was given an emergency appendectomy. This brush with death left her deaf in one ear.

The near-catastrophe only intensified the parental rift. Mother viewed what had happened as a defeat for her position and she did not take it well.

> "I think my mother felt helpless against him after that and I think that's when they turned away from each other.
>
> She had this gorgeous red hair that my father adored. It was beautiful, red and wavy. So what she did, she cut off her hair, and my father was furious.
>
> What he did, he burned up all her religious books, and I think that was the beginning of her depression, and then she made a vow that no matter what was going on, when I reached high school, she was going, she was going to leave the farm.
>
> And that's what happened. But first Mother endured years of depression. Mother did her work but otherwise was withdrawn and alone in her own room." (Robbins, 1979)

The end of overt battling left Satir on neither side, with no one.

> "I did the only thing I could do. Spent time with the animals, outside. I didn't move into other people. I moved into nature and things by myself. Became super-confident. That's one thing I've always been.
>
> In the early years I felt so disconnected and I guess I'm talking emotionally, too, except that I had so much to fill it, that it was not a negative thing - I

suppose - thinking about it. I felt disconnected from other people because I didn't see the connections."

Satir filled the loss of family connectedness with activity. Her mother had always encouraged her to go after whatever she desired to achieve, to take a positive attitude, to find out what would happen by trying. Her skills had been appreciated. Now more than ever she gave her energy to developing competencies. Intellectual giftedness made her a ready learner, an Achievement orientation a superior performer.

Satir took on and mastered one challenge after another. She could do things. She cooked, sewed and mended. She assumed responsibility for her siblings. She grew things. She read the Bible and great books. Whatever came was grist for the mill of her activity and fed her sense of achievement. By 11 she had completed grade school.

When Satir reached adolescence, her mother's retribution came due. The farm had been in Father's family, a tradition going back generations. It was part of his identity as well as the source of his work. Mother's overt reason for pushing to leave the farm was to protect her daughter from the sexual exposure she felt farm life presented, but it also provided revenge for having the traditions and the identity she believed in disregarded by her husband six years earlier.

Satir's father shared his wife's fears about sexuality. Here, unfortunately, they were together. He gave in to his wife's reasoning and took the loss of his way of life. In the midst of the Great Depression he moved his family and had to find a new livelihood. Vengeance exacted, Mother's depression, unrelenting for years, finally lifted. The power battle was over.

For Satir's adolescent body through its own natural development brought Achievement problems. Concerns about sexuality, identity, intimacy and accomplishment emerged, reviving unresolved issues developed in the phase of the Rhythmic Cycle encountered during the Oedipal Period.

Satir, until then a proud, confident, successful young girl, was suddenly exposed to inner and outer demands for which she was completely unprepared. Her emerging sexual feelings aroused profound identity problems. Worth became an issue.

> "I started to exist, on the male-female level, around the dating time. I could hold my own most anywhere, intellectually, in competence; behaviorally, I could do what I needed to do. . . where the big struggles were, occurred in the male-female thing. Feeling one down in relation to pretty women, feeling like the ugly duckling relating to men. That is where the self-esteem business came, and with no joy in my body." (Robbins, 1979)

The Achiever's conflict - accomplishment and position versus intimacy and bodily fulfillment - was manifest. With sexuality tabooed and sexual roles and behaviors confused, experiences of physical closeness were absent. Satir was left vacillating in the "male-female thing."

In her late teens, out of the home, Satir began in earnest the search to find the missing connectedness, to put the pieces together. It was to be a search that would lead to a wealth of understanding and a professional mastery of family dynamics. She graduated college at 19 and began teaching.

> "I taught the sixth and seventh grade. I became principal of the school - to change the traditional school into a progressive school because that's what we were doing. I taught art in the High

School and I taught shorthand and typing. That's
my load." (Robbins, 1979)

Unsatisfied knowing her students and not their families, she
asked them, "Who's going to take me home to see their parents?"
(Robbins, 1979) Her professional search to find and unite the
divided "pieces" of her childhood advanced through observations of
her students in their family relationships.

In her 20's Satir moved toward a family of her own, but
within a month of her marriage, war separated her from her soldier-
husband. Alone, she became sick with violent abdominal pains and
rushed by train to be with her husband who had an ambulance
waiting to carry her to the hospital. There she underwent emergency
surgery. She awoke to find she had undergone a hysterectomy.
The chance for a natural family was over.

When the war ended and her husband returned, their
relationship quickly dissolved. A second marriage also ended in
early failure. Conflict in relation to position and power lie at the
source.

"They were not mean men at all, not at all,
but both men that needed a lot, and I tried to help in
all kinds of different ways. It was just a repetition of
me down there and them up here as I moved through
my male-female thing. I realized how much in caring
for men I insulted them, seeing the ways in which
they couldn't and I could.

I put myself in a trap two ways. If I see you
as somebody who can't, then I am insulting you. If
you accept that I am seeing you this way, then you
are insulting yourself.

Through both these insults I am developing a
grave for myself because everybody in a superior

> position has to have somebody in an inferior
> position, and the one in the superior position has to
> do all the work." (Robbins, 1979)

"Who's on Top," her parents' game, had become incorporated into Satir's own way of interacting. She had identified with the positions in the game. The price for playing it, the loss of a full way of meeting, led to her early marriage failures.

In terms of establishing a natural family, Satir's marriage failures were compounded by a cruel twist. (Fritz Perls, populizer of Gestalt Therapy, had noted the irony of the fact that The Family Therapist had no family. He saw that most outstanding therapeutic theorists came from a place of their own hurts.) Twenty-two years after her hysterectomy, Satir mysteriously experienced vaginal bleeding. The ensuing physical examination revealed that, contrary to what she had believed, only one ovary had been removed.

> "In all those years my body had
> accommodated to the "fact" that there had been a
> hysterectomy. I started menstruating after 40 and for
> 10 years after that. I could have been fertile all along
> but didn't know that." (Robbins, 1979)

The doctor, knowing Satir's ability to achieve, affectionately suggested she had regrown her sexual anatomy.

Satir was unable to have a natural family but did what she could do, adopt children. She further compensated for her loss by becoming the center of a network (called the Avanta Network), a group of loving people who share an interest in the work she does. She suggests that she has "the largest family in the world." (Robbins, 1979)

Still, missing from such a family is the experience of surrender. Leading a network leaves one legitimately in the top position. However, when on top, the ongoing natural flux and flow of the leader's feeling of power is masked by the challenge and expectancy to fulfill the position. Feelings of inadequacy or weakness are often covered, hidden from others, not yielded to no matter the urgency with which they are experienced.

Letting down and sharing truly as equals, without consciousness of goal or purpose, is antithetical to the Achiever's demand for a strong leadership position. In organizations, signs of weakness and vulnerability arouse the competitive urges of others to strive toward replacing them and stir warning feelings of impending defeat and hurtful consequences. Heroes stay the course.

In the 70's, Satir chose to explore beyond the natural reach of her character. She sought out the mystical, the Dreamer aspect of life with its emphasis on vulnerability and surrender. As an Achiever, a "Doer," this part of the Rhythmic Cycle is typically far from familiar.

The Mystic tries to obliterate the Ego, the personal position, to stay close to the gap of energetic nothingness. The Achiever characteristically aims at an opposite target, to develop and advance a strong ego avoiding the vulnerability of emptied places. The Mystic's concerns are otherworldly; the Achiever's are of the real world. While the Achiever strives to be "number one," the mystic seeks to obliterate individual oneness, to be one with "The All."

Exposing herself to the methods of eastern gurus Satir underwent change. A recurring dream, a common one for Achievers, reflects the course of her development.

In the dream Satir climbs to the top of a mountain peak. The dream's content symbolizes the drive to succeed, to gain the top position. Ascent requires heroism, challenges power, strength and competence. Inevitably, when the peak is reached, Satir, as is the case for most Achievers when caught in their character, would see only another summit to be conquered. The reappearing presentment of challenge never allows for the surrender and vulnerability of moments of completion.

On successive occasions Satir's dream has undergone variations, variations that reflect an increasing personal capacity to surrender to the flow of the Rhythmic Cycle in all its phases.

> "Twenty-five years ago I would strive for the top for comfort, for whatever it was, self-worth, maybe, and I would bear the other parts. I would bear the pain to get to the top.
>
> Ten years ago (these were learning points) I would have probably been more focused on the learning that comes from the fall.
>
> Now, I've brought the image much closer to myself in terms of a moment-by-moment thing. It includes some learning but it isn't that focused in a sense. I don't think so much in terms of where I'm rising and where I'm falling, but where I am and what's happening." (Robbins, 1979)

Satir now rides the total pattern of the Rhythmic Cycle more fully, more consciously flowing with the energy wave rather than moving toward "can do" and ego aims. She finds herself more united with the course of energy and more willing to surrender to it. The result is more comfort in her own body.

Near the end of our interview the phone rang. A beau was courting. When the conversation ended Satir moved around the room excitedly checking her appearance and preening her hair. Bubbling with glee and delightful anticipation, she said:

> "...consider the wonder of it. After all these years I am beginning to find the joy of my own body." (Robbins, 1979)

ALEXANDER LOWEN - THE ACHIEVER

Alexander Lowen emphasizes the importance of the body in his life, and in the therapeutic process he developed, Bioenergetic Analysis. Lowen has the Achiever's assertive style, a thrusting style that clearly follows the masculine principle. His energy and vitality are witness to his personal concern for physical dynamics. Vigorous and alert, his excitement and forthright expression reflect aliveness. His voice and movement give off a physical vibrance immediately evident when in his presence.

In his work, Lowen's characteristic aggressive energies are placed in a framework of bold and confident action. He uses his vigor and assertion to challenge his patients' character blocks as they appear within their psychologies and within their muscular systems.

Lowen's moves come from a certainty based on experiences with his body, his understanding of theory and the functioning of his own character. Whether being tough or tender, he dominates the direction of the therapeutic session, striving to make interventions only when he knows the outcome. In this way, he is on top of things, in command and sure of his position with the patient. (Robbins, 1974)

In therapy, Lowen evaluates the person from his understanding of the body and its language. Is the patient in touch and aware of what is happening within? If he believes the answer is "no," the intervention is direct. He is capable of a wide range of responses, from support to confrontation, from empathy to encouragement. The expression of each of his emotional reactions is clear. His energies do not diffuse. His personal boundaries remain firm. Strong expression predominates.

On a popular New York television show Lowen's aggressivity was placed in a public context. The strength of the masculine aspect of the Achiever character was revealed. The program's hostess had an attacking, contradictory, exposing style.

She was not unlike the television host who caused the Creator, Laing, to come apart, badgering him about his personal life. (See Creator Section) This time, assault brought different results. It went something like this:

> After a brief explanation of his theory, Lowen gave two demonstrations. The first was with a patient of his. She was placed over the breathing stool. He worked strongly with her and brought out the expression of intense primal emotions. Screams of a genuine nature, rarely seen on television, were released from her body. The work tapped deep areas, but she was familiar with it and seemed comfortable with the process.
>
> The second demonstration involved the program's announcer, a very different kind of a person, one who showed much vulnerability. Lowen worked carefully with her, observing her body. Gently, tenderly, but still with an honest directness, he told her what he saw. He could read the isolation and pain in her physical movements. As he asked about her feelings of loneliness and estrangement the show's hostess began intruding into what was taking place. She pressed the announcer to refute what Lowen was saying as untrue, directing her to tell what a happy person she really was, how her constant joking proved it.
>
> But the announcer's poignant response carried a truth that affirmed Lowen's interpretations. She spoke of how her jokes were a cover for her feelings. The joking foil she played on television masked who she really was. She revealed that

emotional pain and unhappiness were a prevalent part of her life.

The show moved on to a new segment - questions from the audience. The hostess announced that there "just happened" to be two psychiatric experts sitting in the audience. The "experts' followed her earlier lead. They attacked what Lowen had said and done. They disputed the body's importance, argued that character was not modifiable.

Cutaways to Lowen showed him actively taking in what they were saying, though his internal response to their broadside confrontation was not immediately evident.

The ante was upped when the psychiatrists attacked Lowen's first demonstration, the one that had taken place with his patient. They intimated that only an "exhibitionist" would allow herself to be publicly presented and release the emotions in the way she had. It was then Lowen rose to his feet and announced that this was going to be stopped. If not he was walking off the show.

The pace quickened. The hostess, excited and flustered, claimed he couldn't do that. She cajoled him, saying she knew him, knew that he could handle any situation, certainly this one. He must continue.

Lowen responded that she was partially right. He could handle situations. He said he felt betrayed by her and her people. He had been asked to explain and demonstrate his work but had found himself led into an arena of insult and confrontation. He would handle this situation. He would handle it by exiting.

He was shown getting his hat and coat, then leaving. He had walked off.

Lowen was back on the program the next day. The show began by reviewing what had previously been televised. Then it related what ensued. When off the air, the viewing audience was told, the television staff held a meeting with Lowen and the psychiatrists. As an outcome of the meeting the show acknowledged the unfairness of their procedures. The doctors admitted that they were out-of-bounds professionally. Never working therapeutically with the body they were in no position to make judgmental statements about Lowen's work. Their apologies, too, were announced.

Lowen had encountered a show business excess aggressively. It was Man against System. For the moment, heroically, Man appeared the winner.

The development of Lowen's heroic style highlights the dynamics and issues of the Achiever Phase of the Rhythmic Cycle. The processes of identification are key to understanding his character. Issues of success, gender, sexuality, and the oedipal situation had to be worked through if achievement were to reflect his own nature, rather than simply be something stilted and reactive, impressed upon him by the dreams and desires of those with whom he identified. This working through followed its own Rhythmic Cycle, a cycle focused on the issues of the Achiever Phase.

Though the keystone for Lowen is the body, his parents were in conflict with the value of the physical:

"My father and mother were opposites, that's the real secret of my personality. My father was pleasure-loving and my mother was ambitious and compulsive ... . He was body-oriented, very sexually oriented. My mother was just the opposite, head-oriented and anti-sexual.

My mother believed work came first and then pleasure. My father believed only in pleasure and so he was a failure." (Lowen, 1979)

Lowen's mother was a strong and ambitious woman, rigid in her drive "like a bar of steel." (Robbins, 1979) Her outward thrust manifested in her personality what has been described as the masculine principle. When it came to moving within the world she taught the way was to drive forward. Though this thrust carried through in her son, she felt her own personal striving limited by the restricted cultural role of women. She thought:

"...that the men are more important than women, that the women have a tough life." (Robbins, 1979)

In response, Lowen said:

"I was on my mother's side, designed to save her. I could make it in the world, which being a woman she couldn't do. She hoped for a good life through me. That was clearly stated. My mother was also very ambitious and made statements about the need to rise in the world and be a person and make it." (Robbins, 1979)

"To rise in the world," "to be a person," "to make it"; none of these wishes, dreams of a mother for her son, not uncommon dreams for a Jewish immigrant, none in and of themselves appear injurious. Their accomplishment would be the natural result of the flowering of the Rhythmic Cycle. But the danger in a fixed presentation of such dreams is that natural unfolding is not trusted, a rigid driven quality attempts to force and dominate development. "Making it," achieving position and the goal, becomes the end-all.

The challenge to fulfill mother's dreams for worldly success and to compensate for her own sense of inevitable failure in the world was impressed on Lowen as a charge, indeed a necessity. The dominance of this drive throughout the family is evident in that her push for intellectual accomplishment could even be passed on through Lowen's much more easygoing father:

> "... My father once said to me when I came home with a report card that wasn't all A's, he said, `If you don't get A's don't come back.' ... He didn't mean it... But he put the pressure on. It was out of his personality. I think it was my mother's influence." (Robbins, 1979)

Any aims of accomplishment that Lowen's mother might have desired to displace onto her husband were frustrated. As a child his father had been:

> "... a darling in his family, the youngest son." (Robbins, 1987)

As an adult:

> "He wanted to be indulged and barely eked out a living. At times you weren't sure of it - He

worked in the laundry business and was always
marginal.

When it looked like things might get going,
he'd fall back. There wasn't enough manhood in
him - too masochistic. Holds a position and can't
move. Can't get him down, but he can't get up
either." (Robbins, 1987)

['Masochistic' as used above has a specific
Bioenergetic meaning not to be confused with the
popular use of the word. (See Lowen, 1975) It
corresponds to the pathological expression of the
Solidifier Phase, described earlier. R.R.]

Still, for Lowen, things were significantly different with his
father than with his mother, much more easy and pleasurable:

"Whatever rigidity was in me was
undermined by the softness of my father. ... the
sensitivity, allowing yourself to feel - and sexuality
is soft. It not a hard thing.

The love of a woman, which my father had,
is a very tender and a beautiful quality. I didn't get
that rigid that I cut that off. I got rigid to protect
that." (Robbins, 1987)

Lowen's relationship to his father was played out in their
sharing the more easygoing rhythmical side of life. Father did not
require "striving to make it." Conflicts of fulfilling another's aims
for success were largely absent when with him. Together they
enjoyed bodily feelings and pleasures. Identification with his father
grew in the joint play of sports; throwing a ball, and swimming
together:

"He loved to swim. I still have my father's feeling about the water. I love to swim." (Robbins, 1979)

Lowen's softer more receptive side, and the love for the pleasures of his body that were amplified through his identification with his father, stood against the thrusting drive to succeed, the dominating charge of his mother to be at the top.

Mother's dreams for achievement, unable to be fulfilled either through herself because of cultural limitations, or through her husband because of problems in his character, were given over to her son to fulfill. Lowen could be number one with her and saw himself "favored completely," the "apple of her eye." (Robbins, 1979) This position might have seemed even more valuable when seen against the alternative to which his sister's place gave witness.

The personal difficulties of Lowen's sister provided a vivid example of the danger of being in the unfavored position. Her femaleness gave her no chance to succeed and no chance to be valued by her mother. Rather, it served as a screen for mother to project the frustrations of her own sense of failure to make it fully in her own right. (Robbins, 1979)

But Lowen learned his favored position was not guaranteed simply because he was male. Being number one was conditional, not absolute. For Lowen, in the Achiever Phase of development, success was required for mother's love:

"I'll love you if you try harder - there is love there but also the demand of proving yourself. Then you're not going to reach out for fear that if you haven't proved it, you're going to get rejected and humiliated - meaning you're not good enough.

> Humiliation is a big factor. Most rigid
> people, if they're really rigid, have a tremendous
> sense of pride. I know that's true of me. It's just a
> choice. It dominates you or you dominate it."
> (Robbins, 1979)

Lowen's parents could be together in their love for him, but between themselves with their different orientations:

> "They never got along ... . Never could
> resolve who was the stronger one. They battled on
> issues - fought like cats and dogs.
> At these times my father was stubborn. She
> was attacking." (Robbins, 1988)

> "She held back sexually." (Robbins, 1987)

> "Neither would accept the other's values and
> yet they stayed together. This insecurity in the home
> was frightening." (Robbins, 1975)

The split between mother and father, between mother's masculine, assertive advancing principle and father's generally more easygoing pleasure orientation, divided Lowen's parents and left Lowen with an ongoing creative tension.

> "Father-mother split. Body-mind split. I'm
> pulled in two directions. Brought up with both sides
> of the situation - not sucked in to any one... . But it
> also made it difficult for me to find the full sense of
> my own identity... ." (Robbins, 1975)

After leaving home, Lowen's differing identifications - with the achievement strivings of his mother and the pleasure strivings of his father - had their effects. They provided a tension of the Creative Phase that was played out in his career development and the course of his life. In college, Lowen was interested in mathematics. He saw others getting straight A's, while he received only "mostly A's" - from his mother's side, not good enough.

He went into law, a profession whose practice is deeply intertwined with coming out on top and the rewarding of the masculine aggressive principle that his mother emphasized. He graduated summa cum laude, but "... could not make it in the law profession because the time 1934 was the year of the Great Depression." (Lowen, 1987) Lowen continued on with his studies, receiving the degree Doctorate of Jurisprudence, again with honors. This time magna cum laude. (Lowen 1987)

When Lowen finished his education legal positions were still difficult to find. He taught school and spent some time as athletic director in a summer camp. There, while engaged in the kind of activities he had come to appreciate through his identification with his father, he made a key observation, that provided an impetus that carried throughout his life work. He noticed physical activity affected mental health in positive ways.

Lowen was strongly drawn to this awareness of the mind-body relationship. The power that came to be attached to it was a not unlikely consequence of the oedipal dynamics between him and his divided parents. Mother's priority had been the mental; father's the physical. Identifying with both sides of the conflict, he was left with a tension to bring them together within himself. The split provided the element, the creative tension necessary for working through the damaged aspects of the Achiever Phase that marked his character.

Lowen nourished his observation, gathering information from others about the mind-body relationship. He studied the physically oriented systems of Eurythmics, Progressive Relaxation and Yoga and found that his insight, "... that one could influence mental attitudes by working with the body ... ," was confirmed. Still, though his interest was nourished in this Communicator Phase of his healing, he wrote of what he had taken in; "... their approach didn't entirely satisfy me." (Lowen, 1975)

Pursuing the mind-body issue further, Lowen attended a lecture by psychiatrist Wilhelm Reich. (Lowen, 1975) Reich and his work proved to be pivotal in Lowen's personal and professional development. Lowen was to identify strongly with the charismatic Reich, and to understand his further development, a brief aside about Reich's life is necessary at this point. (For a full discussion of both Reich's life and work, a life of both genius as well as personal and professional tragedy, see Myron Sharaf, Fury on Earth: A Biography of Wilhelm Reich [1983])

As a young professional, Wilhelm Reich contributed powerfully to the field of Psychoanalysis through his understanding of character and its place in therapeutic work. His book, Character Analysis (Reich, 1949), remains a classic in the field today. As he developed his ideas, Reich, showing strong Inspirer characteristics, expanded psychoanalytic concepts beyond their initial boundaries and applied them outside of the traditional context.

Initially, through the Inspirer process of expansion and crossing boundaries, Reich became interested in issues of sexuality and, going further than Freud, studied the function of sexual orgasm in the human being, eventually making it the center of his understanding of disturbed human functioning.

In Europe, Reich carried his ideas outside the clinical context into the political realms of the day, championing the cause of sexual freedom and working to tie it to the agendas of the then current party politics. Later in his career, he would expand his conceptual interest past sexual energies into the exploration of a universal energy he called "orgone." He would apply his inspirations far beyond psychiatric concerns, into the treatment of cancer, atomic radiation, even the making of rain.

Perhaps it was the controversial nature of his interests, but more likely it was the negative aspect of his Inspirer dynamics, the crossing of and disregard for established boundaries, that led to hostile response against him and a continuing succession of controversies that repeatedly stimulated attack from psychoanalytic professionals, political activists, scientists, the popular press and governmental agencies.

The specifics of these encounters are not relevant to the present discussion. It should be noted, though, that when Lowen first came to Reich the hostilities that had surrounded Reich in Europe were not at issue. Later they would arise in their own form in the United States and affect the course of their relationship and Lowen's eventual work.

In 1939, picking up on a suggestion that in America "... he could find a more congenial atmosphere," (Sharaf, 1983), Reich arrived in the United States. A year later, in 1940, Lowen attended a lecture Reich gave in New York.

Lowen was strongly attracted to Reich's presentation of the existence of an underlying identity between the mind and the body. It had remained an identity sharply divided in him personally, by the holdings and rigidities he had developed in childhood.

In practice, Reich worked with the body to break up such holdings. To do so, he encouraged deep breathing and provided opportunity for cathartic release to free the body of neurotic tensions. Later, he came to use hands-on physical pressure to loosen tight muscles that blocked energetic flow. The goal was to aid the person to work through blocks and infantile conflicts, to gain a new sexual economy, to have a sexually fuller response. Reich had written:

"Psychic health depends on orgastic potency. i.e., upon the degree to which one can surrender to and experience the climax of excitation in the natural sexual act. It is founded on the healthy character attitude of the individual's capacity for love. Psychic illnesses are the result of a disturbance of the natural ability to love. In the case of orgastic impotence, from which the overwhelming majority of people suffer, damming-up of biological energy occurs and becomes the source of irrational actions." (Reich, 1973)

In Reich's work with the body, he emphasized and strove for spontaneous physical expression. The benchmark of this expression in therapy, the response that indicated a freedom from neurotic blocks, Reich called the "orgasm reflex". Not a sexual orgasm, lacking genital involvement, Reich identified the orgasm reflex as a specific spontaneous movement in which the body fully and freely participates in a wave-like motion that in fact could occur with each breath. Reich viewed this movement as active in the everyday functioning of healthy individuals. He also saw it as underlying the movement of full sexual orgasm.

Attending Reich's lectures, Lowen soon identified with him, becoming his student with the aim of being a Reichian therapist.

Then at one point in their association, Reich confronted Lowen saying: "... if you are really interested in this work, there is only one way of getting into it, and that is by going into therapy." (Lowen, 1975) Lowen was startled. Perhaps because of the pride of the Achiever character he hadn't considered it:

"I was not in any great trouble when I went to Reich. In fact I went to therapy and didn't think I needed it. ... I was fairly successful within the limits of that time." (Robbins, 1979)

Lowen, however, responded to Reich's suggestion from the part of his personality that still identified with his mother:

> "I am interested, but what I want is to become famous. Reich took this remark seriously for he replied, `I will make you famous.'" (Lowen, 1975)

The totality of Reich's promise touched the Dream Phase in Lowen:

> "Over the years I have regarded Reich's statement as a prophecy. It was the push I needed to overcome my resistance and launch me into my lifework." (Lowen, 1975)

Reich's statement offered a promise that could fulfill the part of Lowen identified with his mother's striving. It provided the lubrication of the psyche needed to allow Lowen to enter therapy.

But it proved to be a deeper, more natural and more consistent motivation than the search for fame, or even the aim to be a Reichian therapist, that provided the real driving power. It was a motivation that reflected his identification with his father's drive for pleasure, but found its true source in the urgings of his own body. Lowen had as a conscious goal fuller orgasmic responsiveness. (Robbins, 1987)

Lowen's first therapy session began with instructions to breathe deeply to increase the strength of any emotional tendencies present. When Lowen's body was charged with energy, Reich directed him to lay his head back and widen his eyes. A full, and for Lowen the Achiever, a surprising scream ensued. Therapy had begun. More was going on than he had known.

Lowen was in therapy with Reich for three years. The process had overtly begun with the Achiever's drive for success. This success attitude that stemmed from identification with his mother eventually put the therapy in jeopardy:

> "Characteristically, I was determined to make the therapy succeed, and it was not until it almost failed that I opened up my feelings to Reich.
>
> ... I was blocked because I couldn't tell Reich my feeling about him. I wanted him to take a fatherly interest in me, not merely a therapeutic one, but knowing this was an unreasonable request, I couldn't express it. Struggling inwardly with the problem, I got nowhere. Reich seemed unaware of my conflict. Try as hard as I could to let my breathing become deeper and fuller, it just didn't work.
>
> I had been in therapy for about a year when this impasse developed. When it seemed to go on indefinitely, Reich suggested I quit. "Lowen," he said, "you are unable to give in to your feelings. Why don't you give up?"
>
> His words were as a sentence of doom. To give up meant failure of all my dreams. I broke down and cried deeply. It was the first time I had sobbed since I was a child. I could no longer hold back my feelings. I told Reich what I wanted from him, and he listened sympathetically." (Lowen, 1975)

In confronting failure with all its weakness, Lowen let go of his rigid attitudinal stance of success. The grasp of his mother identification loosened. Further by expressing his fantasy, the wish that Reich could serve as a father for him, Lowen achieved a loosening of what might be interpreted as a desire to keep his father and the pleasures they had shared together eternally with him. It was a wish that blocked Lowen from realistically advancing in his therapeutic process.

> "Realizing Reich was not going to be my father. I was able to take a more independent position." (Robbins, 1987)

In therapy, now with a more realistic orientation, Lowen went on over the next two years to achieve the orgasmic reflex. At the time in Reich's work this was sufficient to indicate that therapy had reached completion. Lowen was ready for more independence.

> "My therapy with Reich ended in 1945. Shortly before it ended I saw my first patient as a Reichian therapist. At that time there were very few persons who had any real familiarity with Reich's work. Having been a patient for about three years I was able to do some work with people. I worked as a Reichian therapist for two years before going to Switzerland to study medicine." (Robbins, 1988)

Lowen credits his work with Reich powerfully. It provided a crucial key in the evolution of his own identity.

> "It gave me a positive identification with my sexuality which has proved to be the cornerstone of my life." (Lowen, 1975)

It was in 1947 that Lowen left Reich's direct influence in order to further his education and deepen his understanding of the mind-body relationship. That same year an article, "The Strange Case of Wilhelm Reich," by Mildred Edie Brady, appeared in The New Republic. The subheading in large type, ran: "The man who blames both neuroses and cancer on unsatisfactory sexual activities has been repudiated by only one scientific journal." (Sharaf, 1983)

>"Brady's main point could be discerned from the insinuations: the psychoanalytic organization should discipline itself, in other words, do something about "the growing Reich cult," or else it will be 'disciplined by the state'." (Sharaf, 1983)

As traced out by Sharaf (1983), Brady's article proved to be both influential and prophetic. Its negative themes were repeated in popular magazines and one aspect of these reportings caught the attention of the authorities of the Federal Drug Administration. The aura of controversy that Reich had lived with in Europe was now to develop in America.

When he returned to America, in 1951, Lowen found the situation very different than the one he had left four years earlier. Reich was no longer focused on psychotherapy. "Reich had hopes that orgone energy might be helpful as an antidote to nuclear radiation..." (Sharaf, 1983) Some laboratory work he did with radium led to both he and his assistants growing physically and psychologically ill. The mood around Reich was not healthy.

Then too, during the period of Lowen's absence, the critical attacks by the medical and scientific communities and active hostility from a number of psychoanalysts had grown stronger. Lowen questioned the Reichians ability to withstand the onslaught:

"The Reichians' were talking of how they were being persecuted and I was aware that they couldn't handle it in the sense that their work wasn't approved. Obviously there was some sense of justified paranoia. I say 'some sense' because they <u>were</u> persecuted - but the main thing was, they couldn't handle it." (Robbins, 1987)

As a new, yet unlicensed physician, Lowen was vulnerable to be caught in the Reichians' difficulties with the authorities. (Lowen, 1987) Then too, he found a hierarchical structure had developed and he objected to its religious-like nature:

"Reich was at the top of the structure, like God. The Reichian therapists in the structure were like archangels and angels. [How similar to the 4-year-old-play of Inspirer Jacob Moreno, mentioned earlier. (See Inspirer Section) R.R.]

Those who believed in Reich and in the therapy were going to be saved and the rest of the world was damned.

This was how I saw it. Whether true or not, it was how I saw it." (Lowen, 1988)

In this atmosphere, Lowen felt:

"Reich's followers had developed an almost fanatical devotion to him and his work. It was considered presumptuous, if not heretical, to question any of his statements or modify his concepts in the light of one's own experience." (Lowen, 1987)

He now viewed his colleagues as:

> "... too dogmatic. They took his word as if they were biblical statements. I had attended a meeting of the Reichians in 1952. They were beginning to form their own society. The theme was a discussion of contact. They would simply quote statements by Reich. No one offered any independent understanding and when I did it was rejected. (Robbins, 1988)

Lowen chose to no longer directly identify with his colleagues. He had been actively involved with Reich and his work over a 12-year period and now, though still considering himself a Reichian therapist, he moved away from their direct influence. From his experiences with Reich, Lowen took a new conscious identification, one associated with a major life learning:

> "The human being is part of a natural order. When you identify with that natural order you suddenly have a sense of belonging. Belonging didn't depend on connecting to Reich but the larger family of nature and living creatures. I could walk into any group and feel I belonged because on the level of sexuality and the body there are no distinctions." (Robbins, 1987)

The story of Lowen's association with his teacher, Wilhelm Reich, makes manifest Achiever dynamics. His teacher had offered the opportunity to find a way to encompass the conflicting tendencies in his personality, tendencies stemming from the oedipal triangle and what his parents disagreed about, success and pleasure. It involved a period of identification with Reich, dealt with sexuality and inspired advance in his personal solution to the Oedipal situation. He was moving forward again toward his own independent position.

Time revealed that the promise associated with having established the orgasm reflex in therapy was not sufficiently realized in life.

This achievement, with its spontaneous expression, seemed to have been only the peak of an Inspirer Phase in Lowen's therapeutic course. Much of what Lowen achieved during his sessions with Reich did not transfer into improved day-to-day living in the face of its stresses.

Hard work, work of the Solidifier Phase, remained to be done. It took place in therapeutic sessions Lowen underwent in collaboration with his colleague, John Pierrakos. This new therapy had a very different quality from the one Lowen had undergone with Reich. Significantly, each session began in a non-directive, even Rogerian-like way. The first half of the session was patient directed. Lowen worked physically with himself. Only then, in response to what had occurred, would Pierrakos dig into Lowen's tense muscles to allow a streaming of feelings to take place. (Lowen, 1975)

These sessions were less dramatic than those that had occurred under Reich. "There was [sic] fewer of the spontaneously moving experiences." (Lowen, 1975) Hard work, though, paid off in solid gains. Lowen grew in his abilities to contact anger and sadness. The rigidities in his body relaxed so he could use his musculature in a stronger way. An exaggerated fear of pain diminished as feelings of brittleness gave way and he realized that though he could be hurt, he would not break. (Lowen, 1975)

Lowen dealt further with his fear of failure and drive for success. Trying and controlling eased to permit more surrender. His heart opened further. A tendency toward premature ejaculation, still left after his work with Reich, diminished. His response at climax was more satisfying. (Lowen, 1975)

As the end of the therapy approached, Lowen was moving naturally in ways that would result in the achievement of his own position of professional identity. He established, with Pierrakos, the Bioenergetic Institute and he authored <u>Physical Dynamics of Character Structure</u> (1958) which came to serve as a foundation to his approach.

Bioenergetics, as Lowen developed it, maintained a clear, direct and acknowledged relationship to Reich's work. Among the therapists we have discussed Lowen is unique in crediting another as a central contributor to their own development, but there remained a problem: the charismatic nature of Reich's contribution was viewed by the mainstream of professionals as that of a wild but unstable genius.

Reich's behavior appeared to many as eccentric and unbounded. Though his early work on character analysis continued to be held in professional esteem, it was suggested that much of what followed this period was quackery.

The inability to separate what was seen as Reich's psychopathology from what his followers viewed as his real contributions caused a just evaluation of Reich's work to be problematic. The value of his psychological insights and methods, confirmed by those who used them, could have easily been lost to the mainstream of professional practice because of their association with Reich's personal difficulties.

Though Lowen stayed close to his identity with Reich, he found it necessary to move clearly along his own way.

"Bioenergetics took over Reich's basic thinking but did not use a language that would arouse negative thinking in people. For example, 'orgone' we would call 'Bioenergetics'. In this way we could avoid the disputes around the problems of Reich's special language but still have the validity of the view." (Robbins, 1987)

Lowen's commitment, though, stayed with the body. He had been there with his father, before Reich, and remained there when on his own. Building on his teacher's emphasis on the body's potential as a center for the psychotherapuutic process, he further explored character patterns that Reich had initially traced and he went on to describe ones that had not yet been theoretically developed. In the area of technique Lowen added methods useful for therapeutic work on the arms and legs, areas not attended to in Reich's theories.

Reich had worked with patients when they were lying down. This tended to lead them into very regressed expressions where they would rage and scream their infantile conflicts. Lowen expanded the method, placing people on their feet when they were ready to allow exploration of later developmental issues.

Observing that differences in how people stood gave clues to their relationship to reality, Lowen developed the concept of "grounding." Was a person "up in the air?" Could an individual "hold his ground?" Was his or her stance one of a "pushover?" Answers could be observed in bodily posture and energetic movement. New exercises were developed to work with issues that appeared when the client was standing. Achieving a position of full standing could be attained.

Lowen's work on "grounding," as well as the groundedness of his whole approach and personal style, brought Reich's contribution down to earth. In contrast to the "far-out" and expansive character of Reich, Lowen's orientation gave the Bioenergetic Institute a grounded expressive attitude. Through it, conservative and mainstream professional practitioners could allow themselves to make contact and gain therapeutic skills in the areas of bodily dynamics and techniques. It was a possibility largely precluded in more traditional Reichian circles by their checkered history.

Under Lowen's clear personal authority the Institute has grown into the establishment of a strong international association of 45 professional training centers, spread across North and South America as well as Europe. Training fully qualified and professionally recognized therapists, the programs emphasize Bioenergetic training through a four-year core curriculum that includes personal therapy and supervision.

Lowen's success in founding, building and directing a school of psychotherapy that is an influence on the mainstream of therapeutic practice is evidence of the positive aspects and fulfillment of the Achiever position. Late in his 70's he remains a vibrant contributor: his 10th book, <u>Love, Sex and Your Heart</u>, almost ready for publication; his 11th already begun.

Lowen's realistic outlook, emphasis on the whole body and strong position of leadership underly his personal dynamics, values, work and accomplishment. They are the result of a lifelong Rhythmic Cycle of Change that grew out of the dreams and desires of the initial conflict-laden oedipal identifications that came to play in his childhood during the early development of the Achiever Phase:

> "My mother believed the purpose of life was work and success. My father believed the purpose was the pleasure of the body.
>
> I have gained some level of success combining the two - the work of life is pleasure."
> (Robbins, 1979)

••••

Virginia Satir and Alexander Lowen are both Achievers. The contribution of each, grew out of the process of identification with the conflicts and powerfully expressed parental positions they encountered in their early life. Each has a vital, confident, reality oriented personality. Each is strong, aggressive and dominating; each possesses a well-defined ego.

Satir and Lowen differ from the other therapists we have reviewed in that the content of their work stemmed from the positions of their parents, with whom they identified, rather than, more simply, being direct expressions of the major quality of the phase of the Rhythmic Cycle that marked their character.

Generally, the other therapists based their theories on the major quality that marked their character eg; dreams (Jung), creation (Laing), communication (Ellis), inspiration (Moreno), solidification (Rogers).

An exception to this principle is Jacqui Lee Schiff. Schiff's interest in schizophrenics does not express her dynamics as an Inspirer nor does it express an Achiever's identification. It might be considered, as way of explanation, that Inspirers in overrunning of boundaries, have the capacity to draw from many different character styles and interests. This interpretation gains support from the fact that Reich too, developed his interests in the body and in sexuality from expanding on what was around him.

Neither Satir nor Lowen emphasized the major aspect of their character, achievement, as the way of their therapy. Instead, they used their Achiever styles to advance the fields with which they identified.

Though Satir and Lowen differ in the content they work with, for one it's the family for the other the body, in the aim of their own personhood, they share an interest in a common, sexually related, end-point. For Lowen "pleasure" and its relationship to orgasmic reflex is the aim, while Satir speaks of the secrets in the bedroom and "Joy in the body."

For those held in the Achiever Phase of the Rhythmic Cycle experiences of the deepest pleasures and joys of the body can be elusive, sacrificed to maintain a strong ego and the advancement of an identity.

Full pleasure and bodily joy move one to the end of the Achiever Phase. To attain them necessitates surrendering the position with all its authority, pride, and advantage. From the summit of living a vulnerability is required that allows, even invites, intimate moments of meeting, moments when reflexes beyond control move being and body beyond the Achiever position in whatever dance the fates choose in the face of nature's larger currents. From these liberated moments come regeneration. From them, the germ of life springs into growth and love blossoms fresh.

Seeds

Why has the soul fallen
From the highest heights
To the deepest depths below?

Within the fall is contained the resurrection.
(Ansky, 1987)

REQUIEM AND GENESIS

The climax of energy in the final moment of a Rhythmic Cycle brings again the desolate quietness of the void. An epitaph of meaning separates living reality from fading memory.

Like the silent solitude of Nature's winter, the descent toward emptiness is not what it seems. The form that continues is changed by its experiences. No inert vessel, the body contains seeds to start the energetic course again.

A new spring begins. The budding next generation reflects the body's history, adds new dimensions of its own uniqueness.

We have followed the Rhythmic Cycle of Energy, traced its course, portrayed its way-stations. We have seen its movement, the moving of the living spirit as it takes form in human development,

The Rhythmic Cycle of Change

political progression, therapeutic intervention, cultural formation and individual contribution.

We have explored the Rhythmic Cycle from its silent source through six identifiable stages:

Dreamer
Creator
Communicator
Inspirer
Solidifier
Achiever

If we picture the Rhythmic Cycle linearly, and follow its course in quantitative terms, we can trace its amplitude as it passes through time. The Cycle, shown theoretically in Figure 2, appears as a line of energy that increases in distinct segments toward its peak, once there only to fall and start again.

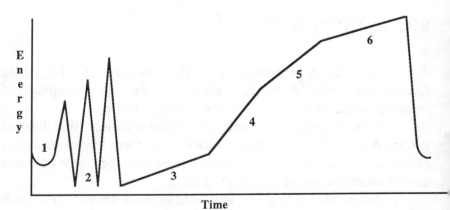

Fig.2 The theoretical phases of the Rhythmic Cycle: (1) Dreamer, (2) Creator, (3) Communicator, (4) Inspirer, (5) Solidifier, & (6) Achiever - followed by the renewing of the Cycle.

The curve of this line has been anticipated elsewhere. It is visible in the ancient oriental symbol of Yin-Yang, the Eastern Mystics' presentation of the flow of change presented in Figure 3 below. Between dark and light, the line of energy courses. Its smooth and graceful shape appears an idealized summary of many Rhythmic Cycles.

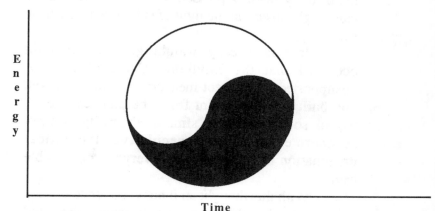

Fig.3 The Yin Yang Symbol of Energy

In the development of this work the Rhythmic Cycle of Energy has been presented as existential, not simply theoretical. Still the author suffered misgivings because, during the time the concept was being defined, the Rhythmic Cycle was not supported by an observable "hard" fact, although it did appear intuitively correct, was bulwarked by numerous examples and proved useful in practice as a therapeutic tool.

It was only an act of fate, one of those mysterious coincidences that sometimes occurs, that as the initial groundwork on the Rhythmic Cycle neared maturation I chanced to watch the television show, The Body in Question. (NET, 1983)

The program was reviewing the history of a number of philosophers' attempts to answer what is known as the "mind-body" question: How does the physical body come to effect the pictures and thoughts of mental consciousness?

Each theory was described as it had historically been expressed and then shown to be laughingly absurd in the light of subsequent scientific evidence.

It wasn't easy watching. The thought occurred that the Rhythmic Cycle of Energy, unsupported by a direct measurable representation, one built point for point from the physical world, would soon smack of similar absurdity, simply another example of speculative theoretical imagination drifting far from everyday observable truth.

With this thought an inner experience of deep pain, a cracking that momentarily teeters the mind over the edge of madness, came over me. All I had developed through meditation, observation, thought, exploration, effort and experience seemed only to be headed toward humiliating overthrow.

For the moment too weak to move, I continued where I was. With little interest I saw the announcer place an electrode on his skin, administer a shock to his nerve, and reflexively move a muscle. The resulting polygraph, shown on the screen, shocked me to alertness. I could hardly believe what I saw.

There on the screen, in a graph that physically portrayed the announcer's experience, was a tracing of the course of energy from nerve excitation through its resultant reflexive muscle movement. It provided the <u>measurable</u> physiological evidence that my description of the Rhythmic Cycle lacked. The intensity of my despair was replaced by an equally exciting overflow of Joy.

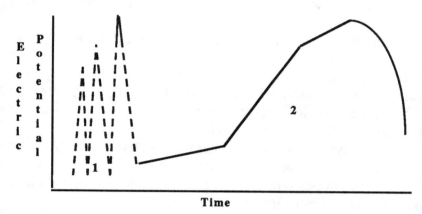

Fig.4 Level of electrical potential from nerve excitation through muscle arousal and release. (1) Nerve (2) Muscle taken from , **Body In Question** NEI, 1983.

What was seen was an almost exact duplicate of the Rhythmic Cycle of Energy as it had been traced out. It differed only in the magnitude of energy spiking that occurred during the phase of the Creator. The author's rendering had been questioned on this point. Therapists had found it inconsistent with their observations. For them, the Creator Phase often seemed to manifest a much higher, if short-lived, energy.

The nerve-muscle reflex arc portrayed on the screen (shown in Figure 4) proved them right. It also provided the missing physical source, the measurable existential base, the building block of the Rhythmic Cycle.

The Rhythmic Cycle of Change

The nerve-muscle reflex is now seen as to be multiplied through the fibers of an individual's bodily systems, then multiplied again through the joint movements of many individuals in larger aggregates. Through this amplification of the nerve-muscle reflex, Nature provides a specific character to humanity's individual and social endeavor, and through it, shape is given to the Rhythmic Cycle of Change.

The Rhythmic Cycle's Phases of Change are, then, at base these reflex arcs expressed through successive areas of human physiology. Scientifically measurable, they allow us an empirical ground for the obtaining of a baseline knowledge that may be fruitful in terms of scientific refinement and the extension of our understanding of the Rhythmic Cycle.

The Rhythmic Cycle of Change can be used too to trace the developmental form of many diverse human activities. What follows is a small potpourri of concepts, examples and applications that have already sprung into being.

• • • • •

The drama of the theater follows the pattern. It begins in the still silence that falls over an audience as the curtain rises. The revealed backdrop of the setting stimulates mood. (Dream) Characters come to life. (Creation) A need or problem is declared. (Communication) Alternative possible solutions arouse a precarious excitement. (Inspiration) The development of a solution begins to be worked through. (Solidification) The action drives toward a climactic cathartic encounter through which the players and the audience share a moment of victory or defeat, of comedy or tragedy. (Achievement) With the final applause emotion drains away. The living experience slips towards the gap of oblivion.

• • • • •

The course of scientific experimentation provides example of a similar process. From a personal, inner motive in an experimenter

276

an area of concern emerges. (Dream) An inconsistency, something split off, unexplained by the current state of the field, is struggled with. (Creation) The terms of the problem are logically defined. (Communication) Alternative hypotheses are developed. (Inspiration) A controlled experimental method is designed, data is collected, statistics calculated and results determined. (Solidification) The experiment is presented, shared with colleagues, with an aim toward either acceptance or rejection into the extant stream of knowledge. (Achievement) Finally effort and energy pass away leaving room for new projects to emerge.

· · · · ·

A sprint race, too, follows the stages of the Rhythmic Cycle. There is the stillness of the ready position (Dream); the explosion of energy as the gun sounds the race's beginning and the runners break from the starting block (Creation); the slow first steps that call upon inner energy reserves to recover from the drain of the start (Communication); the step-by-step rise and building of speed from the crouched to the running position (Inspiration); the systematic working strides of the middle course (Solidification); the spurting lunge and fall at the finish line - the climax that brings the roar of the crowd, victory or defeat (Achievement); and then the exhausting collapse as the runner comes down from the experience.

· · · · ·

The dynamics of the Rhythmic Cycle are present in psychotherapy during each individual session as well as over its whole course. Working with it directly provides a vision of purpose, a direction of movement, a mode of intervention and a frame of reference to evaluate where one has been and where one must go. A life integrated on the Cycle progresses on course as it develops.

The Rhythmic Cycle of Change

A therapy that uses the principles of Rhythmic Integration as a frame of reference seeks out the phases of energy where character patterns disrupt the silent underlying energetic flow. It finds evidence of them in the being, the body and the behavior. They appear as physical disharmonies, distorted emotional responses, and ineffective actions.

Places are noted where energy arrests. The client is aided to become aware of what is happening, to explore and loosen sticking points, to release habitually blocked feelings in order to clear the path for a freer, stronger channel of flow, one that can ripen into a full maturity.

The therapist intervenes to provide assistance appropriate to the Phase that is disturbed. He gets his clue of what to do from the nature of the disturbing Phase itself. He may simply provide space and time to be, directly point out ambivalences that lead nowhere, or nourish with ideas. He may offer support or warning to stimulate or limit excitement. He may push, prod or provoke to get stuck things moving. Finally he may encourage movement toward completion, victory or defeat, and surrender to what is.

As the course of energy flow is freed, the enertgetic path broadens and deepens. Capacities in the less frequently experienced aspects of the Cycle, Phases that have been avoided, come to life. Therapeutic guidance and direction are provided to learn about and strengthen them. A therapy of Rhythmic Integration is on the side of full movement through all phases of the cycle of energy. Whole and rich living demand dreaming, creating, communicating, inspiring, solidifying, and achieving.

• • • • •

Perhaps it's just an idle hope, certainly it hasn't been developed, but understanding the course of change that Cultures and Nations follow stimulates the possibility that perhaps they too could be aided toward development, to move through the extreme blockings that yield sick explosive Societies, or impoverished underdevelopment, or repeated cycling between acting-out and stultifying repression. Such situations afflict the lives of all members caught in these communities.

Fields like anthropology, sociology, social work, and politics all touch on the concerns of the aberrant development of societies. Yet there is no therapeutic resource to turn to, no resource field skilled and trained to identify the cause of disturbance, aid its resolution, stimulate its return to healthy flow along the course of change. Perhaps such a discipline can grow.

• • • • •

Knowledge of the Rhythmic Cycle of Change has been useful in the development of a series of Rhythmic Integration Experiences. Lasting between three hours to five days these Experiences are carefully designed in terms of space, time, and setting to provide a warm and loving atmosphere. Through the use of nature, music, dance, ritual, encounter, interpretation, etc. each of the phases of being, all aspects of the personality, are stimulated and given opportunity for expression in their time.

As participants move through the Rhythmic Integration Experience they discover and therapeutically work with distorting areas and undeveloped parts of themselves. They gain an appreciation of their strengths and have an opportunity to integrate their flow along a balanced path. A participatory knowledge develops that extends and deepens one's living through the wholeness of the course of being.

As one evaluator expressed it, "I have been a psychotherapist for years and have attended many kinds of workshops designed for learning and growth. I want you to know that this experience, with its obvious care and deep human understanding, had a powerful effect for me. I was able quickly and easily to go deeply into places I had never been before and I came out feeling both whole and integrated with my feet on the ground. It's been something really different. I thank you very much for this."

• • • • •

It pretty much happened by chance that the emerging methods of Rhythmic Integration were applied to a 7-foot-tall basketball player, John Donavan. As the local newspaper put it, his only claims to fame were his height and his sister Ann, an All-American athlete who went on to play for the Olympic team.

John had never been a successful player. In the year previous to our working together he had averaged a little over two points per game. As our sessions began he was having problems getting the ball thrown to him even in the local Summer YMCA league. He had difficulties with catching, running, jumping, fouling and shooting.

With three months preseason work on change in both body and feelings, things were vastly different. In the team's opening game the small practically unheard-of school he played for, Marist College, was led toward slaughter against one of the Nation's perennial powerhouse, Notre Dame.

John had improved enough to start the game. His six blocked shots and impressive rebounding sparked his team to a near upset that caught the attention of the national press.

By the following season John was playing professionally in Europe with impressive statistics: near 20 points, 16 rebounds, and six blocked shots per game. He had become a coordinated, confident, integrated contributor. (Robbins, 1984)

The Rhythmic Integration approach was extended the following year to members of the school's women's basketball team. This time there were more participants and they represented widely different skill levels. They ranged in ability from a French national team member who had played against the finest players in the world to players struggling toward an athletic standard of adequacy in even basic skills.

Some players worked briefly on an isolated playing issue. The young woman with the farthest to go, Mary Jo Stempsey, was assigned to the program the longest, for a two month period. In this relatively brief time her improvement was astonishing. She dramatically changed in all levels of functioning, moving from a place deep on the bench into the role of star.

After another three weeks of work in the summer, Stempsey's level of performance advanced and became solid. Through the next year she led the team in every shooting category, as well as in blocked shots. This former poorly coordinated nowhere-to-go player became a regular newspaper headliner. At Season's end, she was rewarded by her team's conference for the outstanding level of her overall play.

Regardless of initial ability level, each participant in the program showed impressive, statistically verified improvement. (Robbins, 1985) Research theorist, Murray Sidman (1960), successfully argues that experimentally controlled change within an individual over an entire process of "rich complexity", one unlikely to occur by chance, meets the rigors of experimental acceptability. Extending the results through replication, as occurred here across a number of individuals, increases the generality of the findings.

This Sports Psychology application of the Rhythmic Cycle buttresses the Cycle's concepts and methods with scientific evidence. Perhaps more important than either research support or improved basketball performance was the demonstration that individuals could learn with relative ease to move more naturally and gracefully. Those with poor coordination, as well as those whose performance was clearly adept, made marked improvements.

All participants improved by consciously attending to hitches and disruptions in basic patterns of physical, emotional, and psychological energetic flow through the stages of the Rhythmic

The Rhythmic Cycle of Change

Cycle. The capacity for natural integrated functioning lies within each of us and was shown to be obtainable to a degree much greater than commonly appreciated.

· · · · ·

This book moves to its close. For the author it is the ending of a rhythmic journey of changes that took place over a period of well over 10 years. For the reader, it is trusted, it has taken less time. A book is a rather unique way for two to meet - a reader and a writer. In a way it hardly seems a meeting at all. Yet I am filled with warmth as I sense that perhaps, maybe you, too, have had a meaningful experience of the Rhythmic Cycle - that in our individual ways we have shared together. I end with a bubbling excitement about the future directions of new beginnings. Thanks for being with me.

· · · · ·

The modern period of dramatic therapeutic advance has passed. Its depositories; its spirits, stories, options, methods and institutions remain to be drawn upon for the next move forward.

Somewhere, the great sea pulsates from the center. At the edge, wave upon wave rolls to shore. Trough rises to crest and spills over. White wash flows onto the sandy beach, the edges of the earth. As the bubbles break and the water recedes, relics of the life of this near former time are left behind to be gathered afresh.

The Rhythmic Cycle that underlies this work comes to an end. Through it, the Cycle itself has been described as an existential fact, a series of phases underlying all human process. With this description complete, new seeds begin to sprout, grow and blossom.

APPENDIX

MAJOR THERAPISTS
AND THERAPEUTIC SCHOOLS IN THIS WORK

Albert Ellis
Institute of Rational-Emotive Therapy
45 E. 65th St.
New York, N.Y. 10021

Jung, Carl (Deceased)
C.G. Jung Institute of New York
28 E. 39th St.
New York, N.Y. 10016

C.G. Jung Institute
Hornweg 28
8700 Kusnacht
Switzerland

Laing, R.D.
Not Available

Lowen, Alexander
International Institute for Bioenergetic Analysis
144 E. 36th St.
New York, N.Y. 10016

Moreno, J.L. (Deceased)
Moreno Academy of Psychodrama
259 Wolcott Ave.
Beacon, N.Y. 12508

The Rhythmic Cycle of Change

Robbins, Ronald
Academy Street Center for Rhythmic Integration
151 Academy St.
Poughkeepsie, N.Y. 12601

Rogers, Carl (Deceased)
Center for Studies of the Person
1125 Torrey Pines Road
La Jolla, Calif. 92037

Satir, Virginia
Anterra Inc.
139 Forest Ave.
Palo Alto, Ca. 94301

Schiff, Jacqui Lee
P.O. Box 1049
Lemon Grove, Ca. 92037

72 Coney Green Dr.
Northfield, Birmingham,
England 3314DU

BIBLIOGRAPHY

Ansky, S. *The Dybbuk.* translated by H. G. Alsberg & W. Katzin). London:Ernest Benn Ltd., 1927.

Ballou, Robert. *Portable World Bible.* New York:Viking. (No date given.)

Bekritsky, Morris. Personal Communication to Ronald Robbins. Poughkeepsie, New York, 1973.

Berne, Eric. "Fritz Perls and Psychodrama." *Group Psychotherapy and Psychodrama*, 25, (3), 1972, 125.

Bisesle, Megan. "Aspects of !Kung Folklore." In Richard Lee & I. Devore (eds.), *Kalahari Hunter-Gatherers: Studies of the Kung San and their Neighbors.* Boston:Harvard University Press, 1976.

Blofeld, John. *The Tantric Mysticism of Tibet..* New York:Dutton, 1970.

Bleek, Wilhelm & Lloyd, L. C. *Specimens of Bushman Folklore.* London:G. Allen and Co., 1911.

Buber, Martin. *Tales of the Hasidim.* New York:Schocken, 1972.

Dornan, S. *Pygmies and Bushmen of the Kalahari.* London:Seeley, Service & Co., 1925.

Ellis, Albert. *The Folklore of Sex.* New York:Grove, 1961.

-----. "Rational-Emotive Therapy." Invited Speech: Auspices of Mid-Hudson Psychological Association. Poughkeepsie, New York, 1975.

-----. "The Use of Rational Humorous Songs in Psychotherapy." In N. F. Fry, Jr., & W. A. Salemeh (eds.) *Handbook of Humor in Psychotherapy*: Advances in the Clincial Use of Humor. Sarasota, Fl: Professional Resource Exchange, Inc., 1987.

-----. Personal communication to Ronald Robbins. Poughkeepsie, 1988.

-----. & Robert Harper. *A Guide to Rational Living*. N. Hollywood:Wilshire Book Co., (No date given.).

Emerson, Ralph Waldo. "Experience." In Brooks Atkinson (ed.), *The Selected Writings of Ralph Waldo Emerson*. New York:Modern Library, 1950.

Evans, Richard I. *Carl Rogers: The Man and His Ideas*. New York:Dutton, 1975.

-----. *R.D. Laing: the Man and His Ideas*. New York:Dutton, 1976.

Farson, R. "Carl Rogers, Quiet Revolutionary." In Richard Evans (ed.), *Carl Rogers: The Man and His Ideas*. New York:Dutton, 1975.

Ghiselin, Brewster (ed.). "Introduction." *The Creative Process*. New York:Mentor Books, 1952.

Goleman, Daniel. "Psychotherapy at 100, Is Marked By Deep Divisions on Approaches." New York Times, 12/17/85, C1.6.

Harner, Michael. *The Way of the Shaman.* New York: Harper and Row, 1980.

Housman, A. E. "The Name and Nature of Poetry." In Brewster Ghiselin (ed.), *The Creative Process.* New York:Mentor Books, 1952.

Jones, Nicholas Blurton & Konner, Melvin J. "!Kung Knowledge of Animal Behavior (or: *The Proper Study of Mankind Is Animals*)." In Richard Lee & I. Devore (eds.), *Kalahari Hunter-Gatherers: Studies of the Kung San and their Neighbors.* Boston:Harvard University Press, 1976.

Jung, Carl. *Memories, Dreams and Reflections.* New York:Vantage, 1961.

Kernberg, Otto. *Borderline Conditions and Pathological Narcissism.* New York:Jason Aronson, 1975.

Kirschenbaum, H. *On Becoming Carl Rogers.* New York:Delacorte Press, 1979.

Konner, Melvin J. "Maternal Care, Infant Behavior and Development Among the !Kung." In Richard Lee & I. Devore (eds.), *Kalahari Hunter-Gatherers: Studies of the Kung San and their Neighbors.* Boston:Harvard University Press, 1976.

Kushner, Harold. *When Bad Things Happen to Good People.* New York:Schoken, 1981.

Laing, R. D. *The Divided Self.* London:Tavistock Publications, 1959.

-----. *The Divided Self.* Baltimore:Pelican, 1965.

-----. *Knots*. New York:Pantheon, 1970.

-----. *The Facts of Life*. New York:Pantheon, 1976.6

Richard Lee & I. Devore (eds.), *Kalahari Hunter-Gatherers: Studies of the Kung San and their Neighbors*. Boston:Harvard University Press, 1976.

Leonard, George. *Education and Ecstasy*. New York:Delacorte, 1966.

Levin, Meyer. *Classic Chassidic Tales*. New York:Citadel Press, 1966.

Lowell, Amy. "The Process of Making Poetry." In Brewster Ghiselin (ed.), *The Creative Process*. New York:Mentor Books, 1952.

Lowen, Alexander. *Physical Dynamics of Character Structure*. New York:Grune & Stratton, 1958.

-----. *Bioenergetics*. New York:Coward, Mc Cann & Geoghegan, 1975.

-----. & Lowen Leslie. *The Way to Vibrant Health: A Manual of Bioenergetic Exercises*. New York:Harper Colophon Books, 1977.

-----. "Introduction to Bioenergetic Analysis.", Invited Speech: Auspices of Vassar College Psychology Department. Poughkeepsie, 1981.

-----. *The Will to Live and the Wish to Die*. New York:International Institute for Bioenergetic Analysis, 1982.

Marshall, Elizabeth. *The Harmless People.* New Hampshire:Thomas Knopf, 1968.

Marshall, Lorna. "Sharing, Talking, and Giving: Relief of Social Tensions among the !Kung." In Richard Lee & I. Devore (eds.), *Kalahari Hunter-Gatherers: Studies of the Kung San and their Neighbors.* Boston:Harvard University Press, 1976.

-----. *The Kung of Nyas Nyase.* Cambridge:Harvard University Press, 1976.

Masterson, James F. *Treatment of the Borderline Adolescent: A Developmental Approach.* New York:Wiley, 1975.

McLean, Don. "American Pie." In *American Pie: The Rainbow Collection.* Los Angeles:United Artist Records, 1971.

Merriam-Webster Dictionary. Pocket Book Edition. New York:Simon and Shuster, 1974.

Miller, Henry. "Reflection on Writing." In Brewster Ghiselin (ed.), *The Creative Process.* New York:Mentor Books, 1952.

Minkin, Jacob S. *The Romance of Hassidism.* North Hollywood:Wilshire Books, 1952.

Moreno, J. L. *Words of the Father.* New York:Beacon House, 1941.

-----. *Who Shall Survive.* Beacon, New York:Beacon House, 1953.

-----. *Words of the Father* (Record). New York:Beacon House, 1961.

Moreno, Zerka. Letter to Ronald Robbins. Poughkeepsie, 1983.

Mozart, W. A. "A Letter." In Brewster Ghiselin (ed.), *The Creative Process*. New York:Mentor Books, 1952.

Neihardt, John G. *Black Elk Speaks*. New York:Pocket Books, 1972.

NET (National Educational Television). *"The Body in Question."* (Shown on WNET, New York), January, 1983.

Nietzche, Friedrich. "Composition of Thus Spake Zarathustra." In Brewster Ghiselin (ed.), *The Creative Process*. New York:Mentor Books, 1952.

Peck, M. Scott. *People of the Lie*. New York:Simon and Schuster, 1983.

Plutarch. In Edmund Fuller (ed.). *Lives of the Noble Greeks*. New York:Dell, 1972.

Poincare, Henri. "Mathematical Creation." In Brewster Ghiselin (ed.), *The Creative Process*. New York:Mentor Books, 1952.

Private Comm. Informer's name witheld at his request. New York, 1975.

Rampa, T. Lobsang. *The Third Eye*. New York:Ballantine, 1964.

Reiter, J. S. *Mozart and his Music*. (Title on cover. Inside title, *Wolfgang Amadeus Mozart*), New York:Time-Life Records, 1975.

Reich, Wilhelm. *Character Analysis*. New York:Orgone Institute Press, 1949.

Reich, Wilhelm. *The Function of the Orgasm.* New York:Ferrar, Straus, and Giroux, 1973.

Robbins, Ronald. Taped Interview with J. L. Moreno. 1970.

-----. Personal communication with Carl Rogers, at Eastern Region for Humanistic Psychology New York, 1975.

-----. Taped Interview with Albert Ellis, 1975.

-----. "The Limb Character and the Psychopathic Personality.", invited address New York Society for Bioenergetic Analysis, 1977.

-----. "Mask, Costume and the Identification Process." Address, Institute for Bioenergetic Analysis, 1980.

-----. Taped Interview with Jacqui Lee Schiff. 1979.

-----. Taped interview with Virginia Satir. 1979.

-----. Taped interview with Alexander Lowen. 1980.

-----. Interview with Alexander Lowen. 1987.

-----. Interview with Alexander Lowen. 1988.

-----. & Robbins, Melvyn. "Bioenergetics and Dream Analysis." in Cassius Joseph (ed.), *Horizons in Bioenergetics.* Memphis:Promethean, 1980.

-----. "Der Rhythmische Zyklus und Widerstand." (The Rhythm of Resistance.), In Ulrich Sollmann (ed.), *Bioenergetische Analyse:Methoden der Korpertherapie.* Essen, West Germany:Synthesis Verlag, 1984.

-----. "Full Play: A Cycle of Change on the Basketball Court." Address delivered Institut fur Bioenergetische Analyse. Rheinland, West Germany, 1984.

-----. "Results '84-'85 Sports Psychology Program: Rhythmic Integration with the Women's Basketball Team". Paper delivered to Marist College Women's Basketball Team. Poughkeepsie, New York, 1985.

Rogers, Carl. "Carl Rogers." In E. G. Boring & Gardiner Lindzey (eds.), *A History of Psychology in Autobiography Vol. 5.* New York:Appleton-Century-Croft, 1967.

-----. "Final Address." Eastern Region for Humanistic Psychology Meeting, New York, 1975.

-----. "In Retrospect: Forty-six Years by Carl Rogers." In Richard Evans (ed.), *Carl Rogers: The Man and His Ideas.* New York:Dutton, 1975.

-----. *On Personal Power.* New York:Delta, 1977.

Rogers, H. (Director of following videotape.). *Eye of Childhood.* Available Cathexis Institute, Lemon Grove, Cal. Rogers Productions, 1979.

Satir, Virginia. *Conjoint Family Therapy.* Palo Alto:Science and Behavior Books, 1965.

-----. *Peoplemaking.* Palo Alto:Science and Behavior Books, 1972.

----. Letter to Ronald Robbins, Poughkeepsie, 1987.

Schapera, I. *The Khoisan People of South Africa - Bushmen and Hottentots*. London:Geo. Routledge and Sons, 1930.

Schiff, Jacqui Lee (with Beth Day). *All My Children*. Philadelphia:Lippencott, 1970.

Schiff, Jacqui Lee. (with nine collaborators). *Cathexis Reader: Transactional Analysis: Treatment of Psychosis*. New York:Harper and Row, 1975.

-----. "One Hundred Children Generate a Lot of TA: History Development and Activities of the Schiff Family in Transactional Analysis after Eric Berne." In Graham Barnes (ed.), *Teaching and Practice of Three TA Schools*. New York:Harper's College Press, 1977.

Scholem, Gershom. *Major Trends in Jewish Mysticism*. New York:Schocken, 1972.

-----. *Kabbalah*. New York:Meridian, 1974.

Sessions, Roger. "The Composer and his Message." In Brewster Ghiselin (ed.), *The Creative Process*. New York:Mentor Books, 1952.

Sharaf, Myron. *Fury on Earth: A Biography of Wilhelm Reich*. New York:St. Martins, 1983.

Shepard, Martin. *Fritz: An Intimate Portrait of Fritz Perls and Gestalt Therapy*. New York:Dutton, 1975.

Shostak, Marjorie. "A !Kung Woman's Memories of Childhood." In Richard Lee & I. Devore (eds.), *Kalahari Hunter-Gatherers:*

Studies of the Kung San and their Neighbors. Boston:Harvard University Press, 1976.

Shostrom, Everett L. (Director of following three films.). *Three Approaches to Psychotherapy: Part 1. Dr. Carl Rogers, Part 2. Dr. Fritz Perls, Part 3. Dr. Albert Ellis.* Santa Anna:Psychological Films, 1965.

Sidman, Murray. *Tactics of Scientific Research: Evaluating Experimental Data in Psychology.* NY:Basic Books, 1960.

Stern, Paul J. C. G. *Jung: The Haunted Prophet.* New York:Delta, 1976.

Stewart, Kilton. *Pygmies and Dream Giants.* New York:Harper and Row, 1975.

Stone, L.J. & Church, J. *Childhood and Adolescence.* New York:Random House, 1968.

Tanaka, Jiro. "Subsistence Ecology of Central Kalahari San." In Richard Lee & I. Devore (eds.), *Kalahari Hunter-Gatherers: Studies of the Kung San and their Neighbors.* Boston:Harvard University Press, 1976.

Van Der Post, L. *The Lost World of the Kalahari.* New York:Morrow, 1958.

-----. *Jung: & the Story of Our Time.* New York:Pantheon, 1975.

Wolfe, Thomas. "The Story of a Novel." In Brewster Ghiselin (ed.), *The Creative Process.* New York:Mentor Books, 1952.

Yeats, W.B. "Three Pieces on the Creative Process." In Brewster Ghiselin (ed.), *The Creative Process.* New York:Mentor Books, 1952.

Yellen John, E. "The Dobe-/Du/da Environment: Background to a Hunting and Gathering Way of Life." In Richard Lee & I. Devore (eds.), *Kalahari Hunter-Gatherers: Studies of the Kung San and their Neighbors.* Boston:Harvard University Press, 1976.

More information about the programs and publications of Rhythmic Integration is available. If you are interested, please write to: Rhythmic Integration, P.O. Box 3240, Poughkeepsie, N.Y. 12601.